Everyday
VEGETARIAN
RECIPES

hinkler

hinkler

Published by Hinkler Books Pty Ltd
45–55 Fairchild Street
Heatherton Victoria 3202 Australia
www.hinkler.com.au

© A.C.N. 144 619 894 Pty Ltd 2011

Cover Illustration: Brijbasi Art Press Limited
Prepress: Splitting Image
Typesetting and internal illustrations: MPS Limited

ISBN: 978 1 7418 4127 5

Printed and bound in China

Contents

Introduction

Vegetarian Cooking

People can be drawn to a vegetarian diet for a variety of reasons. Some have ethical or health concerns, for others it is a matter of religious belief. But for many the decision to stop eating meat could just as easily be an aesthetic or gastronomic one. The variety of fresh seasonal ingredients, abundance of possible dishes and scope that vegetarian cuisine offers for creative cooking and eating are often dismissed or not recognised by confirmed meat-eaters.

For many in the developed world, meat has always been the easy option. Certainly meat dishes have appeared through the ages as the centrepiece of most meals. This tradition has led to a diet often lacking in variety and, consequently, in a beneficial balance of nutrients, as well as to the health consequences of eating too many saturated fats. A diet that over-emphasises meat is a product of affluence, and not necessarily a good one.

Many people have recognised an imbalance in their way of eating and are modifying the amount of flesh foods included in their diets. The discovery of vegetarian food often begins in this way. As people gain confidence, experiment more and discover the pleasures of cooking vegetarian foods they often welcome increased vitality and say goodbye to weight problems. Other benefits might be clearer skin and a more regular and comfortable bowel. Many choose to abandon eating meat altogether.

The term 'vegetarian' is used quite loosely. Some people call themselves vegetarian or 'semi-vegetarian' while still eating a little fish or chicken and no red meat. Many just exclude all meat and fish from their diets. Vegans, on the other hand, exclude all other animal products such as milk, cheese and eggs as well. Most vegetarians, however, are lacto-ovo vegetarians who still eat eggs and dairy products. Some vegetarians also prefer to cook with and eat vegetarian cheeses, which do not contain animal rennet.

This book features no flesh foods, or products from them such as fish sauce or shrimp paste. It is not specifically a vegan cookbook, in that dairy foods such as eggs, butter, cheese and cream are used liberally. However, there are plenty of recipes that are suitable for vegans. Nor is this a book of vegetarian substitutes for a meat-centred diet, offering recipes for pale imitations of meatloaf or burgers, or fake meat flavourings. The recipes are for anyone who loves preparing, serving and eating good food. It is neither a diet nor a health-food book, but is designed to expand the menu of possibilities, to show that one can be a connoisseur of good food, a fine cook and a vegetarian.

Vegetarian Healthy Food

If you were raised a vegetarian (and children thrive on a vegetarian diet), you are probably already in the habit of making sure all your nutritional needs are met. But for those just making the transition, there are a few things to bear in mind. It is just as possible to have a poor diet eating exclusively vegetarian foods as it is eating excessive amounts of animal products. The vegetarian healthy food pyramid is a good starting point if you want to check whether your diet is adequate. Its principles are simple:

Eat Most
- **Grains: wheat, rice, barley, corn, oats, rye, millet, buckwheat**
- **Foods Made From Grains: pasta, bread, wholegrain breakfast cereals**
- **Fruit and Vegetables**

Eat Moderately
- **Dairy: milk, yoghurt, cheese**
- **Pulses: peas, beans of all kinds, lentils**

- **Nuts**
- **Eggs**

Eat Least
- **Sugars: sugar, honey**
- **Fats: butter, cream, margarine, oils, coconut milk**
- **Stimulants: alcohol, tea, coffee**

Meal-planning becomes easier if you make a habit of glancing at the food pyramid as a guide. There should be in each day a majority of foods from the 'Eat Most' group: fruit, cereals and toast for breakfast, bread or bread rolls, salads or cooked vegetable dishes and fruit for lunch or dinner; and pasta or rice-based main course for your largest meal (whether that's at lunchtime or in the evening) with fresh bread or rolls, and more fruit for dessert or snacks.

Small amounts of dairy foods from the 'Eat Moderately' group should form part of the day's meals (unless, or course, you are a vegan): yoghurt with breakfast or lunch, a little cheese with lunch or dinner. Being a vegetarian certainly doesn't mean going hungry: your main meal should include plenty of carbohydrate and protein – dishes and hearty soups made from beans or lentils, as well as egg dishes. Nuts are great for snacking.

The 'Eat Least' category means exactly that – a little butter or margarine on your breakfast toast, a drizzle of virgin olive oil with the salad or to stir-fry (scramble-fry) the evening meal, a glass of wine with dinner. Like most things in life, sugary treats are fine, as long as they are enjoyed in moderation.

You can balance the nutritional content of the day's meals so that the overall pattern easily satisfies the food pyramid guidelines. Compensate for an unavoidably fatty lunch, for example, with an evening meal made up of vegetables, grains and fruit.

The Major Food Groups

Over the following pages you will find more information about the different nutritional groups that make up the foods in the vegetarian healthy eating pyramid (protein, carbohydrates, dietary fibre and fat), including their value to our bodies, their importance in the vegetarian diet and the best sources for finding them. This will help you to be a creative cook and a well-informed vegetarian.

Protein

Nobody needs huge amounts of protein from any source, but everybody needs some. Growing children and pregnant women need a little more than other people. Protein provides the basic structure for the human body – it is the main source of building material for our cells, tissues, muscles, nails, hair, skin, bones, blood and internal organs.

We need protein to make and repair cells and tissues and to create hormones, enzymes, antibodies and other immune-system molecules. It is also needed for the regulation of the body's internal environment, including acid and alkaline balance, water balance and the proper elimination of wastes. However, although it performs all these important tasks, our daily requirements are actually quite small.

What Is It?

Protein is made up of small compounds known as amino acids, which are arranged in chains of varying combinations. There are 23 amino acids, most of which are termed 'non-essential' as they can be made in the body.

But not all amino acids can be manufactured in the body – some must be derived from the diet, and these are termed the 'essential' amino acids. There are eight essential amino acids for adults – isoleucine, leucine, lysine, phenylalanine, methionine, threonine, tryptophan, valine – and an extra one, histidine, for infants.

Sources of these essential amino acids are animal products: meat, poultry, fish and dairy foods. This is why some people worry that a vegetarian diet will be lacking in essential nutrients. But there is no need for concern as there are many good vegetarian and vegan sources of protein: nuts and legumes (beans, peas, lentils, soya beans and products such as soy flour, soy milk, tofu and tempeh). However, these foods don't contain all the essential amino acids in the one food source like animal proteins do.

Protein Sources

- Black beans
- Black-eyed beans
- Broad beans
- Chickpeas (garbanzo beans)
- Kidney beans

- Lentils
- Mung beans
- Cannellini (navy) beans
- Peas
- Soya beans

Plant proteins do have an advantage over animal proteins, as they contain fibre and carbohydrates, which makes them easy to digest as well as being high in vitamins and minerals, and low in saturated fats and kilojoules.

Is Food-Combining Really Necessary?

In the past it was thought that because no one vegetarian source of protein contains all the essential amino acids, it was necessary to carefully combine vegetarian proteins with other foods, such as wholegrains, to provide all the essential amino acids in their correct proportions. This was known as 'food-combining' and, although it sound complicated, it's really very simple... baked beans on toast, or dhal with pitta bread are both ideal examples of food-combining which have evolved into our everyday diet.

However, recent research suggests that as long as there is a healthy mix of legumes, nuts, seeds, wholegrains and vegetables in the diet overall, the body will obtain enough protein for its needs. So, once again, the basic message is to have a balanced diet.

Daily Intake

Our daily requirement of protein is approximately 12–20 per cent of our total kilojoule (calorie) intake, varying according to an individual's size, weight, health and levels of stress and activity. Extra protein is needed during periods of growth: childhood, adolescence, pregnancy and lactation.

Protein Deficiency

It must be noted that Western vegetarians have very little chance of suffering from a protein deficiency. Insufficient protein in the diet can result in physical symptoms such as anaemia, lethargy, muscle weakness and wasting, dry and dull hair, dry skin and poor wound healing.

Protein in Excess

In most Western diets; in fact, there is a much greater chance of consuming an excess of protein than there is of not consuming enough. It is easy to get concerned about protein – this is probably a legacy of the meat-rich diets of the past – but the truth is that most people eat far more protein than they need and if there is too much protein in the diet it is simply converted to body fat.

Carbohydrates

The principal energy source in the diet is carbohydrate. The vital role carbohydrates play cannot be underestimated as they provide fuel for both the muscles and the brain. Carbohydrates occur in the form of starches and sugars from grains and their products (e.g. flour, bread, pasta) as well as potatoes, legumes, fruits and, to a lesser degree, nuts.

What Do They Do?

Carbohydrates break down in the body into glucose and glycogen, both of which are used for energy. The body uses up glucose first and if there is a shortage (for example, during exercise) it converts glycogen, which is stored in the liver, to glucose.

Carbohydrates are generally divided into two categories: simple and complex. A simple carbohydrate is consumed in a form closest to sugar, which takes little breaking down by the body, giving a quick rush of energy, then usually a drop which makes you feel tired or down.

Complex carbohydrates take longer to break down in the body, giving a slower release of sugar and more sustained energy. You probably recognise this phenomenon – you may need a boost, and grab a snack bar or soft drink. Initially you feel better, but soon you will feel worse than you did to start with. Snacking on a complex carbohydrate, such as bread, will give you longer-lasting energy.

Fat or Fiction?

Carbohydrates have gained a bad reputation in the past and have been labelled fattening, mainly because of their bulk. But we now know that this is why they are so valuable – they are filling yet usually contain little or no fat. All carbohydrates have less than half the amount of kilojoules per gram (calories per ounce) than dietary fat and the body converts dietary fat into body fat more efficiently than it does carbohydrates. When you eat carbohydrates, your chance of storing their kilojoules (calories) as fat is 20 per cent lower than if you eat fat.

Some people argue that fresh or dried fruits are sweet and are therefore high in sugar. This may be so, but fruit also contains valuable nutrients and fibre that the body needs. It is processed cane sugar – found in so many snack foods – that should be avoided. It provides no nutritional value and is often accompanied by large quantities of fat.

Daily Intake

It is recommended that about 60 per cent of your daily kilojoules (calories) should come from carbohydrates. (See the table below for further information.)

How Much Carbohydrate Do I Need?

The amount of carbohydrate you need depends on your weight and the amount and level of activity you do. Use this guide to estimate the carbohydrate you should eat each day.

Activity level	Continuous Exercise	Carbohydrate × kg body Weight Per Day	
Light	< 1 hour/day	4.0–4.5 g (0.14–0.16 oz)	Example: A man who weighs
Light–moderate	1 hour/day	4.5–5.5 g (0.16–0.19 oz)	90 kg (198 lb) and does less
Moderate	1–2 hours/day	5.5–6.5 g (0.19–0.23 oz)	than 1 hour's continuous light exercise each day needs
Moderate–heavy	2–4 hours/day	6.5–7.5 g (0.23–0.26 oz)	360–405 grams (12.7–14.3 oz)
Heavy	4–5 hours/day	7.5–8.5 g (0.26–0.30 oz)	of carbohydrate per day.

Value for Vegetarians

In a vegetarian diet, complex carbohydrates give substance to a meal by filling you up and giving a feeling of satisfaction and repleteness. However, take care what you eat with your carbohydrates. It is easy enough to load a jacket potato with butter or sour cream, or dish up a bowl of pasta with a rich creamy sauce. So, in fact, it is the toppings that can make carbohydrates fatty, and not the carbohydrates themselves.

Wherever possible, choose carbohydrates that are the least refined. For instance, use brown rice rather than white, go for wholemeal (whole wheat) instead of white bread, and rolled oats in the form of porridge or muesli at breakfast rather than processed (and often high in added sugar) cereals. These wholegrain products are broken down slowly by the body and therefore give a more sustained release of energy.

Complex carbohydrates are particularly important at breakfast to keep you alert and productive throughout the day, which is why breakfast is traditionally cereal and/or toast. Research has shown that by skipping breakfast, students are less attentive and workers less productive. A hidden danger in missing breakfast is that you'll find you have a craving for sugary snacks later on in the day.

Dietary Fibre

Dietary fibre consists of the cellulose and gums found in fruits, vegetables, grains and legumes – there is no fibre at all in any animal products. Fibre is not a nutrient, but rather a substance that ensures proper digestive functioning. It is a group of food components that is digested (i.e. passes through the stomach and small intestine) but is largely unabsorbed in the process and reaches the large intestine virtually unchanged.

Soluble and Insoluble

Dietary fibre may be classified as soluble or insoluble. Soluble fibre is abundant in legumes, oats, barley and most fruits and vegetables. It has the consistency of a gel and tends to slow digestion time, which has the effect of regulating blood sugar – this is particularly important for diabetics.

Insoluble fibre ('roughage') is found in fruit and vegetable skins and the bran coating around grain kernels. Wholegrains (especially wheat, rice and maize), vegetables and nuts are good sources. Insoluble fibre passes through the digestive tract largely unchanged and speeds up the passage of material through the bowel.

It is important to have a variety of both soluble and insoluble fibre in the diet as each type has a different function: foods that provide both are apples, dried fruits and wholegrains.

Getting Enough Fibre

- Leave the skin on fruit and vegetables, such as apples and potatoes.
- Eat whole pieces of fruit and vegetables rather than consuming them as juices.
- Choose wholegrain products such as breads, breakfast cereals, wholemeal (whole wheat) pasta and brown rice.
- Drink plenty of water during the day to help digest fibre (6–8 glasses is recommended).
- Snack on fresh or dried fruit rather than biscuits (cookies) or cakes.

Benefits

There are many benefits to a high-fibre diet. Both soluble and insoluble fibre readily absorb water, increasing stool bulk and making it softer and easier to expel. However, dietary fibre is not just important for efficient bodily functions and for comfort; it can also help in the prevention of bowel cancer and other bowel disorders, reduce the risk of diabetes, lower cholesterol (which helps prevent heart disease) and reduce the incidence of constipation and haemorrhoids. And, the more unrefined the source of fibre, the more effective it is for improved gastrointestinal health.

Fibre Deficiency

Diets that lack fresh, whole high-fibre foods and instead contain an abundance of refined foods together with animal products (which contain no fibre) have a much higher incidence of diabetes, cardiovascular disease, diverticulitis and bowel and rectal cancer.

Fibre Is Not Boring

There are many misconceptions surrounding the consumption and benefits of fibre. As people turned to 'health foods' in the last few decades, it was thought that large amounts of roughage, such as bran, were needed in the diet. Things were taken to excess and some of the roughage that was consumed was fairly unpalatable – this is probably where health foods and vegetarian diets earned a reputation for being wholesome but boring and unappetising, the worthy fare of the 'the brown rice and lentil brigade'.

With the greater knowledge of the last few years, we now realise just how wrong this perception is. Fibre is present in different forms and in many different foods that we probably already consume on a daily basis. So the addition of 'roughage', such as bran, to other foods is not really necessary, and in fact can be detrimental as it can inhibit the metabolism of other nutrients (for example, iron). Eating a variety of sources of fibre is essential as excessive fibre from a single rather than varied source can inhibit the absorption of other nutrients.

Vegetarians have the edge over meat-eaters when it comes to fibre intake, as the bulk of a vegetarian diet, such as cereals and beans, along with fruit and vegetables, is generally rich in fibre. The main thing to remember is to eat a wide variety of foods, ensuring that a range of fibre is consumed – both soluble and insoluble.

Daily Intake

Nutritionists recommend an intake of 30 grams (1 oz) of fibre per day. A typical serving of grains, fruits or vegetables contains between 1–3 grams (0.04–0.11 oz) of dietary fibre. To get the recommended levels of dietary fibre, you need to consume at least 10 or more servings of fibre-containing foods daily. This should be an easy task for most vegetarians.

Soluble and Insoluble Fibre Foods

Good Sources of Insoluble Fibre
- Cellulose – plant foods, wholegrains, bran, dried fruit, cabbage family
- Lignin – grains, vegetables, fruit
- Hemicellulose – wheat bran, bran cereal

Good Sources of Soluble Fibre
- Pectins – slippery elm, agar, okra, psyllium
- Gums/mucilages – apples, citrus fruit, sugar beet

Fat

Fats are our most concentrated dietary energy source. At 37 kilojoules per gram (250 calories per ounce), they contain more than double the kilojoules of carbohydrates and protein. This is probably what gives this nutrient group its bad reputation, but, of course, no food group is without a specific use to our body and fat is a vital part of our diet.

The Good News

Everyone needs a certain amount of fat in their body to help with growth and development. Fats supply and help absorb the fat-soluble vitamins A, D, E and K, and they are involved in the conversion of beta-carotene to vitamin A. It is not fat itself that is the problem, rather the quantity and type of fat that we eat.

Bad Fats

The fats most commonly linked to health problems are saturated fats. These are usually solid at room temperature and are derived primarily from animal sources – meat and dairy foods – but they are also found in coconut and palm oils.

The body uses saturated fats mainly for storage, insulation and body heat or energy. An excessive consumption of saturated fats in the diet tends to raise blood cholesterol levels and cause fatty deposits in the arteries and blood vessels. This can lead to hardening of the arteries, elevated blood pressure and the formation of blood clots – greatly increasing the risk of heart disease and stroke.

Good Fats

The 'good' fats are unsaturated fats, which are usually liquid at room temperature and are derived from vegetable, nut or seed sources. There are two different types of unsaturated fats – monounsaturated fats and polyunsaturated fats.

Monounsaturated fats are generally considered to be 'good' fats, as they do not increase cholesterol levels. They are found in significant amounts in most nuts, olives and olive oil. Other good vegetarian sources are avocados, chickpeas (garbanzo beans), eggs and sesame seeds.

Polyunsaturated fats are also considered to be 'good'. They are found in nuts, grains and seeds and are usually soft or liquid at room temperature. These fats are the most important group of fats as they are the only source of the two essential fatty acids – omega-3 and omega-6 fats.

It is very important to get an adequate intake of omega-3 and omega-6 because they protect against cardiovascular disease, promote healthy skin and are necessary for normal functioning of the nervous and immune systems. Good vegetarian sources of omega-3 are walnuts and some vegetable oils such as soya, canola, mustard seed and flaxseed. Omega-6 can also be found in vegetable oils such as safflower, sunflower, sesame and soya bean, as well as in evening primrose oil.

Cholesterol

Cholesterol is yet another type of fat. It is a wax-like substance present in all animals but not in plants. It is an essential element for good health and is part of every living cell of the human body. It is not necessary to obtain cholesterol from dietary sources as it is manufactured by the liver and adrenal glands to make stress and sex hormones. It is also required for the nervous system and is essential for the breakdown and elimination of fats. Vegetarian foods that are high in cholesterol include egg yolks and dairy foods. Cholesterol intake should be monitored, but research has shown that it is more important to reduce saturated fat intake, which raises cholesterol, than it is to reduce dietary cholesterol itself.

Tips for Reducing Fat Intake

- Make your meals as filling as possible by choosing foods which take longer to chew and swallow (e.g. whole fruit not fruit juice, whole potatoes, not mashed).
- Don't skip meals or you'll snack later. If you do snack, choose fruits and raw vegetables.
- Spread your food intake over the day to keep you calm and full of energy.
- Become aware of times when you are likely to overeat (stressed, bored, lots of food around) and check your real hunger level before eating.
- Use low-fat plain or skim-milk yoghurt in sauces instead of cream.
- Be careful of hidden fats in snack and processed foods – cakes, biscuits (cookies), french fries, potato chips, corn (nacho) chips, crackers and fast foods. The vegetable oils used in processed foods are the saturated coconut and palm oils.
- Choose polyunsaturated or monounsaturated oils and margarines.

Daily Intake

It is recommended that you try to have no more than 30–40 g (1–1½ oz) of fat per day (30 g for women and small men, 40 g for men and tall women). Nutritionists estimate that most people living on a Western diet consume twice the amount of fat that they actually need. And vegetarians cannot assume that all vegetarian meals are low in fat, particularly if dairy foods are eaten.

Don't Go Hungry – Low-Fat Snack Ideas

- Fresh fruit and vegetables
- Fresh fruit and vegetable juices
- Skim milk and low-fat milk drinks; low-fat yoghurt
- Pasta with tomato-based sauces
- Steamed rice with vegetables
- Baked potato with low-fat yoghurt and cheese
- Wholegrain bread and bread rolls

Finger
Food and
Dips

Greek Cheese Triangles

- **250 g (8¾ oz) Greek feta**
- **180 g (6⅓ oz) Gruyère cheese, grated**
- **2 eggs, lightly beaten**
- **white pepper, to taste**

- **15 sheets filo (phyllo) pastry**
- **½ cup (125 ml/4¼ fl oz) olive oil**
- **125 g (4⅓ oz) butter, melted**

Preheat the oven to moderate 180°C (350°F/Gas 4). Place the feta in a bowl and mash with a fork. Add the Gruyère, egg and pepper, and mix.

Cut the filo (phyllo) sheets in halves widthways. Keep the unused pastry covered with a damp tea towel to prevent it drying out. Place one half of one sheet lengthways on a work surface. Brush with the combined oil and butter, then fold into thirds lengthways. Brush with the oil and butter.

Place 1 tablespoon of the cheese mixture on the corner of the pastry strip. Fold this corner over the filling to edge of pastry to form a triangle. Continue to fold until the filling is enclosed and the end of pastry is reached. Repeat with the remaining pastry and filling.

Place the triangles on a lightly greased baking tray (sheet) and brush them with the oil and butter mixture. Bake for 20 minutes, or until crisp.

Note: You can easily adapt these pastries to suit your personal taste. Try using ricotta instead of Gruyère and adding your favourite fresh herbs, finely chopped. Flat-leaf parsley, mint or thyme are all suitable.

Makes 30

Crispy Cheese and Curry Lentil Balls

- 1 cup (250 g/8¾ oz) red lentils
- 4 spring (green) onions, chopped
- 2 cloves garlic, crushed
- 1 teaspoon ground cumin
- 1 cup (80 g/2¾ oz) fresh breadcrumbs
- 1 cup (125 g/4⅓ oz) grated Cheddar (American) cheese
- 1 large zucchini (courgette), grated
- 1 cup (150 g/5¼ oz) polenta (cornmeal)
- oil, for deep-frying

Place the lentils in a pan and cover with water. Bring to the boil, reduce the heat, cover and simmer for 10 minutes, or until tender. Drain.

Combine half the lentils in a food processor or blender with the spring (green) onion and garlic. Process until smooth. Transfer to a large bowl, then stir in the remaining lentils, cumin, breadcrumbs, cheese and zucchini (courgette) until well combined. Roll level teaspoons of mixture into balls and toss lightly in polenta (cornmeal) to coat.

Fill a heavy-based pan one third full of oil and heat the oil to 180°C (350°F). The oil is ready when a cube of bread dropped into the oil turns golden brown in 15 seconds. Cook small batches of the lentil balls in the oil for 1 minute each batch, or until golden brown, crisp and heated through. Carefully remove with tongs or a slotted spoon and drain on crumpled paper towels. Serve hot.

Makes about 30

Polenta Chillies

- **330 g (11⅔ oz) jar mild, whole chillies**
- **½ cup (60 g/2 oz) grated Cheddar (American) cheese**
- **100 g (3½ oz) soft cream cheese**
- **⅓ cup (40 g/1½ oz) plain (all-purpose) flour**
- **2 eggs, lightly beaten**
- **¾ cup (110 g/3¾ oz) polenta (cornmeal)**
- **¾ cup (75 g/2⅔ oz) dry breadcrumbs**
- **oil, for deep-frying**
- **sour cream, for serving (optional)**

Select twelve large, similar-sized chillies from the jar. Drain well and dry with paper towels. With a sharp knife, cut a slit down the length of one side of each chilli. Remove all the seeds and membrane. Combine the grated Cheddar (American) and cream cheeses; fill each chilli with the cheese mixture.

Place the flour onto a large plate and beaten eggs in a small bowl. Combine the polenta (cornmeal) and breadcrumbs in a small plastic bag; transfer to a large plate. Roll each chilli in flour; shake off excess; dip in egg and roll in crumb mixture to coat chillies thoroughly. Refrigerate for 1 hour. Re-dip in egg and re-roll in the breadcrumbs. Return to the refrigerator for 1 hour.

Heat the oil in a medium pan. Test the oil by frying a small cube of bread; if it browns in 30 seconds, the oil is ready. Deep-fry the prepared chillies in small batches until golden; drain on paper towels.

Note: Delicious served with sour cream and your favourite salsa.

Serves 6

Sweet Potato and Lentil Pastry Pouches

- 2 tablespoons olive oil
- 1 large leek, finely chopped
- 2 cloves garlic, crushed
- 125 g (4⅓ oz) button mushrooms, roughly chopped
- 2 teaspoons ground cumin
- 2 teaspoons ground coriander
- ½ cup (95 g/3⅓ oz) brown or green lentils
- ½ cup (125 g/4⅓ oz) red lentils
- 2 cups (500 ml/17 fl oz) vegetable stock (broth)
- 300 g (10½ oz) sweet potato (yam), diced
- 4 tablespoons finely chopped fresh coriander (cilantro) leaves
- 8 sheets ready-rolled puff pastry
- 1 egg, lightly beaten
- ½ leek, extra, cut into thin strips
- 200 g (7 oz) plain yoghurt
- 2 tablespoons grated Lebanese cucumber
- ½ teaspoon soft brown sugar

Preheat the oven to moderately hot 200°C (400°F/Gas 6). Heat the oil in a saucepan over medium heat and cook the leek for 2–3 minutes, or until soft. Add the garlic, mushrooms, cumin and ground coriander and cook for 1 minute, or until fragrant.

Add the combined lentils and stock (broth) and bring to the boil. Reduce the heat and simmer for 20–25 minutes, or until the lentils are cooked through, stirring occasionally. Add the sweet potato (yam) in the last 5 minutes.

Transfer to a bowl and stir in the coriander (cilantro). Season to taste. Cool.

Cut the pastry sheets into four even squares. Place 1½ tablespoons of filling into the centre of each square and bring the edges together to form a pouch. Pinch together, then tie each pouch with string. Lightly brush with egg and place on lined baking trays (sheets). Bake for 20–25 minutes, or until the pastry is puffed and golden.

Soak the leek strips in boiling water for 30 seconds. Remove the string and re-tie with a piece of blanched leek. Put the yoghurt, cucumber and sugar in a bowl and mix together well. Serve with the pastry pouches.

Makes 32

Salt and Pepper Tofu Puffs

- 2 × 190 g (6⅔ oz) packets fried tofu puffs
- 2 cups (250 g/8¾ oz) cornflour (cornstarch)
- 2 tablespoons salt
- 1 tablespoon ground white pepper
- 2 teaspoons caster (berry) sugar
- 4 egg whites, lightly beaten
- oil, for deep-frying (see Note)
- ½ cup (125 ml/4¼ fl oz) sweet chilli sauce (jalapeno jelly)
- 2 tablespoons lemon juice
- lemon wedges, to serve

Cut the tofu puffs in half and pat dry with paper towels.

Mix the cornflour (cornstarch), salt, pepper and caster (berry) sugar in a large bowl.

Dip the tofu into the egg white in batches, then toss in the cornflour (cornstarch) mixture, shaking off any excess.

Fill a deep heavy-based saucepan or wok one-third full of oil and heat until a cube of bread dropped into the oil browns in 15 seconds. Cook the tofu in batches for 1–2 minutes, or until crisp. Drain well on paper towels.

Place the sweet chilli sauce (jalapeno jelly) and lemon juice in a bowl and mix together well. Serve immediately with the tofu puffs and lemon wedges.

Note: It is best to use a good-quality peanut oil to deep-fry the tofu puffs – the flavour will be slightly nutty.

Serves 4–6

Mini Croissants

- **40 g (1½ oz) butter**
- **3 onions, finely chopped**
- **12 pitted black (ripe) olives, finely sliced**

- **2 tablespoons chopped fresh parsley**
- **3 sheets frozen puff pastry, thawed**
- **1 egg, beaten**

Melt the butter in a frying pan and cook the onions over medium-low heat for 20 minutes, or until golden and sweet tasting. Remove from the heat and stir in the olives, parsley, salt and cracked black pepper, to taste. Allow to cool.

Cut each sheet of pastry in half, then each half into 5 triangles with a base (shortest side) of 8 cm (3 inches). You will have a couple of odd shapes left at each end. Place a little onion mixture at the base of each triangle and roll up towards the point, enclosing the filling. Curl the ends around to form a croissant shape.

Place the croissants on a lightly greased baking tray (sheet) and refrigerate for about 30 minutes. Preheat the oven to moderately hot 200°C (400°F/Gas 6). Brush each croissant with beaten egg, then bake for 20 minutes, or until puffed and golden.

In Advance: Croissants can be prepared up to 6 hours ahead. Bake just before serving.

Makes 30

Nori Cones

- 2 cups (440 g/15½ oz) Japanese short-grain rice
- 2 tablespoons rice vinegar
- 2 tablespoons caster (berry/superfine) sugar
- 10 g (⅓ oz) sliced dried shiitake mushrooms
- 250 g (8¾ oz) choy sum (Chinese flowering cabbage), shredded and blanched
- 1 tablespoon pickled ginger, shredded
- 1 tablespoon sesame seeds, toasted
- 1 tablespoon kecap manis (Indonesian soy sauce)
- ½ teaspoon wasabi paste
- 2 teaspoons mirin
- 1 tablespoon Shoyu (Japanese soy sauce)
- 10 sheets of roasted nori
- ready-made sushi dipping sauce, to serve

Wash the rice under cold running water until the water runs clear, then drain. Drain for an hour. Put in a saucepan with 2 cups (500 ml/17 fl oz) water. Bring to the boil, then reduce the heat and simmer for 10 minutes. Remove from the heat, cover and stand for 15 minutes.

To make the sushi dressing, put the vinegar, sugar, ½ teaspoon salt and 2 tablespoons water in a saucepan and stir over low heat until the sugar and salt have dissolved.

Spread the rice over the base of a non-metallic dish or bowl, pour the sushi dressing over the top and use a rice paddle or spatula to mix the dressing through the rice, separating the grains as you do so. Fan the rice until it cools.

Soak the mushrooms in boiling water for 5 minutes. Drain, squeeze dry and roughly chop.

Put the rice in a bowl and stir in the choy sum, mushrooms, ginger, sesame seeds and the combined kecap manis, wasabi, mirin and Shoyu.

Lay the nori sheets shiny-side down and cut each one into four squares. Brush the joining edge with water and put 1 tablespoon of the mixture in the centre of the square. Roll up on the diagonal to form a cone and top up with 2 teaspoons of filling. Repeat. Serve with the dipping sauce.

Makes 40

Sigara Boregi

- **500 g (1 lb 2 oz) English (common) spinach**
- **1 tablespoon olive oil**
- **4 cloves garlic, crushed**
- **200 g (7 oz) French shallots, finely chopped**
- **½ cup (75 g/2⅔ oz) crumbled feta cheese**
- **1 egg, lightly beaten**
- **3 tablespoons chopped fresh flat-leaf parsley**
- **¼ teaspoon finely grated lemon rind**
- **¼ teaspoon paprika**
- **pinch of nutmeg**
- **6 sheets filo (phyllo) pastry**
- **125 g (4⅓ oz) butter, melted**
- **light olive oil, for deep-frying**

Wash the spinach, leaving a substantial amount of water on the leaves. Place in a large saucepan, cover and briefly cook over low heat until just wilted. Tip the spinach into a colander and press out most of the excess liquid with a wooden spoon. When cool, squeeze dry.

Heat the olive oil in a frying pan, add the garlic and shallots and cook for 2 minutes, or until soft but not browned. Transfer to a bowl and add the crumbled feta cheese, egg, parsley, spinach and lemon rind. Season with the paprika, nutmeg and salt and pepper, and mix well.

Remove a sheet of filo (phyllo) and cover the rest with a damp tea towel to prevent them drying out. Brush the sheet with melted butter, then fold it in half lengthways. It should measure about 33 × 13 cm (13 × 5 inches). Cut it in half widthways. Brush with butter, place about 1 heaped tablespoon of filling at one end of each and spread it to within 1 cm (½ inch) of each side. Fold the sides over to cover the ends of the filling, continuing the folds right up the length of the pastry. Brush with melted butter, then roll up tightly. Brush the outside with butter and seal well. Cover with a damp tea towel while you prepare the rest.

Heat the light olive oil in a deep frying pan to 180°C (350°F), or until a cube of bread browns in 15 seconds. Deep-fry in small batches until golden. Serve warm or at room temperature.

Makes 12

Mini Eggs Florentine

- **8 slices white bread**
- **1–2 tablespoons olive oil**
- **12 quail eggs**
- **2 teaspoons lemon juice**
- **85 g (3 oz) butter, melted, cooled**
- **2 teaspoons finely chopped fresh basil**
- **20 g (⅔ oz) butter, extra**
- **50 g (1¾ oz) baby English (common) spinach leaves**

Preheat the oven to moderate 180°C (350°F/Gas 4). Cut 24 rounds from the bread with a 4 cm (1½ inch) cutter. Brush both sides of the rounds with the oil and bake for 10–15 minutes, or until golden brown.

Add the quail eggs to a small pan of cold water, bring to the boil, stirring gently (to centre the yolk) and simmer for 4 minutes. Drain, then soak in cold water until cool. Peel, then cut in half, remove the yolks and reserve the whites.

Process the quail egg yolks and lemon juice together in a food processor for 10 seconds. With the motor running, add the cooled melted butter in a thin stream. Add the chopped basil and process until combined.

Melt the extra butter in a pan, add the spinach leaves and toss until just wilted. Place a little on each bread round, top each with half a quail egg white and fill the cavity with basil mixture.

Makes 24

Dolmades

- **250 g (8¾ oz) vine leaves in brine**
- **¾ cup (185 ml/6½ fl oz) olive oil**
- **2 large onions, finely chopped**
- **¾ cup (165 g/5¾ oz) short-grain rice**
- **6 spring (green) onions, chopped**
- **4 tablespoons coarsely chopped fresh dill (dill weed)**
- **1 tablespoon finely chopped fresh mint**
- **salt and freshly ground black pepper**
- **1 tablespoon lemon juice**

Rinse the vine leaves in cold water and soak in warm water for 1 hour; drain. Heat ½ cup (125 ml/4¼ fl oz) of the oil in a small heavy-based pan. Add the onions; cook over low heat for 5 minutes. Remove from the heat; set aside, covered, for 5 minutes. Add the rice, spring (green) onions, herbs, salt and pepper to the pan and mix thoroughly.

Lay out a vine leaf, vein-side up. Place 3 teaspoons of the rice mixture onto the centre of the leaf. Fold the sides over the mixture and then roll towards the tip of the vine leaf. Repeat the process with the remaining filling and leaves.

Place five vine leaves over the base of a medium heavy-based pan. Arrange the rolled dolmades in the pan in two layers and drizzle with the remaining oil. Place a heatproof plate on top of the dolmades and cover the dolmades with water. Bring to the boil, reduce the heat and simmer, covered, for 45 minutes. Remove the plate, drain the dolmades and drizzle with lemon juice. Serve warm or cold.

Note: Fresh vine leaves can be used in this recipe if they are available. Use small leaves, blanched briefly in boiling water.

Makes about 35

Corn and Potato Fritters

- 2 large potatoes
- 260 g (9 oz) can corn
  kernels, drained
- 4 eggs, lightly beaten
- 6 spring (green) onions, chopped
- ½ cup (50 g/1¾ oz) dry breadcrumbs
- 1 teaspoon garam masala
- 3 tablespoons oil

Dipping Sauce
- ⅔ cup (160 g/5⅔ oz) natural yoghurt
- 2 tablespoons chopped fresh
  mint leaves
- 2 teaspoons sweet chilli sauce
  (jalapeno jelly)

Peel and coarsely grate the potatoes. Drain on paper towel and squeeze out the excess moisture. Combine in a bowl with the corn, eggs, spring (green) onion, breadcrumbs and garam masala. Mix well.

Heat 2 tablespoons of the oil in a heavy-based frying pan. Cook heaped tablespoons of mixture over medium heat for 2 minutes each side, or until golden. Drain on crumpled paper towel and keep warm. Repeat until all the mixture is used, adding extra oil to the pan if necessary.

For the dipping sauce, combine all the ingredients in a bowl.

Makes about 40

Fresh Vegetable Spring Rolls

- 1 cup (155 g/5½ oz) grated carrot
- 100 g (3½ oz) snow peas (mange tout), sliced
- 1 cup (90 g/3¼ oz) bean sprouts, trimmed
- 30 g (1 oz) rice vermicelli, soaked, drained and cooled
- 2 tablespoons chopped fresh coriander (cilantro)
- 2 tablespoons chopped fresh mint
- ¼ cup (40 g/1½ oz) chopped, dry-roasted peanuts
- 12 rice paper rounds

Dipping Sauce
- 1 tablespoon caster (berry) sugar
- ¼ cup (60 ml/2 fl oz) warm water
- 1 clove garlic, crushed
- ¼ cup (60 ml/2 fl oz) lime juice
- 1 small fresh chilli, finely sliced
- 1 tablespoon chopped fresh coriander (cilantro)

Combine the carrot, snow peas (mange tout) and bean sprouts in a large bowl. Chop the cooked vermicelli roughly and add to the vegetables with the coriander (cilantro), mint and peanuts.

Dip each rice paper round into a bowl of warm water for about 1 minute, until softened. Carefully remove from the water and lay on a clean, flat surface. Place about 2 level tablespoons of vegetable mixture on the lower half of the rice paper; roll up gently but firmly into a spring roll shape. (The moist rice paper will adhere to itself on rolling.) Serve with Dipping Sauce.

To make Dipping Sauce: Place the sugar in a bowl; add water and stir until dissolved. Add the remaining ingredients and stir.

Makes 12

Puris with Relish

- ¾ cup (90 g/3¼ oz) plain (all-purpose) flour
- ¾ cup (110 g/3¾ oz) wholemeal (whole wheat) flour
- 1 teaspoon salt
- 1 tablespoon cracked black pepper
- 3 tablespoons oil or ghee
- 1 teaspoon kalonji (nigella) seeds
- oil, for deep-frying

Coriander Relish
- 60 g (2 oz) fresh coriander (cilantro) leaves
- 20 g (⅔ oz) fresh mint leaves
- ½ small onion
- 1 green chilli
- 2 tablespoons lemon juice

Sift the flours and salt and pepper into a large bowl. Add the oil or ghee and rub it into the flour with your fingertips until it resembles fine breadcrumbs. Stir in the kalonji (nigella) seeds. Make a well, add 3–4 tablespoons hot water and mix with a flat-bladed knife. It should be rough but hold together. Form into a ball.

Divide the dough into 4 and then each portion into 8 pieces, making 32 altogether. On a lightly floured surface, roll one piece at a time into a 6 cm (2½ inch) round. Keep the rest covered with a damp tea towel or plastic wrap. Don't worry about the cracked edges.

Heat 2.5 cm (1 inch) of oil in a wok or large heavy-based frying pan to 180°C (350°F). The oil is ready when a cube of bread dropped into the oil turns golden brown in 15 seconds. Fry 3 or 4 puris at a time, turning them halfway through. They will only take a few seconds to turn golden on each side. Remove from the oil and drain on crumpled paper towel while you fry the remainder.

For the coriander relish, process all the relish ingredients together in a food processor until smooth. Serve with the puris.

Makes 32

Vegetarian Sticky Rice Pockets

- 20 dried bamboo leaves (see Note)
- ½ cup (125 ml/4¼ fl oz) oil
- 6 spring (green) onions, chopped
- 400 g (14 oz) eggplant (aubergine), cut into 1 cm (½ inch) cubes
- ½ cup (90 g/3¼ oz) drained water chestnuts, chopped
- 1 tablespoon mushroom soy sauce
- 3 small red chillies, seeded and finely chopped
- 2 teaspoons sugar
- 3 tablespoons chopped coriander (cilantro)
- 4 cups (800 g/1 lb 12 oz) white glutinous rice, washed and well drained
- 2 tablespoons soy sauce
- 1 teaspoon ground white pepper

Soak the bamboo leaves in boiling water for 10 minutes, or until soft. Drain.

Heat half the oil in a wok and swirl to coat the side. Cook the spring (green) onion and eggplant (aubergine) over high heat for 4–5 minutes, or until golden. Stir in the water chestnuts, soy sauce, chilli, sugar and coriander (cilantro). Allow to cool.

Bring 3 cups (750 ml/26 fl oz) water to a simmer. Heat the remaining oil in a saucepan, add the rice and stir for 2 minutes, or until coated. Stir in ½ cup (125 ml/4¼ fl oz) of the hot water over low heat until it is all absorbed. Repeat until all the water has been added; this should take about 20 minutes. Add the soy sauce and season with white pepper.

Fold one end of a bamboo leaf on the diagonal to form a cone. Hold securely in one hand and spoon in 2 tablespoons of rice. Make an indent in the rice, add 1 tablespoon of the eggplant (aubergine) filling, then top with another tablespoon of rice. Fold the other end of the bamboo leaf over to enclose the filling, then secure with a toothpick. Tie tightly with kitchen string. Repeat with the remaining bamboo leaves, rice and filling.

Put the rice parcels in a single layer inside a double bamboo steamer. Cover with a lid and sit over a wok half filled with simmering water. Steam for 1½ hours, or until the rice is tender, adding more boiling water to the wok as needed. Serve hot.

Note: Bamboo leaves are used to wrap food prior to cooking, but they are not eaten.

Makes 20

Potato Pies

- **6 Roma tomatoes, halved lengthways**
- **3 tablespoons olive oil**
- **50 g (1¾ oz) butter**
- **3 cloves garlic, crushed**
- **800 g (1 lb 12 oz) potatoes, unpeeled and sliced**

- **500 g (1 lb 2 oz) English (common) spinach, trimmed**
- **12 sheets filo (phyllo) pastry**
- **100 g (3½ oz) butter, melted**
- **2 tablespoons sesame seeds**

Preheat the oven to 200°C (400°F/Gas 6). Place the tomato halves, cut-side-up, on a baking tray (sheet), drizzle with 1 tablespoon of the oil and sprinkle with a little salt. Bake for 40 minutes.

Heat the butter and remaining oil in a large non-stick pan and cook the garlic and potato, tossing occasionally, for 10 minutes, or until the potato is tender. Set aside on paper towels. Cook the spinach in the pan for 1–2 minutes, or until wilted. Cool and then squeeze out any excess moisture.

Reduce the oven to 180°C (350°F/Gas 4). Work with one sheet of pastry at a time and cover the rest with a damp tea towel. Brush the pastry with melted butter and place another sheet on top. Brush with butter and repeat with another two layers. Cut in half widthways. Place a few potato slices at one end of each half, leaving a wide border on each side. Top with two tomato pieces and some spinach.

Fold in the sides of the pastry and roll up. Place on a lightly greased baking tray (sheet), brush with melted butter and sprinkle with sesame seeds. Use the remaining filo (phyllo) and filling to make another five parcels. Bake for 25–30 minutes, or until lightly golden.

Makes 6

Spicy Corn Puffs

- 2 corn cobs
- 3 tablespoons chopped fresh coriander (cilantro) leaves
- 6 spring (green) onions, finely chopped
- 1 small fresh red chilli, seeded and finely chopped
- 1 large egg
- 2 teaspoons ground cumin
- ½ teaspoon ground coriander
- 1 cup (125 g/4⅓ oz) plain (all-purpose) flour
- oil, for deep-frying
- sweet chilli sauce (jalapeno jelly), to serve

Cut down the side of the corn cobs with a very sharp knife to release the kernels. Roughly chop the kernels, then place them in a large bowl. Holding the cobs over the bowl, scrape down the sides of the cobs with a knife to release all of the corn juice from the cob.

Add the fresh coriander (cilantro), spring (green) onion, chilli, egg, cumin, ground coriander, 1 teaspoon salt and freshly cracked black pepper to taste to the bowl, and stir well. Add the flour and mix well. The texture of the batter will vary depending on how much juice is released from the corn. If the mixture is too dry, add 1 tablespoon water, but no more than that as the batter should be quite thick and dry. Stand for 10 minutes.

Fill a large heavy-based saucepan or deep-fryer one-third full of oil and heat to 180°C (350°F), or until a cube of bread dropped in the oil browns in 15 seconds. Drop slightly heaped teaspoons of the corn batter into the oil and cook for about 1½ minutes, or until puffed and golden. Drain on crumpled paper towels and serve immediately with a bowl of the sweet chilli sauce (jalapeno jelly) to dip the puffs into.

Note: The batter should be prepared just before serving, or the corn puffs may fall apart when cooked.

Makes about 36

Herb Pepper Lavash with Blue Cheese Dip

- 4 sheets lavash bread
- 90 g (3¼ oz) butter, melted
- 1 small jar herb pepper seasoning
- 1 tablespoon finely chopped fresh chives

Blue Cheese Dip
- 250 g (8¾ oz) blue vein cheese, chopped

- 60 g (2 oz) butter, softened
- 1 tablespoon sweet white wine
- 2 teaspoons chopped fresh mint
- 1 teaspoon chopped fresh rosemary
- 2 teaspoons chopped fresh oregano
- ⅓ cup (90 g/3¼ oz) crème fraîche or sour cream
- salt and pepper

Preheat the oven to moderate 180°C (350°F/Gas 4). Brush each sheet of lavash bread with butter. Sprinkle with herb pepper seasoning and chives.

Cut each sheet into twenty squares. Cut each piece in half to make triangles. Place triangles on baking trays (sheets). Bake for 5 minutes or until crisp. Remove and cool. Serve with Blue Cheese Dip.

To make Blue Cheese Dip: Using electric beaters, beat the cheese and butter in a small bowl until smooth and creamy. Add the wine, mint, rosemary and oregano; mix well. Fold through the crème fraîche or sour cream. Season to taste. Spoon the mixture into serving dishes.

Note: Crisps may be stored in an airtight container for up to 2 weeks. For a variation, combine 2 cloves crushed garlic with melted butter before brushing over lavash bread. Sprinkle with grated Parmesan cheese and chives, cut into squares and triangles and bake.

Serves 10

Potato Noodle Nibbles

- **450 g (15¾ oz) floury potatoes, peeled and chopped**
- **40 g (1½ oz) butter, softened**
- **2 tablespoons grated Parmesan or Pecorino cheese**
- **100 g (3½ oz) besan (chickpea or gram flour)**
- **2 teaspoons ground cumin**
- **2 teaspoons garam masala**
- **1 teaspoon ground coriander**
- **1 teaspoon chilli powder**
- **1 teaspoon cayenne (red) pepper**
- **1½ teaspoons ground turmeric**
- **oil, for deep-frying**

Boil or steam the potato until tender. Drain and cool for 15–20 minutes, then mash with the butter and cheese. Add the besan, cumin, garam masala, coriander, chilli powder, cayenne (red) pepper, turmeric and ¾ teaspoon of salt and mix with a wooden spoon until a soft, light dough forms. Turn out and knead lightly 10–12 times, until quite smooth.

Fill a deep heavy-based pan one third full of oil and heat to 180°C (350°F). Test the temperature by dropping a small ball of dough into the oil. The oil is ready if the dough rises immediately to the surface.

Using a piping bag with a 1 cm (½ inch) star nozzle, pipe short lengths of dough into the oil, cutting the dough off with a knife. Cook in manageable batches. They will rise to the surface and turn golden quickly. Remove with a slotted spoon and drain on crumpled paper towels. Serve the nibbles within 2 hours of cooking.

Serves 6

Beetroot Hummus

- **250 g (8¾ oz) dried chickpeas (garbanzo beans)**
- **1 large onion, chopped**
- **500 g (1 lb 2 oz) beetroot (beets)**
- **½ cup (125 ml/4¼ fl oz) tahini (sesame seed paste)**

- **3 cloves garlic, crushed**
- **¼ cup (60 ml/2 fl oz) lemon juice**
- **1 tablespoon ground cumin**
- **¼ cup (60 ml/2 fl oz) olive oil**

Put the chickpeas (garbanzo beans) in a large bowl, cover with cold water and soak overnight. Drain.

Place the chickpeas (garbanzo beans) and onion in a large heavy-based pan, cover with water and bring to the boil. Cook for 1 hour or until chickpeas are very soft. Drain, reserving 1 cup of cooking liquid; allow to cool.

Cook the beetroot (beets) in a large pan of boiling water until tender. Drain and allow to cool slightly before removing skins.

Chop the beetroot (beets) and place in a food processor, in batches if necessary. Add the chickpea (bean) and onion mixture, tahini, garlic, lemon juice and cumin; process until smooth. Slowly add reserved cooking liquid and olive oil while the machine is running. Process until mixture is thoroughly combined. Drizzle with a little olive oil and serve with Lebanese bread.

Serves 8

White Bean, Chickpea and Herb Dip

- **180 g (6⅓ oz) dried cannellini (haricot) beans**
- **100 g (3½ oz) dried chickpeas (garbanzo beans)**
- **3 slices white bread**
- **3 tablespoons milk**
- **2 spring (green) onions, finely chopped**
- **4 tablespoons thick plain yoghurt**
- **1 tablespoon lemon juice**
- **2 teaspoons finely grated lemon rind**
- **1 tablespoon chopped fresh parsley**
- **2 teaspoons chopped fresh oregano**
- **2 tablespoons olive oil**

Soak the beans and chickpeas in cold water overnight. Rinse well and transfer to a pan. Cover with cold water and bring to the boil. Reduce the heat and simmer for 1 hour, or until very tender, adding more water if needed. Skim any froth from the surface. Drain well, cool and mash.

Remove the crusts from the bread, place in a bowl and drizzle with the milk. Leave for 2 minutes, then mash with your fingertips until very soft. Mix together with the beans.

Add the spring (green) onion, yoghurt, lemon juice, rind, fresh herbs and oil and season well. Mix together well and serve at room temperature.

Serves 12

Tangy Tomato Dip with Pita Crisps

- 2 tablespoons oil
- 1 onion, chopped
- 2 cloves garlic, crushed
- 2 small red chillies, chopped
- 425 g (15 oz) canned tomatoes, crushed
- 2 pimentos (roasted red capsicum/ pepper), chopped
- 2 tablespoons lemon juice
- 4 tablespoons chopped fresh parsley
- 3 pita bread pockets
- 3 tablespoons sour cream

Preheat the oven to moderate 180°C (350°F/Gas 4). Heat oil in a medium pan and add onion, garlic and chillies. Stir over medium heat for 2 minutes or until onion is tender.

Add the tomatoes, pimentos and lemon juice; bring to the boil. Reduce heat to low; simmer, uncovered, for 5 minutes or until reduced and thickened. Remove from heat; stir in parsley.

Split the pita pockets in half and cut each half into eight wedges; brush with a little oil. Place in a single layer on an oven tray (sheet) and bake for 10 minutes or until golden and crisp. Spoon the tomato dip into a bowl and top with sour cream. Serve warm or cold, as a dip for pita crisps.

Makes 2 cups

Tzatziki

- **2 Lebanese cucumbers (about 300 g/10½ oz)**
- **400 g (14 oz) Greek-style natural yoghurt**
- **4 cloves garlic, crushed**
- **3 tablespoons finely chopped fresh mint**
- **1 tablespoon lemon juice**
- **chopped fresh mint, extra, to garnish**

Cut the cucumbers in half lengthways, scoop out the seeds with a teaspoon and discard. Leave the skin on and coarsely grate the cucumber into a small colander. Sprinkle with a little salt and leave to stand over a large bowl for 15 minutes to drain off any bitter juices.

Meanwhile, stir together the yoghurt, garlic, mint and lemon juice in a bowl.

Rinse the cucumber under cold water then, taking small handfuls, squeeze out any excess moisture. Combine the cucumber with the yoghurt mixture and season, to taste. Serve immediately or refrigerate until ready to serve. Garnish with mint. Can be served as a dip with flatbread or as a sauce.

Makes 2 cups

Baba Ghannouj

- **2 large eggplants (aubergines)**
- **3 cloves garlic, crushed**
- **½ teaspoon ground cumin**
- **⅓ cup (80 ml/2¾ fl oz) lemon juice**
- **2 tablespoons tahini**
- **pinch of cayenne (red) pepper**
- **1½ tablespoons olive oil**
- **1 tablespoon chopped fresh flat-leaf parsley**
- **black (ripe) olives, to garnish**

Preheat the oven to moderately hot 200°C (400°F/Gas 6). Prick the eggplants (aubergines) several times with a fork, then cook over an open flame for about 5 minutes, until the skin is black and blistered. Transfer to a baking tin and bake for 40–45 minutes, or until the eggplants (aubergines) are very soft and wrinkled. Place in a colander over a bowl to drain off any bitter juices, leaving them for 30 minutes, or until cool.

Carefully peel the skin from the eggplants (aubergines), chop the flesh and put it in a food processor with the garlic, cumin, lemon juice, tahini, cayenne (red) pepper and olive oil. Process until smooth and creamy. Alternatively, use a potato masher or fork. Season with salt and stir in the parsley. Spread in a flat bowl or on a plate and garnish with the olives. Serve with flatbread or pide for dipping.

Note: If you prefer, you can bake the eggplant (aubergine) in a baking tin in a moderately hot (200°C/400°F/Gas 6) oven for 1 hour, or until very soft.

Makes 1¾ cups

Soups

Roast Pumpkin Soup

- **1.25 kg (2 lb 12 oz) pumpkin, peeled and cut into chunks**
- **2 tablespoons olive oil**
- **1 large onion, chopped**
- **2 teaspoons ground cumin**
- **1 large carrot, chopped**
- **1 celery stick, chopped**
- **1 litre vegetable stock (broth)**
- **sour cream, to serve**
- **finely chopped fresh parsley, to serve**
- **ground nutmeg, to serve**

Preheat the oven to moderate 180°C (350°F/Gas 4). Place the pumpkin chunks on a greased baking tray (sheet) and lightly brush with half the olive oil. Bake for 25 minutes, or until the pumpkin is softened and slightly browned around the edges.

Heat the remaining oil in a large saucepan. Cook the onion and cumin for 2 minutes, then add the carrot and celery and cook for 3 minutes more, stirring frequently. Add the roasted pumpkin and stock (broth). Bring to the boil, then reduce the heat and simmer for 20 minutes.

Allow to cool a little then puree in batches in a blender or food processor. Return the soup to the pan and gently reheat without boiling. Season to taste with salt and cracked black pepper. Top with sour cream and sprinkle with chopped parsley and ground nutmeg before serving.

Note: Butternut pumpkin (squash) is often used in soups as it has a sweeter flavour than other varieties.

Hint: If the soup is too thick, thin it down with a little stock (broth).

Serves 6

Leek and Potato Soup

- cooking oil spray
- 2 leeks, white part only, sliced
- 3 cloves garlic, crushed
- 1 teaspoon ground cumin

- 1 kg (2 lb 3 oz) potatoes, chopped
- 5 cups (1.25 litres/1.3 US qt/1.1 UK qt) vegetable stock (broth)
- ½ cup (125 ml/4¼ fl oz) skim milk

Lightly spray a non-stick frying pan with oil. Add the leek, garlic and 1 tablespoon water to prevent sticking, then cook over low heat, stirring frequently, for 25 minutes, or until the leek turns golden. Add the cumin and cook for 2 minutes.

Put the potato in a large pan with the leek mixture and stock (broth), bring to the boil, reduce the heat and simmer for 10–15 minutes, or until tender. Puree in a processor or blender until smooth. Return to the pan.

Stir in the milk, season and heat through before serving.

Serves 4

Corn Chowder

- 90 g (3¼ oz) butter
- 2 large onions, finely chopped
- 1 clove garlic, crushed
- 2 teaspoons cumin seeds
- 4 cups (1 litre 1.1 US qt/1.75 UK pt) vegetable stock (broth)
- 2 medium potatoes, peeled and chopped
- 1 cup (250 g/8¾ oz) canned creamed-style corn
- 2 cups (400 g/14 oz) fresh corn kernels
- 3 tablespoons chopped fresh parsley
- 1 cup (125 g/4⅓ oz) grated Cheddar (American) cheese
- salt and freshly ground black pepper
- 3 tablespoons cream (optional)
- 2 tablespoons chopped fresh chives, to garnish

Heat the butter in large heavy-based pan. Add the onions and cook over medium-high heat for 5 minutes or until golden. Add garlic and cumin seeds, cook 1 minute, stirring constantly. Add vegetable stock (broth), bring to boil. Add potatoes and reduce heat. Simmer, uncovered, 10 minutes.

Add the creamed corn, corn kernels and parsley. Bring to the boil, reduce heat, simmer for 10 minutes. Stir through the cheese, salt and pepper, to taste, and cream. Heat gently until the cheese melts. Serve immediately, sprinkled with chopped chives.

Serves 8

Chunky Vegetable Soup

- 50 g (1¾ oz) butter
- 1 leek, chopped
- 1 celery stick, chopped
- 1 large carrot, chopped
- 1 large potato, chopped
- 1 parsnip, peeled and chopped
- 1 swede (yellow turnip/rutabaga) or turnip, peeled and chopped
- 225 g (8 oz) sweet potato (yam), chopped
- ½ cup (115 g/4 oz) soup mix (see Note)
- 2 litres (2.1 US qt/1.75 UK qt) vegetable stock (broth) or water
- 1 cup (155 g/5½ oz) frozen peas
- 125 g (4⅓ oz) green beans, chopped
- ¼ cup (15 g/½ oz) chopped fresh mint
- ⅓ cup (20 g/⅔ oz) chopped fresh parsley

Heat the butter in a large heavy-based pan, and cook the leek, celery, carrot, potato, parsnip, swede (yellow turnip/rutabaga) or turnip and sweet potato (yam), stirring, for 5 minutes.

Add the soup mix and stock (broth) or water. Bring slowly to the boil, then reduce the heat and simmer, covered, for 1¼ hours, or until the soup mix has softened.

Add the peas and beans and cook for a further 10 minutes, or until tender. Stir in the chopped mint and parsley. Season to taste with salt and cracked black pepper. Serve hot. Delicious with crusty bread.

Note: Soup mix is a combination of dried beans and pulses.

Serves 6

Italian Tomato Bread Soup

- **750 g (1 lb 10 oz) vine-ripened tomatoes**
- **1 loaf (450 g/15¾ oz) day-old crusty Italian bread**
- **1 tablespoon olive oil**
- **3 cloves garlic, crushed**
- **1 tablespoon tomato paste (tomato puree)**
- **1.25 litres (1.3 US qt/1.1 UK qt) hot vegetable stock (broth) or water**
- **⅓ cup (20 g/⅔ oz) torn fresh basil leaves**
- **2–3 tablespoons extra virgin olive oil**
- **extra virgin olive oil, extra, for serving**

Score a cross in the base of each tomato. Place the tomatoes in a bowl of boiling water for 10 seconds, then plunge into cold water and peel the skin away from the cross. Cut the tomatoes in half and scoop out the seeds with a teaspoon. Roughly chop the tomato flesh.

Discard most of the crust from the bread and tear the bread into 3 cm (1¼ inch) pieces.

Heat the oil in a large saucepan. Add the garlic, tomato and tomato paste (tomato puree), then reduce the heat and simmer, stirring occasionally, for 10–15 minutes, or until reduced. Add the stock (broth) and bring to the boil, stirring for 2–3 minutes. Reduce the heat to medium, add the bread pieces and cook, stirring, for 5 minutes, or until the bread softens and absorbs most of the liquid. Add more stock (broth) or water if the soup is too thick. Remove the saucepan from the heat.

Stir in the basil leaves and extra virgin olive oil, and leave for 5 minutes so the flavours have time to develop. Serve drizzled with a little extra virgin olive oil.

Serves 4

Yoghurt Soup

- **1.5 litres (1.6 US qt/1.3 UK qt) vegetable stock (broth)**
- **⅓ cup (75 g/2⅔ oz) short-grain white rice**
- **80 g (2¾ oz) butter**
- **50 g (1¾ oz) plain (all-purpose) flour**
- **250 g (8¾ oz) natural yoghurt**
- **1 egg yolk**
- **1 tablespoon finely sliced fresh mint**
- **¼ teaspoon cayenne (red) pepper**

Put the stock (broth) and rice in a saucepan and bring to the boil over high heat. Reduce the heat to medium-low and simmer for 10 minutes, then remove from the heat and set aside.

In another saucepan, melt 60 g (2 oz) of the butter over low heat. Stir in the flour and cook for 2–3 minutes, or until pale and foaming. Gradually add the stock (broth) and rice mixture, stirring constantly, and cook over medium heat for 2 minutes, or until the mixture thickens slightly. Reduce the heat to low.

In a small bowl, whisk together the yoghurt and egg yolk, then gradually pour into the soup, stirring constantly. Remove from the heat and stir in the mint and ½ teaspoon salt.

Just before serving, melt the remaining butter in a small saucepan over medium heat. Add the cayenne (red) pepper and cook until the mixture is lightly browned. Pour over the soup.

Serves 4–6

Soupe au Pistou

- 3 stalks fresh flat-leaf parsley
- 1 large sprig of fresh rosemary
- 1 large sprig of fresh thyme
- 1 large sprig of fresh marjoram
- ¼ cup (60 ml/2 fl oz) olive oil
- 2 onions, thinly sliced
- 1 leek, thinly sliced
- 1 bay leaf
- 375 g (13¼ oz) pumpkin, cut into small pieces
- 250 g (8¾ oz) potato, cut into small pieces
- 1 carrot, cut in half lengthways and thinly sliced
- 2 litres (2.1 US qt/1.75 UK qt) vegetable stock (broth) or water
- ½ cup (90 g/3¼ oz) fresh or frozen broad beans
- ½ cup (80 g/2¾ oz) fresh or frozen peas
- 2 small zucchinis (courgettes), finely chopped
- 2 ripe tomatoes, peeled and roughly chopped
- ½ cup (60 g/2 oz) short macaroni or shell pasta

Pistou
- ½ cup (25 g/¾ oz) fresh basil leaves
- 2 large cloves garlic, crushed
- ⅓ cup (35 g/1¼ oz) grated Parmesan
- ⅓ cup (80 ml/2¾ fl oz) olive oil

Tie the parsley, rosemary, thyme and marjoram together with string. Heat the oil in a heavy-based saucepan and add onion and leek. Cook over low heat for 10 minutes, or until soft.

Add the herb bunch, bay leaf, pumpkin, potato, carrot, 1 teaspoon salt and the stock (broth). Cover and simmer 10 minutes, or until vegetables are almost tender.

Add the broad beans, peas, zucchini (courgettes), tomato and pasta. Cover and cook for 15 minutes, or until the vegetables are very tender and the pasta is cooked. Add more water if necessary. Remove the herbs, including the bay leaf.

For the pistou, finely chop the basil and garlic in a food processor. Pour in the oil gradually, processing until smooth. Stir in the Parmesan and ½ teaspoon freshly ground black pepper and serve spooned over the soup.

Note: The flavour of this soup improves if refrigerated overnight, then gently reheated.

Serves 8

Spicy Tomato and Pea Soup

- **5 large very ripe tomatoes, chopped**
- **2 cups (500 ml/17 fl oz) water**
- **2 tablespoons ghee or butter**
- **1 large onion, thinly sliced**
- **1 clove garlic, crushed**
- **2 teaspoons ground coriander**
- **2 teaspoons ground cumin**
- **½ teaspoon fennel seeds**
- **2 bay leaves**
- **1 green chilli, seeded and sliced**
- **1½ cups (375 ml/13 fl oz) coconut cream**
- **1½ cups (240 g/8½ oz) frozen peas**
- **1 tablespoon sugar**
- **1 tablespoon chopped fresh mint**

Simmer the tomato in the water until very tender, then blend the tomato and water in a food processor.

Heat the ghee in a large pan; add the onion and garlic and cook over medium heat until very soft. Add the coriander, cumin, fennel seeds, bay leaves and chilli, and cook, stirring, for 1 minute.

Add the coconut cream and the pureed tomatoes, and bring to the boil. Reduce the heat, add the peas and cook until tender. Remove the bay leaves, add the sugar and mint, and season with freshly ground pepper to taste. Serve with hot toasted chapattis brushed with ghee.

Serves 6

49

Chickpea Soup

- 1½ cups (330 g/11⅔ oz) dried chickpeas (garbanzo beans)
- ½ onion
- 1 bay leaf
- ½ head garlic, unpeeled (8 cloves)
- 2 tablespoons olive oil
- 1 celery stick, chopped
- 1 large onion, extra, finely chopped
- 3 cloves garlic, extra, chopped
- 1 teaspoon ground cumin
- 1 teaspoon paprika
- ¼ teaspoon dried chilli powder
- 3 teaspoons chopped fresh oregano
- 1 litre (1.1 US qt/1.75 UK pt) vegetable stock (broth)
- 2 tablespoons lemon juice
- olive oil, extra to drizzle

Place the chickpeas (garbanzo beans) in a bowl and cover with water. Soak overnight, then drain. Transfer to a saucepan and add the onion, bay leaf, garlic and 1.5 litres (1.6 US qt/1.3 UK qt) water. Bring to the boil, then reduce the heat and simmer for 1 hour, or until the chickpeas (garbanzo beans) are tender. Drain, reserving 2 cups (500 ml/17 fl oz) cooking liquid. Discard the onion, bay leaf and garlic.

Heat the oil in the same saucepan, add the celery and extra onion, and cook over medium heat for 5 minutes, or until golden. Add the extra garlic and cook for a further 1 minute. Add the cumin, paprika, chilli powder and 2 teaspoons of the oregano, and cook, stirring, for 1 minute. Return the chickpeas (garbanzo beans) to the pan and stir to coat with the spices.

Pour in the vegetable stock (broth) and reserved cooking liquid, bring to the boil, then reduce the heat and simmer for 20 minutes. Stir in the lemon juice and remaining oregano and serve drizzled with olive oil.

Serves 4

Spinach and Lentil Soup

- 2 cups (370 g/13 oz) brown lentils
- 5 cups (1.25 litres (1.3 US qt/1.1 UK qt)) water
- 2 teaspoons olive oil
- 1 medium onion, finely chopped
- 2 cloves garlic, crushed
- 20 English (common) spinach leaves, stalks removed and leaves finely shredded
- 1 teaspoon ground cumin
- 1 teaspoon finely grated lemon rind
- 2 cups (500 ml/17 fl oz) vegetable stock (broth)
- 2 cups (500 ml/17 fl oz) water
- 2 tablespoons finely chopped fresh coriander (cilantro)

Place the lentils in a large pan with water. Bring to the boil and then simmer, uncovered, for 1 hour. Rinse and drain, then set aside. In a separate pan heat the oil; add the onion and garlic. Cook over medium heat until golden. Add spinach and cook for another 2 minutes.

Add the lentils, cumin, lemon rind, stock (broth) and water to the pan. Simmer, uncovered, for 15 minutes. Add the coriander (cilantro) and stir through. Serve immediately.

Serves 4–6

Summer Soup

- 4 medium red capsicums (peppers)
- 4 medium tomatoes
- ¼ cup (60 ml/2 fl oz) oil
- ½ teaspoon dried marjoram
- ½ teaspoon dried mixed herbs
- 2 cloves garlic, crushed
- 1 teaspoon mild curry paste (jerk seasoning paste)
- 1 medium red (Spanish) onion, sliced
- 1 medium leek, sliced (white part only)
- 250 g (8¾ oz) green cabbage, chopped
- 4 cups (1 litre (1.1 US qt/ 1.1 UK pt)) water
- 1 teaspoon sweet chilli sauce (jalapeno jelly)
- salt and freshly ground black pepper

Cut the red capsicums (peppers) into quarters. Remove the seeds and membrane. Grill (broil) until the skin blackens and blisters. Place on a cutting board, cover with a tea towel and allow to cool before peeling. Mark a small cross on the top of each tomato. Place in a bowl and cover with boiling water for about 2 minutes. Drain and cool. Peel skin off downwards from the cross and discard. Cut the tomatoes in half and gently scoop out the seeds using a small spoon.

Heat the oil in a large pan; add the herbs, garlic and curry paste (jerk seasoning paste). Stir over low heat for 1 minute, or until aromatic. Add the onion and leek and cook for 3 minutes or until golden. Add the cabbage, tomatoes, red capsicums (peppers) and water. Bring to the boil, reduce heat and simmer for 20 minutes. Remove from the heat; allow to cool slightly.

Place the soup in small batches in a food processor bowl. Process for 30 seconds or until smooth. Return the soup to a clean pan, stir through chilli sauce (jalapeno jelly) and season with salt and pepper. Reheat gently and serve hot.

Serves 6

Mexican Bean Chowder

- ¾ cup (155 g/5½ oz) dried red kidney beans
- ¾ cup (165 g/5¾ oz) dried Mexican black beans (see Note)
- 1 tablespoon oil
- 1 onion, chopped
- 2 cloves garlic, crushed
- ½–1 teaspoon chilli powder
- 1 tablespoon ground cumin
- 2 teaspoons ground coriander
- 2 × 400 g (14 oz) cans chopped tomatoes
- 3 cups (750 ml/26 fl oz) vegetable stock (broth)
- 1 red capsicum (pepper), chopped
- 1 green capsicum (pepper), chopped
- 440 g (15½ oz) can corn kernels
- 2 tablespoons tomato paste (tomato puree)
- grated Cheddar (American) cheese, to serve
- sour cream, to serve

Soak the kidney beans and black beans in separate bowls in plenty of cold water overnight. Drain. Place in a large saucepan, cover with water and bring to the boil. Reduce the heat and simmer for 45 minutes, or until tender. Drain.

Heat the oil in a large saucepan, add the onion and cook over medium heat until soft. Add the garlic, chilli powder, cumin and coriander, and cook for 1 minute. Stir in the tomato, stock (broth), capsicum (peppers), corn and tomato paste (tomato puree). Cook, covered, for 25–30 minutes. Add the beans during the last 10 minutes of cooking. Stir occasionally.

Serve topped with the grated Cheddar (American) cheese and a spoonful of sour cream.

Note: Mexican black beans are also known as black turtle beans.

Serves 6

Japanese Vegetable Ramen Noodle Soup

- 250 g (8¾ oz) fresh ramen noodles
- 1 tablespoon vegetable oil
- 1 tablespoon finely chopped fresh ginger (ginger root)
- 2 cloves garlic, crushed
- 150 g (5¼ oz) oyster mushrooms, halved
- 1 small zucchini (courgette), thinly sliced
- 1 leek, halved lengthways and thinly sliced
- 100 g (3½ oz) snow peas (mange tout), halved on the diagonal
- 100 g (3½ oz) fried tofu puffs, cut into julienne strips
- ⅓ cup (80 g/2¾ oz) white miso paste
- ⅓ cup (80 ml/2¾ fl oz) light soy sauce
- ¼ cup (60 ml/2 fl oz) mirin
- 1 cup (90 g/3¼ oz) bean sprouts, tailed
- ½ teaspoon sesame oil
- 4 spring (green) onions, thinly sliced
- 100 g (3½ oz) enoki mushrooms

Bring a large saucepan of lightly salted water to the boil. Add the noodles and cook, stirring to prevent them sticking together, for 2 minutes, or until just tender. Drain, rinse under cold running water, then drain again.

Heat a wok over medium heat, add the vegetable oil and swirl to coat. Add the ginger (ginger root) and garlic and stir-fry (scramble-fry) for 30 seconds, then add the oyster mushrooms, zucchini (courgette), leek, snow peas (mange tout) and sliced tofu puffs and stir-fry (scramble-fry) for 4 minutes. Pour in 1.5 litres (1.6 US qt/1.3 UK qt) water and bring to the boil, then reduce the heat and simmer. Stir in the miso paste, soy sauce and mirin until heated through, but don't let it boil. Just before serving, stir in the bean sprouts and sesame oil.

Place the noodles in the bottom of six serving bowls, then pour the broth over the top. Sprinkle with the sliced spring (green) onion and enoki mushrooms.

Serves 6

54

Red Gazpacho

- 1 kg (2 lb 3 oz) vine-ripened tomatoes
- 2 slices day-old white Italian bread, crust removed, broken into pieces
- 1 red capsicum (pepper), seeded, roughly chopped
- 2 cloves garlic, chopped
- 1 small fresh green chilli, chopped, optional
- 1 teaspoon sugar
- 2 tablespoons red wine vinegar
- 2 tablespoons extra virgin olive oil
- 8 ice cubes

Garnish
- ½ Lebanese cucumber, seeded, diced
- ½ red capsicum (pepper), seeded, diced
- ½ green capsicum (pepper), seeded, finely diced
- ½ red onion, finely diced
- ½ ripe tomato, diced

Score a cross in the base of each tomato. Place in a bowl of boiling water for 10 seconds, then plunge into cold water and peel away from the cross. Cut the tomatoes in half and scoop out the seeds with a teaspoon. Chop the tomatoes.

Soak the bread in cold water for 5 minutes, then squeeze out any excess liquid. Place the bread in a food processor with the tomato, capsicum (pepper), garlic, chilli, sugar and vinegar, and process until combined and smooth.

With the motor running, add the oil to make a smooth creamy mixture. Season, to taste. Refrigerate for at least 2 hours. Add a little extra vinegar, if desired.

For the garnish, mix the ingredients in a bowl. Put 2 ice cubes in each bowl of soup and serve the garnish in the separate bowls.

Serves 4

Country Pumpkin and Pasta Soup

- 1 large onion
- 750 g (1 lb 10 oz) pumpkin
- 2 medium potatoes
- 1 tablespoon olive oil
- 30 g (1 oz) butter
- 2 cloves garlic, crushed
- 12 cups (3 litres/3.2 US qt/2.6 UK qt) vegetable stock (broth)
- 125 g (4⅓ oz) miniature pasta or risoni
- 1 tablespoon chopped fresh parsley, for serving (optional)

Peel the onion and chop finely. Peel pumpkin and potatoes and chop into small cubes. Heat oil and butter in a large pan. Add onion and garlic and cook, stirring, for 5 minutes over low heat.

Add the pumpkin, potatoes and stock (broth). Increase heat, cover pan and cook for 10 minutes or until vegetables are tender.

Add pasta and cook, stirring occasionally, for 5 minutes or until just tender. Serve immediately. Sprinkle with chopped parsley, if desired.

Serves 4–6

Tomato Soup with Pasta and Basil

- **3 large ripe tomatoes (750 g/1 lb 10 oz)**
- **2 tablespoons olive oil**
- **1 medium onion, finely chopped**
- **1 clove garlic, crushed**
- **1 small red capsicum (pepper), finely chopped**
- **4 cups (1 litre/1.1 US qt/1.75 UK pt) vegetable stock (broth)**
- **3 tablespoons tomato paste (tomato puree)**
- **salt and pepper**
- **1 teaspoon sugar**
- **¼ cup (7 g/¼ oz) basil leaves, or 1½ teaspoons dried basil**
- **1 cup (155 g/5½ oz) small shell pasta or macaroni**
- **fresh basil leaves, extra**

Cut a small cross in the top of each tomato. Place in a bowl and cover with boiling water for about 2 minutes; drain and cool. Peel skin downward from the cross and discard. Roughly chop flesh. Heat oil in a large heavy-based pan. Add onion, garlic and red capsicum (pepper); cook, stirring, for 10 minutes or until all ingredients are soft. Add tomatoes and cook another 10 minutes.

Add the stock (broth), tomato paste (tomato puree), salt, pepper and sugar. Cover and simmer for 15 minutes. Remove from the heat, add the basil. Allow to cool. Process in batches, in a food processor or blender, until smooth. Return the mixture to the pan and reheat gently.

Cook the pasta separately in boiling salted water until tender; drain. Add to soup and heat through. Serve sprinkled with fresh basil leaves.

Serves 4

Chilli and Corn Soup

- **1 coriander (cilantro) sprig**
- **4 corn cobs**
- **30 g (1 oz) butter**
- **2 red capsicums (peppers), diced**
- **1 small onion, finely chopped**

- **1 small red chilli, finely chopped**
- **1 tablespoon plain (all-purpose) flour**
- **2 cups (500 ml/17 fl oz)**
  vegetable stock (broth)
- **½ cup (125 ml/4¼ fl oz) cream**

Trim the leaves off the coriander (cilantro) and finely chop the root and stems. Cut the kernels off the corn cobs.

Heat the butter in a large saucepan over medium heat. Add the corn kernels, capsicum (peppers), onion and chilli and stir to coat the vegetables in the butter. Cook, covered, over low heat, stirring occasionally, for 10 minutes, or until the vegetables are soft. Increase the heat to medium and add the coriander (cilantro) root and stem. Cook, stirring, for 30 seconds, or until fragrant. Sprinkle with the flour and stir for a further minute. Remove from the heat and gradually add the vegetable stock (broth), stirring together. Add 2 cups (500 ml/17 fl oz) water and return to the heat. Bring to the boil, reduce the heat to low and simmer, covered, for 30 minutes, or until the vegetables are tender. Cool slightly.

Ladle about 2 cups (500 ml/17 fl oz) of the soup into a blender and puree until smooth. Return the puree to the soup in the saucepan, pour in the cream and gently heat until warmed through. Season to taste with salt. Sprinkle with the coriander (cilantro) leaves to serve. Delicious with grilled cheese on pitta bread.

Serves 4

Carrot and Orange Soup

- **500 g (1 lb 2 oz) carrots**
- **30 g (1 oz) butter**
- **½ cup (125 ml/4¼ fl oz) orange juice**
- **4–5 cups (1–1.25 litres/1.1–1.3 US qt/ 0.9–1.1 UK qt) vegetable stock (broth)**
- **1 small onion, roughly chopped**
- **3–4 teaspoons chopped fresh thyme, or 1 teaspoon dried**
- **salt and pepper**
- **sour cream and nutmeg, for serving**

Peel and slice the carrots. Place carrots and butter in a large heavy-based pan and cook over medium heat for 10 minutes, stirring occasionally.

Add the orange juice, stock (broth) and onion. Bring to the boil, add thyme, salt and pepper. Reduce heat; cover and cook for 20 minutes, or until the carrots are tender. Allow to cool.

Process the mixture in batches, in a food processor or blender, until smooth. Return mixture to the pan and reheat. Serve in individual bowls. Top each with a dollop of sour cream sprinkled with nutmeg. Garnish with a small sprig of thyme, if desired.

Serves 4

Potato and Broccoli Soup

- **500 g (1 lb 2 oz) broccoli**
- **cooking oil spray**
- **2 onions, finely chopped**
- **2 cloves garlic, finely chopped**
- **2 teaspoons ground cumin**
- **1 teaspoon ground coriander**
- **750 g (1 lb 10 oz) potatoes, cubed**
- **2 small vegetable stock (bouillon) cubes**
- **1½ cups (375 ml/13 fl oz) skim milk**
- **3 tablespoons finely chopped fresh coriander (cilantro)**

Cut the broccoli into small pieces. Lightly spray the base of a large saucepan with cooking oil, then place over medium heat and add the onion and garlic. Add 1 tablespoon water to prevent sticking. Cover and cook, stirring occasionally, over low heat for 5 minutes, or until the onion has softened and is lightly golden. Add the ground cumin and coriander and cook for 2 minutes.

Add the potato and broccoli to the pan, stir well and add the stock (bouillon) cubes and 1 litre (1.1 US qt/1.75 UK pt) of water. Slowly bring to the boil, reduce the heat, cover and simmer over low heat for 20 minutes, or until the vegetables are tender. Allow to cool slightly.

Blend the soup in batches in a food processor or blender until smooth. Return to the pan and stir in the milk. Slowly reheat, without boiling. Stir the chopped coriander (cilantro) through and season well before serving.

Serves 6

Soba Noodle Soup

- **250 g (8¾ oz) packet soba noodles**
- **2 dried shiitake mushrooms**
- **2 litres (2.1 US qt/1.75 UK qt) vegetable stock (broth)**
- **120 g (4¼ oz) snow peas (mange tout), cut into thin strips**
- **2 small carrots, cut into thin strips**
- **2 cloves garlic, finely chopped**
- **6 spring (green) onions, cut into 5 cm (2 inch) lengths and sliced lengthways**
- **3 cm (1¼ inch) piece ginger (ginger root), cut into julienne strips**
- **⅓ cup (80 ml/2¾ fl oz) soy sauce**
- **¼ cup (60 ml/2 fl oz) mirin or sake**
- **1 cup (90 g/3¼ oz) bean sprouts**
- **fresh coriander (cilantro), to garnish**

Cook the noodles according to the packet instructions. Drain.

Soak the mushrooms in ½ cup (125 ml/4¼ fl oz) boiling water until soft. Drain, reserving the liquid. Remove the stalks and finely slice the mushrooms.

Combine the vegetable stock (broth), mushrooms, reserved liquid, snow peas (mange tout), carrot, garlic, spring (green) onion and ginger (ginger root) in a large saucepan. Bring slowly to the boil, then reduce the heat to low and simmer for 5 minutes, or until the vegetables are tender. Add the soy sauce, mirin and bean sprouts. Cook for a further 3 minutes.

Divide the noodles among four large serving bowls. Ladle the hot liquid and vegetables over the top and garnish with coriander (cilantro).

Serves 4

Spiced Carrot Soup Sip

- ⅓ cup (80 ml/2¾ fl oz) olive oil
- 2 teaspoons honey
- 3 teaspoons ground cumin
- 3 teaspoons coriander seeds, lightly crushed
- 2 cinnamon sticks, broken in half
- 1.5 kg (3 lb 5 oz) carrots, cut into even chunks (about 3 cm/1¼ inches)
- 3 cups (750 ml/26 fl oz) vegetable stock (broth)
- 100 ml (3½ fl oz) cream
- ¾ cup (185 g/6½ oz) sour cream
- 3 tablespoons fresh coriander (cilantro) leaves

Preheat the oven to moderately hot 200°C (400°F/Gas 6). Combine the oil, honey, cumin, coriander seeds, cinnamon sticks, 1 teaspoon salt and plenty of cracked black pepper in a roasting tin. Add the chunks of carrot and mix well to ensure that all the carrot is coated in the spice mixture.

Roast for 1 hour, or until the carrot is tender, shaking the pan occasionally during cooking. Remove from the oven, discard the cinnamon sticks with tongs and allow the carrot to cool slightly.

Transfer half the carrot chunks, 1½ cups (375 ml/13 fl oz) of the stock (broth) and 1 cup (250 ml/8½ fl oz) water to a food processor or blender and blend until smooth. Strain through a fine sieve into a clean saucepan. Repeat with the remaining carrots, stock (broth) and another 1 cup (250 ml/8½ fl oz) water. Bring the soup to a simmer and cook for 10 minutes. Add the cream and season to taste. Ladle into a jug, then pour into shot glasses or espresso cups. Garnish each with ¼ teaspoon sour cream and a coriander (cilantro) leaf.

Think Ahead: The soup can be refrigerated for 2 days or frozen before the cream is added for up to 8 weeks.

Makes 36 serves

Pie-Crust Mushroom Soup

- **400 g (14 oz) large field (meadow) mushrooms**
- **60 g (2 oz) butter**
- **1 onion, finely chopped**
- **1 clove garlic, crushed**
- **¼ cup (30 g/1 oz) plain (all-purpose) flour**

- **3 cups (750 ml/26 fl oz) vegetable stock (broth)**
- **2 tablespoons fresh thyme leaves**
- **2 tablespoons sherry**
- **1 cup (250 ml/8½ fl oz) cream**
- **1 sheet frozen puff pastry, thawed**
- **1 egg, lightly beaten**

Preheat the oven to moderately hot 200°C (400°F/Gas 6). Peel and roughly chop the mushrooms, including the stems. Melt the butter in a large saucepan, add the onion and cook over medium heat for 3 minutes, or until soft. Add the garlic and cook for another minute. Add the mushrooms and cook until soft. Sprinkle with the flour and stir for 1 minute.

Stir in the stock and thyme and bring to the boil. Reduce the heat and simmer, covered, for 10 minutes. Cool before processing in batches. Return the soup to the pan, stir in the sherry and cream, then pour into 4 ovenproof bowls (use small deep bowls rather than wide shallow ones, or the pastry may sag into the soup).

Cut rounds of pastry slightly larger than the bowl tops and cover each bowl with pastry. Seal the pastry edges and brush lightly with the egg. Place the bowls on a baking tray (sheet) and bake for 15 minutes, or until golden and puffed.

Serves 4

Lentil and Vegetable Soup with Spiced Yoghurt

- 2 tablespoons olive oil
- 1 small leek (white part only), chopped
- 2 cloves garlic, crushed
- 2 teaspoons curry powder
- 1 teaspoon ground cumin
- 1 teaspoon garam masala
- 1 litre (1.1 US qt/1.75 UK pt) vegetable stock (broth)
- 1 fresh bay leaf
- 1 cup (185 g/6½ oz) brown lentils
- 450 g (15¾ oz) butternut pumpkin (squash), peeled and cut into 1 cm (½ inch) cubes
- 400 g (14 oz) can chopped tomatoes
- 2 zucchini (courgettes), cut in half lengthways and sliced
- 200 g (7 oz) broccoli, cut into small florets
- 1 small carrot, diced
- ½ cup (80 g/2¾ oz) peas
- 1 tablespoon chopped fresh mint

Spiced Yoghurt
- 1 cup (250 g/8¾ oz) thick plain yoghurt
- 1 tablespoon chopped fresh coriander (cilantro) leaves
- 1 clove garlic, crushed
- 3 dashes hot chilli (pepper) sauce

Heat the oil in a saucepan over medium heat. Add the leek and garlic and cook for 4–5 minutes, or until soft and golden. Add the curry powder, cumin and garam masala and cook for 1 minute, or until fragrant.

Add the stock (broth), bay leaf, lentils and pumpkin (squash). Bring to the boil, then reduce the heat to low and simmer for 10–15 minutes, or until the lentils are tender. Season well.

Add the tomatoes, zucchini (courgettes), broccoli, carrot and 2 cups (500 ml/17 fl oz) water, and simmer for 10 minutes, or until the vegetables are tender. Add the peas and simmer for 2–3 minutes.

Combine the yoghurt, coriander (cilantro), garlic and hot chilli (pepper) sauce in a bowl. Add a dollop of the yoghurt to each serving of soup and garnish with the mint.

Serves 6

Starters

Grilled Vegetables with Garlic Mayonnaise

- 2 medium eggplants (aubergines), cut into thin slices
- salt
- 4 small leeks, halved lengthways
- 2 medium red capsicums (peppers), cut into eighths
- 4 small zucchinis (courgettes), halved lengthways
- 8 large flat mushrooms

Dressing
- 1 tablespoon balsamic vinegar
- 2 tablespoons Dijon mustard

- 2 teaspoons dried oregano leaves
- 1 cup (250 ml/8½ fl oz) olive oil

Garlic Mayonnaise
- 2 egg yolks
- 1 tablespoon lemon juice
- 2 cloves garlic, crushed
- 1 cup (250 ml/8½ fl oz) olive oil
- 1 tablespoon chopped fresh chives
- 1 tablespoon chopped fresh parsley
- 1 tablespoon water

Sprinkle eggplant (aubergine) slices with salt and allow to stand for 30 minutes. Rinse under cold water, then pat dry with paper towels.

Place eggplants (aubergines), leeks, red capsicums (peppers) and zucchinis (courgettes) in a single layer on a flat grill tray (broiler sheet); brush with dressing. Cook under preheated grill on high for 5 minutes, turning once; brush occasionally with dressing. Add mushrooms, cap-side up, to grill tray (broiler sheet) and brush with dressing. Continue cooking vegetables for 10 minutes or until tender, turning mushrooms once. Brush vegetables with dressing during cooking. Serve with Garlic Mayonnaise.

To make Dressing: Combine vinegar, mustard and oregano in bowl; gradually whisk in oil.

To make Garlic Mayonnaise: Place egg yolks, lemon juice and garlic in a food processor or blender, blend for 5 seconds until combined. With motor running, add oil slowly in a thin, steady stream until it is all added and mayonnaise is thick and creamy. Add chives, parsley and water and blend for 3 seconds until combined.

Note: Garlic mayonnaise can be made several days ahead and refrigerated. Do not worry if the dressing separates – simply brush on as required.

Serves 8

Two-Cheese Rice Fritters

- 3¼ cups (810 ml/27 fl oz) vegetable stock (broth)
- 1 tablespoon olive oil
- 20 g (⅔ oz) butter
- 1 small onion, finely chopped
- 1¼ cups (275 g/9⅔ oz) short-grain rice
- ⅓ cup (35 g/1¼ oz) freshly grated Parmesan cheese
- 30 g (1 oz) fresh mozzarella cheese, cut into 1 cm (½ inch) cubes
- 35 g (1¼ oz) sun-dried tomatoes, chopped
- oil, for deep-frying
- 70 g (2½ oz) mixed salad leaves, to serve

Pour the vegetable stock (broth) into a small saucepan and bring to the boil. Reduce the heat a little, cover the pan with a lid and keep at a low simmer until needed.

Heat the oil and butter in a large saucepan. Cook the onion until softened but not brown. Stir in the rice until well coated. Add a quarter of the stock (broth) to the pan. Stir for 5 minutes, or until all the liquid has been absorbed.

Repeat the process until all the stock (broth) has been added and the rice is almost tender, stirring constantly. Stir in the Parmesan. Remove from heat. Transfer to a bowl to cool, then refrigerate for 1 hour.

With wet hands, roll 2 tablespoonfuls of rice mixture into a ball. Make an indentation into the ball, and press in a cube of mozzarella and a couple of pieces of sun-dried tomato. Reshape the ball to completely encase the tomato, then flatten slightly into a disc. Refrigerate for 15 minutes.

Fill a deep-fat fryer or large pot one-third full of oil and heat to 180°C (350°F), or until a cube of bread dropped into the oil browns in 15 seconds. Gently lower the rice fritters a few at a time into the oil and cook for 1–2 minutes, or until golden brown. Remove with a slotted spoon, then drain on crumpled paper towels. To serve, arrange salad leaves on each plate and place three rice fritters on top.

Note: These fritters can be prepared up to 24 hours in advance. Store, uncooked, in the refrigerator and fry just before serving.

Serves 6

Grilled Tomatoes with Bruschetta

- 1 loaf Italian bread
- 4 large ripe tomatoes
- ½ teaspoon dried marjoram leaves
- salt and freshly ground black pepper
- ⅓ cup (80 ml/2¾ fl oz) olive oil
- 2 tablespoons red wine vinegar
- 1 teaspoon soft brown sugar
- 1 clove garlic, cut in half
- ½ cup (110 g/3¾ oz) chopped, marinated artichokes
- 1 tablespoon finely chopped flat-leaf parsley

Cut bread into thick slices. Preheat grill (broiler). Cut the tomatoes in half; gently squeeze out seeds. Place tomatoes, cut side down, in a shallow, ovenproof dish. Place marjoram, salt and pepper, oil, vinegar and sugar in a small screw-top jar; shake well. Pour half over the tomatoes.

Cook the tomatoes under a hot grill (broiler) for 30 minutes; turn halfway during cooking. Pour remaining oil mixture over the tomatoes. Remove from heat and keep warm.

Brush the bread slices liberally with some oil, on both sides, and toast until golden. Rub cut surface of garlic over bread. Place cooked tomatoes onto bread, top with artichokes and sprinkle with parsley.

Serves 4

Spinach and Water Chestnut Dumplings

Filling
- 1 tablespoon peanut oil
- 1 teaspoon sesame oil
- 1 clove garlic, crushed
- 2.5 cm (1 inch) piece fresh ginger (ginger root), grated
- 2 tablespoons chopped fresh garlic chives
- 30 g (1 oz) water spinach, chopped into 1 cm (½ inch) lengths
- 120 g (4¼ oz) can water chestnuts, drained, finely chopped
- 1 tablespoon soy sauce

Pastry
- 2 cups (350 g/12¼ oz) rice flour
- ⅔ cup (85 g/3 oz) tapioca starch
- 2 tablespoons arrowroot flour
- 1 tablespoon glutinous rice flour
- tapioca flour, for dusting
- tapioca flour, for dusting

Dipping Sauce
- ½ teaspoon sesame oil
- ½ teaspoon peanut oil
- 1 tablespoon soy sauce
- 1 tablespoon lime juice
- 1 small red chilli, seeded and finely chopped

For the filling, heat the oils over medium-low heat in a wok. Add the garlic and ginger (ginger root) and cook, stirring, for 1 minute, or until fragrant but not brown. Add the chives, water spinach, water chestnuts and soy sauce and cook for 2 minutes. Remove from the pan and cool for about 5 minutes. Drain away any liquid.

Combine the pastry ingredients in a large pan with 2½ cups (600 ml/20 fl oz) water, stirring to remove any lumps. Stir over low heat for 10 minutes, or until thick. Cook stirring, for another 5 minutes, or until the liquid is opaque. Turn onto a work surface dusted liberally with tapioca flour and cool for 10 minutes. (You will need to use the tapioca flour to continually dust the surface and your hands while kneading.) With floured hands, knead the dough for 10 minutes. Divide into two, covering one half with plastic wrap.

Roll out the dough to 2 mm (1/16 inch) thick. Cut out 9 cm (3½ inch) rounds with a cutter. Place a heaped teaspoon of filling in the centre of each circle, dampen the edge, fold over and pleat to seal. This is very easy with a dumpling press. Place on a lightly floured board or tray and repeat with the remaining dough and filling. Do not re-roll any pastry scraps. Before steaming, lightly brush the dumplings with oil.

Half fill a wok or pan with water, cover and bring to the boil. Place the dumplings, leaving a gap between each, in a bamboo steamer lined with lightly oiled baking paper. Cover and steam for 10 minutes, or until the pastry is opaque. Repeat until all the dumplings are done, then serve with the dipping sauce on the side.

For the sauce, whisk all the ingredients together in a small bowl.

Note: Water spinach, also known as kangkung, is available at Asian greengrocers. Rice flour, tapioca starch, arrowroot flour and glutinous rice flour are available from large Asian food stores and some supermarkets.

Makes 30

Marinated Antipasto

- **750 g (1 lb 10 oz) slender eggplant (aubergine)**
- **¼ cup (60 ml/2 fl oz) olive oil**
- **2 tablespoons balsamic vinegar**
- **2 cloves garlic, crushed**
- **pinch of salt (to taste)**
- **2 tablespoons chopped fresh parsley**

Cut the eggplant (aubergine) into thick diagonal slices, place in a colander and sprinkle well with salt. After 30 minutes, rinse and pat dry.

Whisk the oil, vinegar, garlic and salt until smooth. Season, to taste.

Heat a little oil in a frying pan and brown the eggplant (aubergine) in batches. Transfer to a bowl, toss with the dressing and parsley and marinate for 4 hours. Serve at room temperature.

Serves 6–8

Saganaki Haloumi

- **400 g (14 oz) haloumi cheese**
- **olive oil, for shallow-frying**
- **2 tablespoons lemon juice**

Pat the haloumi dry with paper towels and cut into 1 cm (½ inch) slices.

Pour oil into a large frying pan to 5 mm (¼ inch) depth and heat over medium heat. Add the cheese and fry for 1 minute each side, or until golden. Remove the pan from the heat and pour the lemon juice over the cheese. Season with ground black pepper. Serve straight from the pan or on a serving plate, as part of a meze spread, with crusty bread to mop up the lemon and olive oil mixture.

Note: Saganaki refers to the two-handled frying pan in which this dish is traditionally served.

Serves 6

Spicy Cabbage Rolls

- **6 large green cabbage leaves**

Filling
- **2 teaspoons olive oil**
- **4 spring (green) onions, finely chopped**
- **1 clove garlic, crushed**
- **2 tablespoons tomato paste (tomato puree)**
- **½ cup (75 g/2⅔ oz) dried currants**
- **2 tablespoons slivered almonds**
- **1 teaspoon cumin seeds**
- **½ teaspoon ground cinnamon**

- **2 tablespoons finely chopped fresh parsley**
- **2½ cups (470 g/16½ oz) cooked long-grain rice**
- **1 cup (250 ml/8½ fl oz) vegetable stock (broth)**

Yoghurt Sauce
- **¾ cup (185 g/6½ oz) plain yoghurt**
- **1 teaspoon ground cumin**
- **1 tablespoon finely chopped fresh mint**

Preheat the oven to moderately hot 190°C (375°F/Gas 5). Brush a deep ovenproof dish with melted butter or oil.

Blanch the cabbage leaves in boiling water for 10 seconds or until they are soft and pliable. Drain; remove and discard the hard stalk from the leaves. Set leaves aside.

To make Filling: Heat the oil in a large pan. Add the spring (green) onions and garlic and cook over medium heat for 30 seconds. Add the tomato paste (tomato puree), dried currants, almonds, cumin seeds, cinnamon, parsley and rice; stir until well combined. Remove from heat and cool slightly.

Place 3 tablespoons of filling on the edge of one cabbage leaf. Roll into a neat parcel, folding in the edges while rolling. Repeat with the remaining filling and leaves. Place the cabbage parcels, flap-side down, in prepared dish and pour the stock (broth) over them. Invert an ovenproof plate on top of the cabbage parcels to prevent them from falling apart. Cover with a lid or foil; bake for 20–25 minutes or until heated through.

To make Yoghurt Sauce: Mix together the yoghurt, cumin and mint in a bowl. Serve the cabbage rolls warm or cold with Yoghurt Sauce.

Serves 6

Mini Lentil Burgers with Tomato Relish

- 1 cup (185 g/6½ oz) brown lentils
- 1 bay leaf
- 1 onion, roughly chopped
- 1 clove garlic, crushed
- 1 small leek, finely sliced
- 1 small carrot, finely grated
- 1 cup (80 g/2¾ oz) fresh breadcrumbs

- 2 egg yolks
- 2 tablespoons chopped fresh coriander (cilantro)
- 2 tablespoons oil
- 8 slices bread, cut into 4 cm (1½ inch) squares
- ready-made tomato relish, for serving

Place the lentils and bay leaf in a pan, cover with plenty of water, bring to the boil and simmer for 20–30 minutes, or until tender; drain well and discard the bay leaf.

Combine half the cooked lentils with the onion and garlic in a food processor until the mixture forms a smooth paste. Transfer to a bowl and mix with the remaining lentils, leek, carrot, breadcrumbs, egg yolks and coriander (cilantro); season with salt and freshly ground black pepper. Form level tablespoons of the mixture into mini burgers.

Heat some of the oil in a non-stick frying pan and fry the mini burgers in batches until browned on both sides, adding more oil as necessary. Drain on paper towels and serve warm, on the bread squares (or toast), with a dollop of tomato relish on top. Garnish with fresh herbs.

Makes 32

Cheesey Tomato Boats

- **5 large zucchini (courgettes)**
- **1 large tomato, finely chopped**
- **2 spring (green) onions, finely chopped**
- **1 tablespoon chopped fresh parsley**
- **½ cup (60 g/2 oz) grated Cheddar (American) cheese**

Cut each zucchini (courgette) into three equal pieces, about 4 cm (1½ inches) long. Cut each piece in half lengthways.

Using a teaspoon, scoop a small hollow from each piece. Add the zucchini (courgette) to a pan of simmering water for about 3 minutes, or until tender; drain. Refresh under cold water, then pat dry with paper towels.

Combine the tomato, onion, parsley and cheese in a small bowl. Spoon the filling into the zucchini (courgette) boats. Cook under a preheated grill (broiler) until the cheese has melted and the boats are warmed through. Serve immediately.

Makes 30

75

Golden Nugget Soufflés

- **4 golden nugget pumpkins (squash)**
- **60 g (2 oz) butter**
- **3 tablespoons plain (all-purpose) flour**
- **⅔ cup (170 ml/5¾ fl oz) milk**
- **3 eggs, separated**
- **½ cup (65 g/2⅓ oz) grated Gruyère cheese**

Preheat oven to hot 210°C (415°F/Gas 6–7). Cut the tops from each pumpkin (squash) and scoop out all the seeds and fibre. Place the pumpkins (squash) in an ovenproof dish; cover the dish with foil; bake for 1 hour. Remove from the dish; invert onto a wire rack to drain away any liquid.

Using a metal spoon, scoop most of the softened flesh from the pumpkins (squash), leaving a little behind to support the skin. Mash the flesh in a bowl. Let cool.

Melt the butter in a small pan; add the flour and stir for 1 minute, or until golden and bubbling. Add milk gradually, stirring until smooth between each addition. Stir constantly over medium heat until mixture thickens; cook for another minute, then remove from heat. Stir the egg yolks and cheese into the milk mixture; add the pumpkin (squash) and mix together until smooth and creamy. Season with salt and pepper.

Beat the egg whites with electric beaters until stiff peaks form; fold whites into pumpkin (squash) mixture with a metal spoon. Make sure the egg white is mixed in thoroughly so that no white streaks are visible but, at the same time, fold in gently and quickly, to retain the volume.

Spoon mixture into pumpkin (squash) shells, filling to just below the rim. Don't overfill or pumpkins (squash) will overflow while cooking. If there is any filling remaining, bake it in a small ramekin at the same time the pumpkins (squash) are baked. Place filled pumpkins (squash) in a baking dish; bake 20–25 minutes, or until puffed and golden. Serve immediately.

Serves 4

Vegetable Strudel

- 12 English (common) spinach leaves
- 2 tablespoons olive oil
- 1 medium onion, finely sliced
- 1 medium red capsicum (pepper), cut into strips
- 1 medium green capsicum (pepper), cut into strips
- 2 medium zucchinis (courgettes), sliced
- 2 slender eggplants (aubergines), sliced
- salt and pepper
- 6 sheets filo (phyllo) pastry
- 40 g (1½ oz) butter, melted
- ⅓ cup (20 g/⅔ oz) finely sliced fresh basil leaves
- ½ cup (60 g/2 oz) grated Cheddar (American) cheese
- 2 tablespoons sesame seeds

Preheat oven to hot 210°C (415°F/Gas 6–7). Brush an oven tray (sheet) with melted butter or oil. Wash the spinach leaves thoroughly and steam or microwave them until they are just softened. Squeeze out excess moisture and spread the leaves out to dry.

Heat the oil in a frying pan, add the onion and cook over medium heat for 3 minutes. Add the capsicums (peppers), zucchinis (courgettes) and eggplants (aubergines); cook, stirring, for another 5 minutes or until vegetables have softened. Season and then set aside to cool.

Brush 1 sheet of filo (phyllo) pastry with melted butter, top with a second sheet. Repeat with remaining pastry, brushing with butter between each layer. Place the spinach, cooled vegetable mixture, basil and cheese along one long side of pastry, about 5 cm (2 inches) in from the edge. Fold the sides over the filling, fold short end over and roll up tightly.

Place the strudel, seam-side down, on prepared tray (sheet). Brush with remaining melted butter and sprinkle with sesame seeds. Bake for 25 minutes, or until golden brown and crisp.

Serves 4–6

Borek

- **400 g (14 oz) feta**
- **2 eggs, lightly beaten**
- **¾ cup (25 g/¾ oz) chopped fresh flat-leaf parsley**
- **375 g (13¼ oz) filo (phyllo) pastry**
- **⅓ cup (80 ml/2¾ fl oz) good-quality olive oil**

Preheat the oven to moderate 180°C (350°F/Gas 4). Lightly grease a baking tray (sheet). Crumble the feta into a large bowl using a fork or your fingers. Mix in the eggs and parsley and season with freshly ground black pepper.

Cover the filo (phyllo) pastry with a damp tea towel so it doesn't dry out. Remove one sheet at a time. Brushing each sheet lightly with olive oil, layer 4 sheets on top of one another. Cut the pastry into four 7 cm (2¾ inch) strips.

Place 2 rounded teaspoons of the feta mixture in one corner of each strip and fold diagonally, creating a triangle pillow. Place on the baking tray (sheet), seam-side-down, and brush with olive oil. Repeat with the remaining pastry and filling to make 24 parcels. Bake for 20 minutes, or until golden. Serve these as part of a large meze plate.

Note: Fillings for borek are versatile and can be adapted to include your favourite cheeses such as haloumi, Gruyère, Cheddar (American) cheese or mozzarella.

Makes 24

Baked Ricotta

- **1 whole fresh ricotta (2 kg/4⅖ lb)**
- **¾ cup (185 ml/6½ fl oz) olive oil**
- **¾ cup (185 ml/6½ fl oz) lemon juice**
- **2 tablespoons thin strips of lemon rind**
- **2 cloves garlic, crushed**
- **6 tablespoons fresh basil leaves, finely shredded**
- **50 g (1¾ oz) semi-dried tomatoes, roughly chopped**

Remove any paper from the base of the ricotta and put the ricotta in a plastic colander. Place over a bowl, ensuring the base of the colander is not touching the base of the bowl. Cover with plastic wrap and leave overnight in the refrigerator, to drain.

Preheat the oven to very hot 260°C (500°F/Gas 10). Line a baking tray (sheet) with baking paper. Transfer the ricotta to the tray (sheet) and brush with a little of the olive oil. Bake for 30 minutes, or until golden brown. Allow to cool slightly.

Mix the remaining olive oil, lemon juice and rind, garlic and basil in a bowl. Season, to taste, with salt and pepper. Place the whole ricotta on a platter, pour on the dressing and scatter with the semi-dried tomatoes. Serve with thin slices of Italian-style bread or bruschetta.

Serves 8–10

Tomato and Basil Croustades

- 1 day-old unsliced white bread loaf
- 3 tablespoons olive oil
- 2 cloves garlic, crushed
- 3 tomatoes, diced
- 250 g (8¾ oz) bocconcini, cut into small chunks
- 1 tablespoon tiny capers, rinsed and dried
- 1 tablespoon extra virgin olive oil
- 2 teaspoons balsamic vinegar
- 4 tablespoons shredded fresh basil

Preheat the oven to moderate 180°C (350°F/Gas 4). Remove the crusts from the bread and cut the loaf into 4 even pieces. Using a small serrated knife, cut a square from the centre of each cube of bread, leaving a border of about 1.5 cm (⅝ inch) on each side. You should be left with 4 'boxes'. Combine the oil and garlic and brush all over the croustades. Place them on a baking tray (sheet) and bake for about 20 minutes, or until golden and crisp. Check them occasionally to make sure they don't burn.

Meanwhile, combine the tomato and bocconcini with the tiny capers in a bowl. In a jug, stir together the oil and balsamic vinegar, then gently toss with the tomato mixture. Season with salt and freshly ground black pepper, then stir in the basil. Spoon into the croustades, allowing any excess to tumble over the sides.

Note: This recipe is a delicious first course for serving in summer. Choose very ripe tomatoes for maximum flavour. You can substitute diced feta for the bocconcini.

Serves 4

Grilled Mushrooms with Sesame Seeds

- **1 tablespoon sesame seeds**
- **400 g (14 oz) medium, flat mushrooms or shiitake mushrooms**
- **2 tablespoons teriyaki sauce**
- **2 tablespoons mirin or sweet sherry**
- **1 tablespoon sugar**
- **1 tablespoon finely chopped chives**
- **1 teaspoon sesame oil**
- **10 chives, cut into short lengths**

Preheat the oven to moderate 180°C (350°/Gas 4). Sprinkle the sesame seeds on a baking tray (sheet) and bake for 10 minutes, or until golden. Remove from the tray (sheet).

Wipe the mushrooms with a damp cloth and discard the stalks. Put the mushrooms in a shallow dish. Combine the teriyaki sauce, mirin, sugar, chives and sesame oil, pour over the mushrooms and leave for 5 minutes.

Put the mushrooms on a greased baking tray (sheet), brush with half the marinade and grill (broil) under a preheated hot grill (broiler) for 5 minutes. Turn the mushrooms over, brush with the remaining marinade and grill (broil) for another 5 minutes or until browned. Garnish the mushrooms with the roasted sesame seeds and chopped chives.

Makes 30–35

81

Mushrooms with Two Sauces

- **750 g (1 lb 10 oz) button mushrooms**
- **⅓ cup (40 g/1½ oz) plain (all-purpose) flour**
- **1 cup (100 g/3½ oz) dry breadcrumbs**
- **3 eggs**
- **olive oil, for deep-frying**

- **1 teaspoon Dijon mustard**
- **1 tablespoon lemon juice**
- **1 cup (250 ml/8½ fl oz) olive oil**
- **1 small clove garlic, crushed**
- **2 tablespoons natural yoghurt**
- **2 teaspoons finely chopped fresh parsley**

Sauces
- **1 small red capsicum (pepper)**
- **2 egg yolks**

Wipe the mushrooms with paper towel and remove the stems. Measure the flour into a large plastic bag and the breadcrumbs into a separate bag. Lightly beat the eggs in a bowl.

Put the mushrooms in with the flour and shake until evenly coated. Shake off any excess flour, then dip half the mushrooms in egg to coat well. Transfer to the bag with the breadcrumbs and shake to cover thoroughly. Place on a tray (sheet) covered with baking paper. Repeat with the rest of the mushrooms, then refrigerate them all for 1 hour.

Cut the red capsicum (pepper) into large flattish pieces, discarding the membranes and seeds. Cook, skin-side-up, under a hot grill (broiler) until the skin blackens and blisters. Cool in a plastic bag, then peel. Process in a food processor or blender to a smooth paste.

Place the egg yolks, mustard and half the lemon juice in a bowl. Beat together for 1 minute with electric beaters. Add the oil, a teaspoon at a time, beating constantly until thick and creamy. Continue beating until all the oil is added, then add the remaining lemon juice. (If you prefer, you can make the mayonnaise in a blender.) Divide the mayonnaise between two bowls. Into one, stir the garlic, yoghurt and parsley and into the other, the red capsicum (pepper) mixture.

Fill a heavy-based saucepan one third full of oil and heat the oil to 180°C (350°F), or until a cube of bread dropped into the oil browns in 15 seconds. Gently lower batches of the mushrooms into the oil and cook for 1–2 minutes, or until golden brown. Remove with a slotted spoon and drain on paper towels.

To serve, arrange the mushrooms on serving plates and spoon a little of each sauce into each mushroom. If you prefer, you can keep the sauces separate, filling each mushroom with either one or the other.

Note: Cook the mushrooms just before serving. The sauces can be made up to 1 day ahead and refrigerated, covered.

Serves 8

Cheese and Spinach Roulade Bruschetta

- **1 French bread stick**
- **2 tablespoons oil**
- **500 g (1 lb 2 oz) English (common) spinach**
- **90 g (3¼ oz) spreadable cream cheese**
- **90 g (3¼ oz) goat's cheese**
- **3 tablespoons canned pimento (roast red capsicum/pepper), drained and finely chopped**

Preheat the oven to moderately hot 200°C (400°F/Gas 6). Cut the bread into 24 thin slices and lightly brush both sides with oil. Bake in a single layer on a baking tray (sheet) for 10 minutes, or until lightly browned, turning once. Remove and allow to cool.

Remove the stalks from the spinach and place the leaves in a bowl. Cover with boiling water and leave for a couple of minutes, or until the leaves have wilted. Drain and leave to cool. Squeeze out the excess liquid and drain on crumpled paper towels.

Lay the spinach leaves flat, overlapping, on a piece of plastic wrap, to form a 25 × 20 cm (10 × 8 inch) rectangle. Beat the cheeses together until soft and smooth. Spread the cheese mixture evenly and carefully over the spinach. Top the cheese evenly with pimento (roasted red capsicum/pepper). Using the plastic wrap as a guide, carefully roll up the spinach to enclose the cheese. Remove the plastic wrap and cut the log into thin slices using a sharp knife. Serve on the toast.

Note: Be sure to thoroughly drain the spinach and pimento (roasted red capsicum/pepper) to avoid a watery result.

Makes about 24

Vegetable Ramekins with Relish

- 1 large eggplant (aubergine), cut into 1 cm (½ inch) cubes
- 1 tablespoon salt
- 200 g (7 oz) fresh ricotta cheese
- 1¼ cups (310 g/11 oz) sour cream
- 3 eggs
- 1 tablespoon cornflour (cornstarch)
- 1 cup (135 g/4¾ oz) grated zucchini (courgette)
- ½ teaspoon cracked black pepper

Capsicum (Pepper) Relish
- ¾ cup (185 ml/6½ fl oz) brown vinegar
- ⅓ cup (90 g/3¼ oz) sugar
- 1 teaspoon yellow mustard seeds
- 1 green apple, peeled and chopped
- 1 pear, peeled and chopped
- 1 red capsicum (pepper), chopped
- 1 green capsicum (pepper), chopped

Preheat the oven to hot 210°C (415°F/Gas 6–7). Brush six ½ -¾ cup capacity ramekins with oil. Place the eggplant (aubergine) in a colander, sprinkle with salt and set aside for 20 minutes. Rinse under cold water; drain well.

Using electric beaters, beat ricotta and sour cream in a small bowl until light and creamy. Add eggs and cornflour (cornstarch) and beat until smooth. Transfer to large bowl and gently fold in the eggplant (aubergine), zucchini (courgette) and black pepper.

Spoon the mixture evenly into prepared ramekins. Arrange in a deep baking dish. Fill dish two-thirds up the side of ramekins with warm water; cover baking dish loosely with foil. Bake for 40 minutes or until a skewer comes out clean when inserted into the centre of ramekins. When ready to serve, top or accompany with Capsicum (Pepper) Relish.

To make Capsicum (Pepper) Relish: Heat vinegar, sugar and mustard seeds in a pan for 5 minutes or until sugar dissolves and mixture boils. Add remaining ingredients. Bring to boil, reduce heat and simmer, uncovered, for 30 minutes.

Makes 6

Nachos with Guacamole

- **440 g (15½ oz) canned red kidney beans, rinsed and drained**
- **4 tablespoons ready-made tomato salsa**
- **250 g (8¾ oz) corn (nacho) chips**
- **2 cups (250 g/8¾ oz) grated Cheddar (American) cheese**
- **1½ cups (375 g/13¼ oz) ready-made tomato salsa, extra**
- **4 tablespoons sour cream**

Guacamole
- **1 large avocado**
- **1 spring (green) onion, finely chopped**
- **1 small tomato, finely chopped**
- **1 tablespoon lemon juice**
- **freshly ground black pepper**

Preheat oven to moderate 180°C (350°F/Gas 4). Combine kidney beans and salsa; divide mixture between four ovenproof serving plates. Cover with corn (nacho) chips and grated cheese. Place in the oven for 3–5 minutes, until cheese has melted.

To assemble, spoon the extra salsa onto melted cheese; top with guacamole and sour cream.

To make Guacamole: Cut the avocado in half, discard the skin and stone. Mash the flesh lightly with a fork and combine with spring (green) onion, tomato, lemon juice and pepper.

Serves 4

Timballo of Leeks and Basil

- **pinch of saffron threads**
- **½ cup (125 ml/4¼ fl oz) dry white wine**
- **3 cups (750 ml/26 fl oz) vegetable stock (broth)**
- **50 g (1¾ oz) butter**
- **1 onion, finely chopped**
- **2 garlic cloves, crushed**
- **1⅔ cups (360 g/12¾ oz) risotto rice**
- **leaves from 2 thyme sprigs**
- **½ cup (50 g/1¾ oz) freshly grated Parmesan cheese**

- **2 tablespoons olive oil**
- **2 leeks (white part only), thinly sliced**
- **400 g (14 oz) thin zucchini (courgettes), thinly sliced on the diagonal**
- **¼ teaspoon freshly grated nutmeg**
- **10 basil leaves, shredded**
- **⅓ cup (80 g/2¾ oz) sour cream**

Soak the saffron in the wine. Pour the stock (broth) and ½ cup (125 ml/4¼ fl oz) water into a saucepan and bring to the boil. Reduce the heat, cover with a lid and keep at a low simmer.

Melt half the butter in a large saucepan wider than it is high. Add the onion and garlic and cook over low heat for about 5 minutes, or until softened but not browned. Add the rice and stir until well coated. Stir in the thyme and season well. Stir in the saffron-infused wine, then increase the heat and cook, stirring constantly, until it is absorbed. Stir ½ cup (125 ml/4¼ fl oz) of the stock (broth) into the rice, then reduce the heat and cook until it is absorbed. Continue adding more liquid, ½ cup (125 ml/4¼ fl oz) at a time until all the liquid is absorbed and the rice is tender and creamy. This will take around 25–30 minutes. Remove from the heat and stir in the remaining butter and the Parmesan.

Heat the oil in a frying pan and cook the leeks without browning over low heat for 5 minutes. Add the zucchini (courgette) slices and cook for about 5 minutes, or until softened. Add the nutmeg and season well with salt and freshly ground black pepper. Stir in the basil and sour cream. Cook, stirring, for 2–3 minutes, or until the sauce thickens.

Preheat the oven to moderate 180°C (350°F/Gas 4) and grease a 1.5 litre (1.6 US qt/1.3 UK qt) pudding basin or rounded ovenproof bowl. Cut out a piece of greaseproof paper the size of the basin's base and line the base.

Cover with half the rice mixture, pressing it down firmly. Spoon in two-thirds of the zucchini (courgette) mixture, keeping the remaining one-third warm in the pan. Press in the last of the rice mixture. Cover with foil and transfer to the oven.

Bake for 20 minutes. Remove from the oven and rest for 5 minutes. Carefully unmould onto a serving plate. Serve the reserved zucchini (courgette) on the side and serve at once.

Serves 4–6

Sides
and
Salads

Garden Salad

- **1 green oak-leaf lettuce**
- **150 g (5¼ oz) rocket (arugula)**
- **1 small radicchio (red chicory)**
- **1 large green capsicum (pepper), cut into thin strips**
- **zest of 1 lemon**

Dressing
- **2 tablespoons roughly chopped fresh coriander (cilantro)**
- **¼ cup (60 ml/2 fl oz) lemon juice**
- **2 teaspoons soft brown sugar**
- **2 tablespoons olive oil**
- **1 clove garlic, crushed (optional)**

Wash and dry the salad greens thoroughly; tear into bite-size pieces. Combine salad greens, green pepper and lemon zest in a large serving bowl.

To make Dressing: Whisk all ingredients in a small mixing bowl for 2 minutes or until well combined. Pour dressing over salad and toss to combine. Serve chilled.

Note: Make dressing and salad just before serving. Choose a selection of your favourite salad greens for this recipe. This is delicious served in summer with a chilled frascati or a light red wine.

Serves 4–6

Coleslaw

- ½ green (savoy) cabbage
- ¼ red cabbage
- 3 carrots, coarsely grated
- 6 radishes, coarsely grated
- 1 red capsicum (pepper), chopped
- 4 spring (green) onions, sliced
- 3 tablespoons chopped fresh flat-leaf parsley
- 1 cup (250 g/8¾ oz) good-quality mayonnaise

Remove the hard cores from the cabbages and thinly shred the leaves with a sharp knife. Place in a large bowl and add the carrot, radish, red capsicum (pepper), spring (green) onion and parsley.

Add the mayonnaise, season with salt and freshly ground black pepper and toss well.

Note: The vegetables can be chopped and refrigerated for up to 3 hours before serving. Add the mayonnaise just before serving.

Serves 10

Haloumi with Salad and Garlic Bread

- 4 firm, ripe tomatoes
- 1 Lebanese cucumber
- 140 g (5 oz) rocket (arugula)
- ½ cup (80 g/2¾ oz) Kalamata olives
- 1 loaf crusty unsliced white bread

- 5 tablespoons olive oil
- 1 large clove garlic, cut in half
- 400 g (14 oz) haloumi cheese
- 1 tablespoon lemon juice
- 1 tablespoon chopped fresh oregano

Preheat the oven to moderate 180°C (350°F/Gas 4). Heat the grill (broiler) to high.

Cut the tomatoes and cucumber into bite-sized chunks and place in a serving dish with the rocket (arugula) and olives. Mix well.

Slice the bread into eight 1.5 cm (⅝ inch) slices, drizzle 1½ tablespoons of the olive oil over the bread and season with salt and pepper. Grill (broil) until lightly golden, then rub each slice thoroughly with a cut side of the garlic. Wrap loosely in foil and keep warm in the oven.

Cut the haloumi into 8 slices. Heat ½ tablespoon of the oil in a shallow frying pan and fry the haloumi slices for 1–2 minutes on each side, until crisp and golden brown.

Whisk together the lemon juice, oregano and remaining olive oil to use as a dressing. Season, to taste. Pour half the dressing over the salad and toss well. Arrange the haloumi on top and drizzle with dressing. Serve immediately with the warm garlic bread.

Serves 4

92

Chinese Vegetables

- **500 g (1 lb 2 oz) Chinese green vegetables (see Note)**
- **2 teaspoons peanut oil**
- **½ teaspoon finely chopped garlic**
- **1 tablespoon vegetarian oyster sauce**
- **½ teaspoon caster (berry) sugar**
- **2 tablespoons water**
- **1 teaspoon sesame oil**

Bring a large pan of water to the boil.

Wash Chinese greens. Remove any tough leaves and trim stems. Chop greens into 3 equal portions.

Add the greens to the pan of boiling water. Cook for 1 to 2 minutes, or until just tender but still crisp. Use tongs to remove greens from the pan, drain well and place on a heated serving platter.

Heat the peanut oil in a small pan and cook the garlic briefly. Add the vegetarian oyster sauce, sugar, water and sesame oil and bring to the boil. Pour over the greens and toss to coat. Serve immediately.

Note: Use choy sum, bok choy or Chinese broccoli (gai lan), or a combination of any two.

Serves 4

Tabbouleh

- ¾ cup (130 g/4½ oz) burghul
- 3 ripe tomatoes
- 1 telegraph cucumber
- 4 spring (green) onions, sliced
- 4 cups (120 g/4¼ oz) chopped fresh flat-leaf parsley
- ½ cup (25 g/¾ oz) chopped fresh mint

Dressing
- ⅓ cup (80 ml/2¾ fl oz) lemon juice
- ¼ cup (60 ml/2 fl oz) olive oil
- 1 tablespoon extra virgin olive oil

Place the burghul in a bowl, cover with 2 cups (500 ml/17 fl oz) water and leave for 1½ hours.

Cut the tomatoes in half, squeeze gently to remove any excess seeds and cut into 1 cm (½ inch) cubes. Cut the cucumber in half lengthways, remove the seeds with a teaspoon and cut the flesh into 1 cm (½ inch) cubes.

To make the dressing, place the lemon juice and 1½ teaspoons salt in a bowl and whisk until well combined. Season well with freshly ground black pepper and slowly whisk in the olive oil and extra virgin olive oil.

Drain the burghul and squeeze out any excess water. Spread the burghul out on a clean tea towel or paper towels and leave to dry for about 30 minutes. Put the burghul in a large salad bowl, add the tomato, cucumber, spring (green) onion, parsley and mint, and toss well to combine. Pour the dressing over the salad and toss until evenly coated.

Serves 6

Herbed Feta Salad

- **2 slices thick white bread**
- **200 g (7 oz) feta cheese**
- **1 clove garlic, crushed**
- **1 tablespoon finely chopped fresh marjoram**
- **1 tablespoon finely chopped fresh chives**
- **1 tablespoon finely chopped fresh basil**
- **2 tablespoons white wine vinegar**
- **⅓ cup (80 ml/2¾ fl oz) olive oil**
- **1 red coral lettuce**
- **1 butter, coral or oak-leaf lettuce**

Preheat oven to moderate 180°C (350°F/Gas 4). Remove crusts from bread and cut bread into cubes. Place on an oven tray (sheet) in a single layer; bake for 10 minutes, or until crisp and lightly golden; cool completely.

Cut feta into small cubes; place in a bowl. Combine garlic, marjoram, chives, basil, vinegar and oil in small screw-top jar and shake for 30 seconds. Pour over feta and cover with plastic wrap. Leave for at least 30 minutes, stirring occasionally. Wash and dry lettuces. Tear leaves into pieces and place in a bowl. Add feta with dressing, and bread cubes; toss.

Serves 6–8

Insalata Caprese

- **3 large vine-ripened tomatoes**
- **250 g (8¾ oz) bocconcini**
- **12 fresh basil leaves**

- **¼ cup (60 ml/2 fl oz) extra virgin olive oil**
- **4 fresh basil leaves, roughly torn, extra**

Slice the tomato into twelve 1 cm (½ inch) slices. Slice the bocconcini into 24 slices the same thickness as the tomato.

Arrange the tomato slices on a serving plate, alternating them with 2 slices of bocconcini and placing a basil leaf between the bocconcini slices.

Drizzle with the olive oil, sprinkle with the torn basil and season well with salt and freshly ground black pepper.

Note: You could use whole cherry tomatoes and toss them with the bocconcini and basil.

Serves 4

Vietnamese Salad

- **200 g (7 oz) dried rice vermicelli**
- **1 cup (140 g/5 oz) crushed peanuts**
- **½ cup (10 g/⅓ oz) fresh Vietnamese mint leaves, torn**
- **½ cup (15 g/½ oz) firmly packed fresh coriander (cilantro) leaves**
- **½ red onion, cut into thin wedges**
- **1 green mango, cut into julienne strips**
- **1 Lebanese cucumber, halved lengthways and thinly sliced on the diagonal**

Lemon Grass Dressing
- **½ cup (125 ml/4¼ fl oz) lime juice**
- **1 tablespoon shaved palm sugar**
- **¼ cup (60 ml/2 fl oz) seasoned rice vinegar**
- **2 stems lemon grass, finely chopped**
- **2 red chillies, seeded and finely chopped**
- **3 kaffir lime leaves, shredded**

Place the rice vermicelli in a bowl and cover with boiling water. Leave for 10 minutes, or until soft, then drain, rinse under cold water and cut into short lengths.

Place the vermicelli, three-quarters of the peanuts, the mint, coriander (cilantro), onion, mango and cucumber in a large bowl and toss together.

To make the dressing, place all the ingredients in a jar with a lid and shake together. Toss the salad and dressing and refrigerate for 30 minutes. Sprinkle with the remaining nuts to serve.

Serves 4–6

Sprout and Pear Salad with Sesame Dressing

- **250 g (8¾ oz) snow pea (mange tout) sprouts**
- **250 g (8¾ oz) fresh bean sprouts**
- **30 g (1 oz) fresh chives**
- **100 g (3½ oz) snow peas (mange tout)**
- **1 celery stick**
- **2 firm pears, not green**
- **fresh coriander (cilantro) sprigs**
- **sesame seeds, for garnish**

Sesame Dressing
- **2 tablespoons soy sauce**
- **1 teaspoon sesame oil**
- **1 tablespoon soft brown sugar**
- **2 tablespoons peanut oil**
- **1 tablespoon rice vinegar**

Wash and drain the snow pea (mange tout) sprouts. Remove the brown tips from the bean sprouts. Cut the chives into 4 cm (1½ inch) lengths and cut the snow peas (mange tout) and celery into thin matchstick strips. Peel and core the pears. Cut them into thin strips, slightly wider than the celery and snow peas (mange tout). Place in a bowl and cover with water to prevent discoloration.

To make Sesame Dressing: Combine all the ingredients in a small screw-top jar and shake them well.

Drain the pears. Combine all salad ingredients and the coriander (cilantro) sprigs in a large serving bowl. Pour the dressing over and toss lightly. Sprinkle with sesame seeds and serve immediately.

Serves 6

Asparagus Salad

- **2 red capsicums (peppers)**
- **⅓ cup (80 ml/2¾ fl oz) virgin olive oil**
- **1 clove garlic, crushed**
- **2 tablespoons lemon juice**
- **2 tablespoons chopped basil**
- **2 tablespoons pine nuts**
- **310 g (11 oz) fresh asparagus**
- **small black (ripe) olives**

Cut the capsicums (peppers) into large pieces, removing the seeds and white membrane. Place, skin-side-up, under a hot grill (broiler) until the skin blackens and blisters. Cool under a tea towel or in a plastic bag, then carefully peel away and discard the skin. Finely dice the capsicum (pepper) flesh.

Put the olive oil, garlic, lemon juice and basil in a small bowl and whisk to combine. Add the capsicum (pepper) and pine nuts, and season with salt and pepper.

Remove the woody ends from the asparagus (hold each spear at both ends and bend gently – the woody end will snap off at its natural breaking point). Plunge the asparagus into a large frying pan of boiling water and cook for 3 minutes, or until just tender. Drain and plunge into a bowl of iced water, then drain again and gently pat dry with paper towels.

Arrange the asparagus on a large serving platter and spoon the dressing over the top. Garnish with the black (ripe) olives and perhaps a few lemon wedges to squeeze over the top.

Serves 4

Spicy Lentil Salad

- 1 cup (220 g/7¾ oz) brown rice
- 1 cup (185 g/6½ oz) brown lentils
- 1 teaspoon turmeric
- 1 teaspoon ground cinnamon
- 6 cardamom pods
- 3 star anise
- 2 bay leaves
- ¼ cup (60 ml/2 fl oz) sunflower oil
- 1 tablespoon lemon juice
- 250 g (8¾ oz) broccoli florets
- 2 carrots, cut into julienne strips
- 1 onion, finely chopped
- 2 cloves garlic, crushed

- 1 red capsicum (pepper), finely chopped
- 1 teaspoon garam masala
- 1 teaspoon ground coriander
- 1½ cups (250 g/8¾ oz) fresh or frozen peas, thawed

Mint and Yoghurt Dressing
- 1 cup (250 g/8¾ oz) plain yoghurt
- 1 tablespoon lemon juice
- 1 tablespoon chopped fresh mint
- 1 teaspoon cumin seeds

Put 3 cups (750 ml/26 fl oz) water with the rice, lentils, turmeric, cinnamon, cardamom, star anise and bay leaves in a pan. Stir well and bring to the boil. Reduce the heat, cover and simmer gently for 50–60 minutes, or until the liquid is absorbed. Remove the whole spices. Transfer the mixture to a large bowl. Whisk 2 tablespoons of the oil with the lemon juice and fork through the rice mixture.

Boil, steam or microwave the broccoli and carrots until tender. Drain and refresh in cold water.

Heat the remaining oil in a large pan and add the onion, garlic and capsicum (pepper). Stir-fry for 2–3 minutes, then add the garam masala and coriander, and stir-fry (scramble-fry) for a further 1–2 minutes. Add the vegetables and toss to coat in the spice mixture. Add to the rice and fork through to combine. Cover and refrigerate until cold.

To make the dressing mix the yoghurt, lemon juice, mint and cumin seeds together, and season with salt and pepper. Spoon the salad into individual serving bowls or onto a platter and serve with the dressing.

Serves 6

South-Western Bean Salad

- 1 cup (220 g/7¾ oz) dried black beans
- 1 cup (200 g/7 oz) white cannellini (white kidney) beans
- 1 medium red (Spanish) onion
- 1 medium red capsicum (pepper)
- 270 g (9½ oz) canned corn kernels, drained
- 3 tablespoons chopped fresh coriander (cilantro)
- 1 clove garlic, crushed
- ½ teaspoon ground cumin
- ½ teaspoon French mustard
- 2 tablespoons red wine vinegar
- ¼ cup (60 ml/2 fl oz) olive oil
- salt and pepper

Soak the beans in separate bowls in cold water overnight. Drain the beans; place them in separate pans and cover with water. Bring both pans of water to the boil, reduce heat and simmer for 45 minutes or until tender. Drain, rinse and allow to cool.

Chop the onion and red capsicum (pepper). Place in a bowl and add the beans, corn and coriander (cilantro). Stir until well combined.

Combine the garlic, cumin, mustard and vinegar in a small jug; gradually whisk in the oil. Season lightly with salt and pepper. Pour over the bean mixture and toss lightly to combine.

Note: South-Western Bean Salad can be made up to a day in advance. It is a great dish to serve at a barbecue or take on a picnic, as it can be made ahead of time and will carry well. Black beans are also known as turtle beans and are available at good delicatessens. They are not to be confused with Chinese black beans.

Serves 4–6

Tunisian Carrot Salad

- **500 g (1 lb 2 oz) carrots, thinly sliced**
- **3 tablespoons finely chopped fresh flat-leaf parsley**
- **1 teaspoon ground cumin**
- **⅓ cup (80 ml/2¾ fl oz) olive oil**
- **¼ cup (60 ml/2 fl oz) red wine vinegar**
- **2 cloves garlic, crushed**
- **¼ to ½ teaspoon harissa (Indonesian hot chilli [pepper] sauce)**
- **12 black (ripe) olives**
- **2 hard-boiled eggs, quartered**

Bring 2 cups (500 ml/17 fl oz) water to the boil in a saucepan. Add the carrot and cook until tender. Drain and transfer to a bowl. Add the parsley, cumin, olive oil, vinegar and garlic. Season with harissa and salt and pepper. Stir well.

To serve, place the carrots in a serving dish and garnish with the olives and eggs.

Note: If the carrots are not sweet, you can add a little honey to the dressing. See page 279 for a harissa recipe.

Serves 6

102

Goat's Cheese Salad

- **12 slices white bread**
- **4 × 100 g (3½ oz) rounds goat's cheese**
- **60 g (2 oz) mixed salad leaves (mesclun)**
- **60 g (2 oz) rocket (arugula)**
- **250 g (8¾ oz) cherry tomatoes, halved**
- **1 tablespoon white wine vinegar**
- **¼ cup (60 ml/2 fl oz) olive oil**
- **½ teaspoon wholegrain mustard**

Preheat the oven to moderate 180°C (350°F/Gas 4). Using a biscuit (cookie) cutter, cut a round out of each slice of bread. (The bread must not be larger than the cheese or the edges will burn under the grill [broiler].) Place the bread on a baking tray (sheet) and bake for 10 minutes. Slice each cheese into three.

Place a slice of cheese on each piece of bread. Arrange a bed of salad leaves and rocket (arugula) on small individual serving plates; top with several tomato halves. Cook cheese and bread rounds under a preheated hot grill (broiler) for 5 minutes or until the cheese turns golden and bubbles. Drizzle salad leaves with dressing and place 3 cheese rounds on top of each salad. Sprinkle with chopped chives to serve, if desired.

To make dressing: Combine vinegar, oil and mustard in a small screw-top jar; shake vigorously for a minute or so until well combined.

Serves 4

Fresh Beetroot and Goat's Cheese Salad

- 1 kg (2 lb 3 oz) fresh beetroot (beets) (4 bulbs with leaves)
- 200 g (7 oz) green beans
- 1 tablespoon red wine vinegar
- 2 tablespoons extra virgin olive oil
- 1 clove garlic, crushed
- 1 tablespoon drained capers, coarsely chopped
- 100 g (3½ oz) goat's cheese

Trim the leaves from the beetroot (beets). Scrub the bulbs and wash the leaves well. Add the whole bulbs to a large saucepan of salted water, bring to the boil, then reduce the heat and simmer, covered, for 30 minutes, or until tender when pierced with the point of a knife.

Meanwhile, bring a saucepan of water to the boil, add the beans and cook for 3 minutes, or until just tender. Remove with a slotted spoon and plunge into a bowl of cold water. Drain well. Add the beetroot (beet) leaves to the same saucepan of water and cook for 3–5 minutes, or until the leaves and stems are tender. Drain, plunge into a bowl of cold water, then drain well.

Drain and cool the beetroots (beets), then peel the skins off and cut the bulbs into thin wedges.

For the dressing, put the red wine vinegar, oil, garlic, capers, ½ teaspoon each of salt and pepper in a screw top jar and shake.

To serve, divide the beans, beetroot (beet) leaves and bulbs among four serving plates. Crumble goat's cheese over the top of each and drizzle with dressing. Delicious served with fresh crusty bread.

Serves 4

Summer Salad

- 1½ cups (330 g/11⅔ oz) dried chickpeas (garbanzo beans)
- 1 small Lebanese cucumber
- 2 medium tomatoes
- 1 small red (Spanish) onion
- 3 tablespoons chopped fresh parsley
- ½ cup (60 g/2 oz) pitted black (ripe) olives
- 1 tablespoon lemon juice
- 3 tablespoons olive oil
- 1 clove garlic, crushed
- 1 teaspoon honey

Place the chickpeas (garbanzo beans) in a large bowl and cover with cold water. Leave to soak overnight. Drain the chickpeas (garbanzo beans), place in a pan, cover with fresh water and cook for 25 minutes or until just tender. Drain and allow to cool.

Cut the cucumber in half lengthways, scoop out seeds and cut into 1 cm (½ inch) slices. Cut the tomatoes into cubes roughly the same size as the chickpeas (garbanzo beans), and chop onion finely. Combine the chickpeas (garbanzo beans), cucumber, tomato, onion, parsley and olives in a serving bowl.

Place the lemon juice, oil, garlic and honey in a small screw-top jar and shake well. Pour the dressing over the salad and toss lightly to combine. Serve at room temperature.

Serves 6

Orange and Date Salad

- 6 navel oranges
- 2 teaspoons orange blossom water
- 8 dates, pitted and thinly
  sliced lengthways
- 90 g (3¼ oz) slivered almonds,
  lightly toasted
- 1 tablespoon shredded fresh mint
- ¼ teaspoon ras el hanout or cinnamon

Peel the oranges, removing all the pith. Section them by cutting away all the membranes from the flesh. Place the segments in a bowl and squeeze the juice from the remainder of the orange over them. Add the orange blossom water and stir gently to combine. Cover with plastic wrap and refrigerate until chilled.

Place the segments and the juice on a large flat dish and scatter the dates and almonds over the top. Sprinkle the mint and ras el hanout or cinnamon over the orange segments. Serve chilled.

Serves 4–6

Green Olive, Walnut and Pomegranate Salad

- **1 cup (100 g/3½ oz) walnut halves**
- **½ cup (125 ml/4¼ fl oz) olive oil**
- **1½ tablespoons pomegranate syrup**
- **½ teaspoon chilli flakes**
- **2 cups (350 g/12¼ oz) green olives, pitted and cut in halves**
- **1 cup (175 g/6¼ oz) pomegranate seeds**
- **1 large red onion, chopped**
- **1 cup (20 g/⅔ oz) fresh flat-leaf parsley leaves**

Soak the walnut halves in boiling water for 3–4 minutes, or until the skins peel off readily. Drain, peel and pat dry. Lightly toast under a medium grill (broiler) and when cool, roughly chop.

Combine the olive oil, pomegranate syrup and chilli flakes in a screw top jar and shake well.

Place the olives, pomegranate seeds, onion, walnuts and parsley in a bowl and toss. Just before serving, pour the dressing over, season, to taste, and combine well.

Serves 4

Stuffed Mushroom Salad

- **20 button mushrooms**
- **¼ cup (60 g/2 oz) pesto, chilled**
- **100 g (3½ oz) rocket (arugula) leaves**
- **1 green oak-leaf lettuce**
- **12 small black (ripe) olives**
- **⅓ cup (50 g/1¾ oz) sliced semi-dried or sun-dried tomatoes**
- **1 tablespoon roughly chopped basil**
- **Parmesan shavings, to serve**

Dressing
- **⅓ cup (80 ml/2¾ fl oz) olive oil**
- **1 tablespoon white wine vinegar**
- **1 teaspoon Dijon mustard**

Trim the mushroom stalks level with the caps and scoop out the remaining stalk with a melon baller. Spoon the pesto into the mushrooms.

To make the dressing, whisk together all the ingredients. Season with salt and pepper, to taste.

Arrange the rocket (arugula) and lettuce leaves on a serving plate and top with the mushrooms, olives, tomato and basil. Drizzle the dressing over the salad and top with the Parmesan shavings. Serve immediately.

Hint: Home-made pesto is preferable for this recipe. To make your own, process 1 cup (30 g/1 oz) loosely packed basil leaves, 2 tablespoons pine nuts and ¼ cup (25 g/¾ oz) grated Parmesan in a food processor to form a smooth paste. Gradually pour in ¼ cup (60 ml/2 fl oz) olive oil in a steady stream with the motor running. Process until combined.

Serves 4

Salata Horiatiki

- 1 telegraph cucumber, peeled
- 2 green capsicums (peppers)
- 4 vine-ripened tomatoes, cut into wedges
- 1 red onion, finely sliced
- 16 Kalamata olives
- 250 g (8¾ oz) Greek feta, cubed

- 24 fresh flat-leaf parsley leaves
- 12 whole fresh mint leaves
- ½ cup (125 ml/4¼ fl oz) good-quality olive oil
- 2 tablespoons lemon juice
- 1 clove garlic, crushed

Cut the cucumber in half lengthways and discard the seeds. Cut into bite-sized pieces. Cut each capsicum (pepper) in half lengthways, remove the membrane and seeds and cut the flesh into 1 cm (½ inch) wide strips. Gently mix the cucumber, green capsicum (pepper), tomato, onion, olives, feta, parsley and mint leaves in a large salad bowl.

Place the oil, lemon juice and garlic in a screw top jar, season and shake well. Pour over the salad and serve.

Serves 4

Lentil Salad

- 1 small onion
- 2 cloves
- 1½ cups (300 g/10½ oz) puy lentils (see Note)
- 1 strip lemon rind
- 2 cloves garlic, peeled
- 1 fresh bay leaf
- 2 teaspoons ground cumin
- 2 tablespoons red wine vinegar
- ¼ cup (60 ml/2 fl oz) olive oil
- 1 tablespoon lemon juice
- 2 tablespoons finely chopped fresh mint leaves
- 3 spring (green) onions, finely chopped

Stud the onion with the cloves and place in a saucepan with the lentils, rind, garlic, bay leaf, 1 teaspoon cumin and 3½ cups (875 ml/30 fl oz) water. Bring to the boil and simmer gently over medium heat for 25–30 minutes, or until the lentils are tender. Drain off any excess liquid and discard the onion, rind and bay leaf. Reserve the garlic and finely chop.

Whisk together the vinegar, oil, juice, garlic and remaining cumin. Stir the dressing through the lentils with the mint and spring (green) onion. Season well, then leave for 30 minutes to allow the flavours to develop. Serve at room temperature.

Note: Puy lentils are small green lentils, available from gourmet food stores.

Serves 4–6

Warm Bean Salad

- **2 tablespoons olive oil**
- **1 medium onion, finely chopped**
- **1 clove garlic, crushed**
- **1 small red capsicum (pepper), cut into short strips**
- **90 g (3¼ oz) green beans**
- **60 g (2 oz) button mushrooms, sliced**
- **1 tablespoon balsamic vinegar**
- **440 g (15½ oz) canned mixed beans**
- **chopped fresh parsley, for serving**

Heat half the oil in a medium pan. Add the onions and cook for 2 minutes over medium heat. Add the garlic, red capsicum (pepper), green beans, mushrooms and vinegar. Cook for another 5 minutes, stirring occasionally.

Thoroughly rinse and drain the mixed beans. Add to the vegetables with the remaining oil and stir until just warmed through. Sprinkle with chopped parsley for serving.

Serves 4

Mexicana Salad

- **250 g (8¾ oz) dried black-eyed beans**
- **250 g (8¾ oz) dried red kidney beans**
- **500 g (1 lb 2 oz) sweet potato (yam)**
- **1 large red onion, chopped**
- **1 large green capsicum (pepper), chopped**
- **3 ripe tomatoes, chopped**
- **3 tablespoons chopped fresh basil**
- **3 flour tortillas**
- **1 tablespoon oil**
- **2 tablespoons grated Parmesan**
- **¼ cup (60 g/2 oz) sour cream**

Dressing
- **1 clove garlic, crushed**
- **1 tablespoon lime juice**
- **2 tablespoons olive oil**

Guacamole
- **3 ripe avocados**
- **2 tablespoons lemon juice**
- **1 clove garlic, crushed**
- **1 small red onion, finely chopped**
- **1 small red chilli, seeded and chopped**
- **¼ cup (60 g/2 oz) sour cream**
- **2 tablespoons hot taco sauce**

Soak the beans in a large bowl of cold water overnight. Drain and cook in a large pan of rapidly boiling water for 30 minutes, or until just tender. Skim off any scum that appears on the surface during cooking. Do not overcook or the beans will be mushy. Drain and set aside to cool.

Chop the sweet potato (yam) into small cubes and cook in boiling water for 5 minutes, or until tender. Drain and allow to cool, then combine with the onion, capsicum (pepper), tomato and beans. Stir in the basil.

For the dressing, combine all the ingredients in a jar and shake well until combined. Pour over the salad and toss gently to coat.

Preheat the oven to moderate 180°C (350°F/Gas 4). Using a small knife or shaped cutter, cut Christmas tree shapes out of the tortillas, brush lightly with the oil, place on baking trays (sheets) and sprinkle with grated Parmesan. Bake for 5–10 minutes, or until crisp and golden.

To make the guacamole, mash the avocados with the lemon juice. Add the garlic, onion, chilli, sour cream and taco sauce and mix well.

Put the salad in a large bowl or on a platter, pile the guacamole in the centre, top with the sour cream and arrange the Christmas tree shapes on top.

Serves 10–12

Pasta

Pasta Pronto

- 2 tablespoons extra virgin olive oil
- 4 garlic cloves, finely chopped
- 1 small red chilli, finely chopped
- 3 × 400 g (14 oz) cans crushed tomatoes
- 1 teaspoon sugar
- ⅓ cup (80 ml/2¾ fl oz) dry white wine
- 3 tablespoons chopped herbs such as basil or parsley
- 400 g (14 oz) vermicelli (see Note)
- ⅓ cup (35 g/1¼ oz) shaved Parmesan cheese

Heat the oil in a large deep frying pan and cook the garlic and chilli for 1 minute. Add the tomato, sugar, wine, herbs and 1¾ cups (440 ml/15 fl oz) water. Bring to the boil and season.

Reduce the heat to medium and add the pasta, breaking the strands if the pieces are too long. Cook for 10 minutes, or until the pasta is cooked, stirring often to stop the pasta from sticking. The pasta will thicken the sauce as it cooks. Season to taste and serve in bowls with shaved Parmesan.

Note: Vermicelli is a pasta similar to spaghetti, but thinner. You can also use spaghettini or angel hair pasta for this recipe.

Serves 4

114

Farmhouse Pasta

- **375 g (13¼ oz) pasta**
- **1 large potato, cut into small cubes**
- **400 g (14 oz) broccoli**
- **⅓ cup (80 ml/2¾ fl oz) olive oil**
- **3 cloves garlic, crushed**
- **1 small fresh red chilli, finely chopped**
- **2 × 400 g (14 oz) cans diced tomatoes**
- **¼ cup (30 g/1 oz) grated Pecorino cheese**

Bring a large saucepan of salted water to the boil and cook the pasta and potato together for 8–10 minutes, or until the pasta is al dente. Drain and return to the saucepan. Meanwhile, trim the broccoli into florets and discard the stems. Place in a saucepan of boiling water and cook for 1–2 minutes, then drain and plunge into iced water. Drain and add to the cooked pasta and potato.

Heat the oil in a saucepan, add the garlic and chilli and cook for 30 seconds. Add the tomato and simmer for 5 minutes, or until slightly reduced and thickened. Season to taste with salt and cracked black pepper.

Pour the tomato mixture over the pasta, potato and broccoli. Toss well and stir over low heat until warmed through. Serve sprinkled with grated Pecorino cheese.

Serves 4

Blue Cheese with Walnut Lasagnette

- **375 g (13¼ oz) lasagnette**
- **1 cup (100 g/3½ oz) walnuts**
- **40 g (1½ oz) butter**
- **3 French shallots, finely chopped**
- **1 tablespoon brandy or cognac**
- **1 cup (250 ml/8½ fl oz) crème fraîche**
- **200 g (7 oz) gorgonzola cheese, crumbled**
- **70 g (2½ oz) baby English (common) spinach leaves**

Preheat the oven to 200°C (400°F/Gas 6). Cook the pasta in a large saucepan of boiling salted water until al dente. Drain, return to the pan and keep warm.

Meanwhile, place the walnuts on a baking tray (sheet) and roast for 5 minutes, or until golden and toasted. Cool, then roughly chop.

Heat the butter in a large saucepan, add the shallots and cook over medium heat for 1–2 minutes, or until soft, taking care not to brown. Add the brandy and simmer for 1 minute, then stir in the crème fraîche and gorgonzola. Cook for 3–4 minutes, or until the cheese has melted and the sauce has thickened.

Stir in the spinach and toasted walnuts, reserving 1 tablespoon for garnish. Heat gently until the spinach has just wilted. Season with salt and cracked black pepper. Gently mix the sauce through the pasta. Divide among serving plates and sprinkle with the reserved walnuts.

Note: The gorgonzola needs to be young as this gives a sweeter, milder flavour to the sauce.

Serves 4

Macaroni Cheese

- **225 g (8 oz) macaroni**
- **80 g (2¾ oz) butter**
- **1 onion, finely chopped**
- **3 tablespoons plain (all-purpose) flour**
- **2 cups (500 ml/17 fl oz) milk**
- **2 teaspoons wholegrain mustard**
- **250 g (8¾ oz) Cheddar (American) cheese, grated**
- **30 g (1 oz) fresh breadcrumbs**

Cook the pasta in rapidly boiling salted water until al dente. Drain. Preheat the oven to moderate 180°C (350°F/Gas 4) and grease a casserole dish.

Melt the butter in a large pan over low heat and cook the onion for 5 minutes, or until softened. Stir in the flour and cook for 1 minute, or until pale and foaming. Remove from the heat and gradually stir in the milk. Return to the heat and stir until the sauce boils and thickens. Reduce the heat and simmer for 2 minutes. Stir in the mustard and about three-quarters of the cheese. Season to taste.

Mix the pasta with the cheese sauce. Spoon into the dish and sprinkle the breadcrumbs and remaining cheese over the top. Bake for 15 minutes, or until golden brown and bubbling.

Serves 4

Penne with Olive and Pistachio Pesto

- **500 g (1 lb 2 oz) penne**
- **125 g (4⅓ oz) unsalted, shelled pistachio nuts**
- **4 cloves garlic**
- **1 tablespoon green peppercorns**
- **2 tablespoons lemon juice**
- **150 g (5¼ oz) pitted black (ripe) olives**
- **1½ cups (150 g/5¼ oz) freshly grated Parmesan plus extra, shaved, for serving**
- **½ cup (125 ml/4¼ fl oz) light olive oil**

Cook the penne in a large pan of rapidly boiling salted water until al dente. Drain and return to the pan.

While the penne is cooking, combine the pistachio nuts, garlic, peppercorns, lemon juice, black (ripe) olives and Parmesan in a food processor for 30 seconds, or until roughly chopped.

While the motor is running, gradually pour in the olive oil in a thin stream. Blend until the mixture is smooth. Toss the pesto through the hot pasta and serve topped with extra Parmesan.

Serves 4

Fresh Vegetable Lasagne with Rocket

- 1 cup (150 g/5¼ oz) fresh or frozen peas
- 16 asparagus spears, trimmed and cut into 5 cm (2 inch) lengths
- 2 large zucchini (courgettes), cut into thin ribbons
- 2 fresh lasagne sheets (noodles), each 24 cm × 35 cm (9½ inch × 14 inch)
- 100 g (3½ oz) rocket (arugula) leaves
- 1 cup (30 g/1 oz) fresh basil, torn
- 2 tablespoons extra virgin olive oil
- 250 g (8¾ oz) low-fat ricotta
- 150 g (5¼ oz) semi-dried tomatoes
- Parmesan shavings, to garnish

Balsamic Syrup
- ⅓ cup (80 ml/2¾ fl oz) balsamic vinegar
- 1½ tablespoons brown sugar

To make the syrup, place the vinegar and sugar in a saucepan and stir over medium heat until the sugar dissolves. Reduce the heat and simmer for 3 minutes, or until the sauce becomes syrupy. Remove from the heat.

Bring a saucepan of salted water to the boil. Blanch the peas, asparagus and zucchini (courgettes) in separate batches until just tender, removing each batch with a slotted spoon and refreshing in cold water. Reserve the cooking liquid and return to the boil.

Cook the lasagne sheets (noodles) in the boiling water for 1–2 minutes, or until al dente. Refresh in cold water and drain. Cut each in half lengthways.

Toss the vegetables and the rocket (arugula) with the basil and olive oil. Season.

To assemble, place one strip of pasta on a serving plate – one-third on the centre of the plate and two-thirds overhanging one side. Place some of the salad on the centre one-third, topped with some ricotta and tomato. Season and fold over one-third of the lasagne sheet (noodle). Top with another layer of salad, ricotta and tomato. Fold back the final layer of pasta and garnish with a little salad and tomato. Repeat with the remaining pasta, salad, ricotta and tomato to make four servings. Just before serving, drizzle with balsamic syrup and garnish with Parmesan.

Serves 4

Sweet Potato Ravioli

- **500 g (1 lb 2 oz) orange sweet potato (yam), cut into large pieces**
- **¼ cup (60 ml/2 fl oz) olive oil**
- **150 g (5¼ oz) ricotta cheese**
- **1 tablespoon chopped fresh basil**
- **1 clove garlic, crushed**
- **2 tablespoons grated Parmesan**
- **2 × 250 g (8¾ oz) packets egg won ton wrappers**
- **60 g (2 oz) butter**
- **4 spring (green) onions, sliced on the diagonal**
- **2 cloves garlic, crushed, extra**
- **300 ml (10 fl oz) cream**
- **baby basil leaves, to serve**

Preheat the oven to hot 220°C (425°F/Gas 7). Place the sweet potato (yam) on a baking tray (sheet) and drizzle with oil. Bake for 40 minutes, or until tender.

Transfer the sweet potato (yam) to a bowl with the ricotta, basil, garlic and Parmesan and mash until smooth.

Cover the won ton wrappers with a damp tea towel. Place 2 level teaspoons of the sweet potato (yam) mixture into the centre of one wrapper and brush the edges with a little water. Top with another wrapper. Place onto a baking tray (sheet) lined with baking paper and cover with a tea towel. Repeat with the remaining ingredients to make 60 ravioli, placing a sheet of baking paper between each layer.

Melt the butter in a frying pan. Add the spring (green) onion and garlic and cook over medium heat for 1 minute. Add the cream, bring to the boil, then reduce the heat and simmer for 4–5 minutes, or until the cream has reduced and thickened. Keep warm.

Bring a large saucepan of water to the boil. Cook the ravioli in batches for 2–4 minutes, or until just tender. Drain well. Ladle the hot sauce over the top of the ravioli, garnish with the basil leaves and serve immediately.

Serves 4

Spinach and Ricotta Gnocchi

- **4 slices white bread**
- **½ cup (125 ml/4¼ fl oz) milk**
- **500 g (1 lb 2 oz) frozen spinach, thawed**
- **250 g (8¾ oz) ricotta cheese**
- **2 eggs**

- **½ cup (50 g/1¾ oz) freshly grated Parmesan, plus some shaved Parmesan, for serving**
- **¼ cup (30 g/1 oz) plain (all-purpose) flour**

Remove the crust from the bread and soak the bread in the milk, in a shallow dish, for 10 minutes. Squeeze out all the excess liquid. Then squeeze excess liquid from the spinach.

Combine the bread in a bowl with the spinach, ricotta cheese, eggs, Parmesan and salt and pepper. Use a fork to mix thoroughly. Cover and refrigerate for 1 hour.

Lightly dust your hands in flour. Roll heaped teaspoonsful of the mixture into dumplings. Lower batches of the gnocchi into a large pan of boiling salted water. Cook for about 2 minutes, or until the gnocchi rise to the surface. Transfer to serving plates. Drizzle with foaming butter, if you wish, and serve with shaved Parmesan.

Serves 4–6

Spaghettini with Asparagus and Rocket

- **100 ml (3½ fl oz) extra virgin olive oil**
- **16 thin asparagus spears, cut into 5 cm (2 inch) lengths**
- **375 g (13¼ oz) spaghettini**
- **120 g (4½ oz) rocket (arugula), shredded**
- **2 small fresh red chillies, finely chopped**
- **2 teaspoons finely grated lemon rind**
- **1 clove garlic, finely chopped**
- **1 cup (100 g/3½ oz) grated Parmesan**
- **2 tablespoons lemon juice**

Bring a large saucepan of water to the boil over medium heat. Add 1 tablespoon of the oil and a pinch of salt to the water and blanch the asparagus for 3–4 minutes. Remove the asparagus with a slotted spoon, refresh under cold water, drain and place in a bowl. Return the water to a rapid boil and add the spaghettini. Cook the pasta until al dente. Drain and return to the pan.

Meanwhile, add the rocket (arugula), chilli, lemon rind, garlic and ⅔ cup (65 g/2⅓ oz) of the Parmesan to the asparagus and mix well. Add to the pasta, pour on the lemon juice and remaining olive oil and season with salt and freshly ground black pepper. Stir well to evenly coat the pasta with the mixture. Divide among four pasta bowls, top with the remaining Parmesan and serve.

Note: You can use other types of pasta such as tagliatelle, macaroni or spiral-shaped pasta.

Serves 4

Gnocchi Romana

- **3 cups (750 ml/26 fl oz) milk**
- **½ teaspoon ground nutmeg**
- **⅔ cup (85 g/3 oz) semolina**
- **1 egg, beaten**
- **1½ cups (150 g/5¼ oz) freshly grated Parmesan**

- **60 g (2 oz) butter, melted**
- **½ cup (125 m/4¼ fl oz) cream**
- **½ cup (75 g/2⅔ oz) freshly grated mozzarella cheese**

Line a deep Swiss roll tin with baking paper. Combine the milk, half the nutmeg, and salt and freshly ground pepper, to taste, in a medium pan. Bring to the boil, reduce the heat and gradually stir in the semolina. Cook, stirring occasionally, for 5–10 minutes, or until the semolina is stiff.

Remove the pan from the heat, add the egg and 1 cup of the Parmesan. Stir to combine and then spread the mixture in the tin. Refrigerate for 1 hour, or until the mixture is firm.

Preheat the oven to moderate 180°C (350°F/Gas 4). Cut the semolina into rounds using a floured 4 cm (1½ inch) cutter and arrange in a greased shallow casserole dish.

Pour the melted butter over the top, followed by the cream. Combine the remaining grated Parmesan with the mozzarella cheese and sprinkle them on the rounds. Sprinkle with the remaining nutmeg. Bake for 20–25 minutes, or until the mixture is golden. You can serve garnished with a sprig of fresh herbs.

Note: Some claim that this traditional dish from Rome can be traced as far back as Imperial Roman times. A crisp garden salad is the ideal accompaniment for this lovely rich recipe.

Serves 4

Pasta with Pesto and Parmesan

- **500 g (1 lb 2 oz) linguine or taglierini**
- **¼ cup (40 g/1½ oz) pine nuts**
- **2 firmly packed cups (100 g/3½ oz) fresh basil leaves**
- **2 cloves garlic, chopped**
- **¼ cup (25 g/¾ oz) freshly grated Parmesan plus shavings, to garnish**
- **½ cup (125 ml/4¼ fl oz) extra virgin olive oil**

Cook the pasta in a large pan of rapidly boiling salted water until al dente. Drain and return to the pan.

While the pasta is cooking, mix the pine nuts, fresh basil leaves, garlic and Parmesan in a food processor until finely chopped. With the motor running, add the extra virgin olive oil in a slow stream until a smooth paste is formed. Season with salt and freshly ground black pepper, to taste. Toss the pesto through the hot pasta until it is thoroughly distributed. Garnish with shavings of fresh Parmesan.

Serves 4

Spaghetti Mediterranean

- **500 g (1 lb 2 oz) spaghetti**
- **750 g (1 lb 10 oz) tomatoes**
- **½ cup (125 ml/4¼ fl oz) extra virgin olive oil**
- **2 garlic cloves, crushed**
- **4 spring (green) onions, finely sliced**
- **salt (to taste)**
- **½ teaspoon grated lemon rind**
- **1 tablespoon fresh thyme leaves**
- **12 stuffed green olives, thinly sliced**
- **shredded fresh basil, for serving**

Cook the spaghetti in a large pan of rapidly boiling salted water until al dente. Drain and return to the pan.

While the pasta is cooking, score small crosses in the bases of the tomatoes. Add to a pan of boiling water for 1–2 minutes, drain and plunge into cold water. Peel down from the cross and discard the skin. Cut the tomatoes in half horizontally. Place a sieve over a small bowl and squeeze the tomato seeds and juice into it; discard the seeds. Chop the tomatoes roughly and set aside.

In a bowl, combine the olive oil, garlic, spring (green) onion, salt, lemon rind, thyme leaves and stuffed green olives. Add the chopped tomato and tomato juice, mix well and season with salt and freshly ground black pepper, to taste. Add the sauce to the pasta, toss to combine and sprinkle with shredded fresh basil.

Serves 4-6

Potato Gnocchi with Tomato and Basil Sauce

Tomato Sauce
- 1 tablespoon oil
- 1 onion, chopped
- 1 celery stick, chopped
- 2 carrots, chopped
- 2 × 425 g (15 oz) cans crushed tomatoes
- 1 teaspoon sugar
- ½ cup (30 g/1 oz) fresh basil, chopped

Potato Gnocchi
- 1 kg (2 lb 3 oz) old potatoes
- 30 g (1 oz) butter
- 2 cups (250 g/8¾ oz) plain (all-purpose) flour
- 2 eggs, beaten
- freshly grated Parmesan, for serving

To make the tomato sauce, heat the oil in a large frying pan, add the onion, celery and carrot and cook for 5 minutes, stirring regularly. Add the tomato and sugar and season with salt and pepper, to taste. Bring to the boil, reduce the heat to very low and simmer for 20 minutes. Cool slightly and process, in batches, in a food processor until smooth. Add the basil; set aside.

To make the potato gnocchi, peel the potatoes, chop roughly and steam or boil until very tender. Drain thoroughly and mash until smooth. Using a wooden spoon, stir in the butter and flour, then beat in the eggs. Cool.

Turn onto a floured surface and divide into two. Roll each into a long sausage shape. Cut into short pieces and press each piece with the back of a fork.

Cook the gnocchi, in batches, in a large pan of boiling salted water for about 2 minutes, or until the gnocchi rise to the surface. Using a slotted spoon, drain the gnocchi, and transfer to serving bowls. Serve with the tomato sauce and freshly grated Parmesan. Garnish with herbs.

Serves 4–6

126

Garlic Bucatini

- **500 g (1 lb 2 oz) bucatini**
- **⅓ cup (80 ml/2¾ fl oz) olive oil**
- **8 garlic cloves, crushed**

- **2 tablespoons chopped fresh parsley**
- **freshly grated Parmesan, for serving**

Cook the bucatini in a large pan of rapidly boiling water until al dente. Drain and return to the pan.

When the pasta is almost finished cooking, heat the olive oil over low heat in a frying pan and add the garlic. Cook for 1 minute before removing from the heat. Add the garlic oil and the parsley to the pasta and toss to distribute thoroughly. Serve with Parmesan.

Note: Olives or diced tomato can be added. Do not overcook the garlic or it will be bitter.

Serves 4

Mushroom Ravioli

- ½ cup (70 g/2½ oz) hazelnut kernels, toasted and skinned
- 90 g (3¼ oz) unsalted butter
- 150 g (5¼ oz) mushrooms
- 1 tablespoon olive oil
- 200 g (7 oz) packet won ton wrappers

Chop the hazelnuts in a food processor. Heat the butter in a pan over medium heat until it sizzles and turns nutty brown. Remove from the heat, stir in the chopped hazelnuts and season with salt and pepper, to taste.

Wipe the mushrooms with paper towel. Chop the stems and caps finely. Heat the oil in a pan, add the mushrooms and stir until soft. Add salt and pepper, and cook until the liquid has evaporated. Allow to cool.

Lay 12 won ton wrappers on a work surface and put a small teaspoonful of the mushroom filling on six of them. Brush the edges of the wrappers with water and place another wrapper on top. Press firmly to seal. If desired, trim the edges with a pasta cutter. Lay the ravioli on a tray lined with a clean tea towel and cover with another tea towel. Repeat with 12 more squares. Filling and sealing a few at a time prevents the ravioli from drying out.

When all the ravioli are made, cook in batches in a large pan of rapidly boiling salted water. Don't crowd the pan. Very thin pasta will be done in about 2 minutes after the water returns to the boil, so lift out with a slotted spoon and drain in a colander while the next batch is cooking. Serve with the hazelnut sauce.

Note: If you can't get toasted and skinned hazelnuts from your health food store, spread the nuts on a baking tray (sheet) and roast in a moderate oven for 10–12 minutes. Cool, then rub in a tea towel to remove as many of the skins as possible.

Serves 4

Cotelli with Capers, Bocconcini and Basil Oil

- ½ cup (125 ml/4¼ fl oz) olive oil
- 125 g (4⅓ oz) jar capers in brine, drained
- 500 g (1 lb 2 oz) cotelli
- 2 tablespoons lemon juice
- 2 cups (100 g/3½ oz) firmly packed fresh basil
- ⅓ cup (35 g/1 oz) grated Parmesan
- 250 g (8¾ oz) cherry tomatoes, quartered
- 8 bocconcini, quartered
- extra virgin olive oil, for serving

Heat half the olive oil in a pan, add the capers and cook over high heat for 3–4 minutes, or until crisp and golden. Drain on paper towels and set aside.

Cook the pasta in a large pan of rapidly boiling salted water until al dente. Drain and return to the pan to keep warm. Meanwhile, mix the lemon juice, 1½ cups (75 g/2⅔ oz) of the basil and the remaining olive oil in a food processor until smooth. Season.

Roughly tear the remaining basil leaves, then toss through the warm pasta with the basil mixture, 2 tablespoons of the Parmesan and the cherry tomatoes. Spoon into warmed bowls and top with the bocconcini and capers. Drizzle with extra virgin olive oil and garnish with the remaining grated Parmesan. Serve immediately.

Serves 4

Tortellini with Mushroom Sauce

Pasta
- 2 cups (250 g/8¾ oz) plain (all-purpose) flour
- pinch salt
- 3 eggs
- 1 tablespoon olive oil
- ¼ cup (60 ml/2 fl oz) water

Filling
- 125 g (4⅓ oz) packet frozen spinach, thawed, excess liquid removed
- ½ cup 125 g (4⅓ oz) ricotta cheese
- 2 tablespoons freshly grated Parmesan cheese
- 1 egg, beaten
- salt and freshly ground black pepper

Sauce
- 1 tablespoon olive oil
- 1 clove garlic, crushed
- 125 g (4⅓ oz) mushrooms, sliced
- 1 cup (250 ml/8½ fl oz) cream
- 3 tablespoons freshly grated Parmesan cheese
- salt and freshly ground black pepper

To make Pasta: Sift the flour and salt onto a board. Make a well in the centre of the flour. In a jug, whisk together eggs, oil and 1 tablespoon of the water. Add the egg mixture gradually to the flour, working in with your hands until the mixture forms a ball. Add extra water if necessary. Knead on a lightly floured surface for 5 minutes or until dough is smooth and elastic. Place the dough in a lightly oiled bowl. Cover with plastic wrap and set aside for 30 minutes.

To make Filling: In a bowl, combine the drained spinach, ricotta and Parmesan cheeses, egg, salt and pepper. Set aside.

To make Sauce: Heat the oil in a frying pan. Add the garlic and stir over low heat for 30 seconds. Add the mushrooms and cook for 3 minutes. Pour in the cream and set aside.

Roll the dough out on a lightly floured surface until it is very thin. Using a floured cutter, cut into 5 cm (2 inch) rounds. Spoon about ½ teaspoon of filling in the centre of each round. Brush a little water around the edge of each round. Fold the rounds in half to form a semi-circle. Press the edges together firmly. Wrap each semi-circle around your forefinger to form a ring. Press the ends of the dough together firmly.

Cook the tortellini in batches in a large pan of rapidly boiling water for about 8 minutes each batch, until just tender. Drain well and return to the pan. Keep warm.

Return sauce to medium heat. Bring to the boil. Reduce heat and simmer for 3 minutes. Add the Parmesan cheese, salt and pepper and stir well. Add the sauce to the tortellini and toss until well combined. Divide the tortellini and sauce between individual warmed serving bowls.

Serves 4

Fettucine with Zucchini and Crisp-Fried Basil

- **1 cup (250 ml/8½ fl oz) olive oil**
- **a handful of fresh basil leaves**
- **500 g (1 lb 2 oz) fettucine or tagliatelle**
- **60 g (2 oz) butter**
- **2 cloves garlic, crushed**
- **500 g (1 lb 2 oz) zucchini (courgettes), grated**
- **¾ cup (75 g/2⅔ oz) freshly grated Parmesan**

To crisp-fry the basil leaves, heat the oil in a small pan, add 2 leaves at a time and cook for 1 minute, or until crisp. Remove with a slotted spoon and drain on paper towels. Repeat with the remaining basil leaves.

Cook the pasta in a large pan of rapidly boiling salted water until al dente. Drain and return to the pan.

While the pasta is cooking, heat the butter in a deep heavy-based pan over low heat until the butter is foaming. Add the garlic and cook for 1 minute. Add the zucchini (courgettes) and cook, stirring occasionally, for 1–2 minutes or until softened. Add to the hot pasta. Add the Parmesan and toss well. Serve the pasta garnished with the crisp basil leaves.

Note: The basil leaves can be fried up to 2 hours in advance. Store in an airtight container after cooling.

Serves 6

132

Ricotta and Basil with Tagliatelle

- **500 g (1 lb 2 oz) tagliatelle**
- **1 cup (20 g/⅔ oz) fresh flat-leaf parsley**
- **1 cup (50 g/1¾ oz) fresh basil leaves**
- **1 teaspoon olive oil**
- **⅓ cup (50 g/1¾ oz) chopped sun-dried capsicum (pepper)**
- **1 cup (250 g/8¾ oz) sour cream**
- **250 g (8¾ oz) fresh ricotta cheese**
- **¼ cup (25 g/¾ oz) freshly grated Parmesan**

Cook the tagliatelle in a large pan of rapidly boiling salted water until al dente. Drain and return to the pan.

While the pasta is cooking, process the parsley and basil in a food processor or blender until just chopped.

Heat the oil in a pan. Add the sun-dried capsicum (pepper) and fry for 2–3 minutes. Stir in the sour cream, ricotta and Parmesan and stir over low heat for 4 minutes, or until heated through. Do not allow to boil.

Add the herbs and sauce to the pasta, toss to combine and serve.

Serves 4

Ravioli with Herbs

- **2 tablespoons olive oil**
- **1 clove garlic, halved**
- **800 g (1 lb 12 oz) ricotta-filled ravioli**
- **60 g (2 oz) butter, chopped**
- **2 tablespoons chopped fresh parsley**
- **⅓ cup (20 g/⅔ oz) chopped fresh basil**
- **2 tablespoons chopped fresh chives**

Combine oil and garlic in a small bowl; set aside. Add ravioli to a large pan of rapidly boiling water and cook until tender.

Drain ravioli well in a colander and return to pan. Add oil to pasta; discard garlic. Add butter and herbs to ravioli and toss well. As a variation, use fresh coriander (cilantro) instead of parsley. Season with salt and pepper. Sprinkle with Parmesan when serving, if you wish.

Serves 6

Creamy Asparagus Linguine

- **200 g (7 oz) fresh full-fat ricotta cheese**
- **1 cup (250 ml/8½ fl oz) cream**
- **¾ cup (75 g/2⅔ oz) freshly grated Parmesan**
- **freshly ground nutmeg, to taste**
- **500 g (1 lb 2 oz) linguine**
- **500 g (1 lb 2 oz) fresh asparagus spears, cut into short lengths**
- **½ cup (45 g/1⅔ oz) toasted flaked almonds, for serving**

Put the ricotta in a bowl and stir until smooth. Stir in the cream, Parmesan and nutmeg and season with salt and freshly ground black pepper, to taste.

Cook the linguine in a large pan of rapidly boiling salted water until not quite tender. Add the asparagus to the pan and cook for another 3 minutes.

Drain the pasta and asparagus, reserving 2 tablespoons of the cooking water. Return the pasta and asparagus to the pan.

Add the reserved cooking water to the ricotta mixture, stirring well to combine. Spoon the mixture over the pasta and toss gently. Serve sprinkled with the toasted almonds.

Note: To toast flaked almonds, you can heat them under a moderately hot grill (broiler) for about 2 minutes. Stir them occasionally and be careful to avoid burning them.

Serves 4

Ravioli with Peas and Artichokes

- **650 g (1 lb 7 oz) fresh cheese and spinach ravioli**
- **1 tablespoon olive oil**
- **8 marinated artichoke hearts, quartered**
- **2 large cloves garlic, finely chopped**
- **½ cup (125 ml/4¼ fl oz) dry white wine**
- **½ cup (125 ml/4¼ fl oz) vegetable stock (broth)**
- **2 cups (310 g/11 oz) frozen peas**
- **¼ cup (7 g/¼ oz) chopped fresh flat-leaf parsley**
- **½ teaspoon seasoned cracked pepper**

Cook the ravioli in a large pan of rapidly boiling salted water until al dente. Drain.

While the ravioli is cooking, heat the olive oil in a pan and cook the artichoke hearts and garlic over medium heat for 2 minutes, stirring frequently. Add the wine and stock (broth) and stir until well mixed. Bring to the boil, reduce the heat slightly and simmer for 5 minutes. Add the peas (they don't need to be thawed first) and simmer for another 2 minutes.

Stir the parsley and pepper into the artichoke mixture. Serve the ravioli topped with the artichoke mixture.

Note: You can buy marinated artichoke hearts in jars from supermarkets and delicatessens.

Serves 4

Roasted Vegetable Lasagne

- 1 red capsicum (pepper)
- 1 large eggplant (aubergine), sliced lengthways, salted, rinsed and well-drained
- 2 large zucchinis (courgettes), sliced thinly lengthways
- 400 g (14 oz) sweet potato (yam), peeled and sliced thinly lengthways
- 6 egg (Roma) tomatoes, quartered
- 375 g (13¼ oz) fresh lasagne sheets (noodles)
- ⅓ cup (90 g/3¼ oz) good-quality pesto
- 300 g (10½ oz) bocconcini, finely sliced

- olive oil
- 1 cup (100 g/3½ oz) freshly grated Parmesan cheese

Marinade
- ½ cup (125 ml/4¼ fl oz) olive oil
- 2 tablespoons red wine vinegar
- 1 tablespoon finely chopped capers
- 1 tablespoon finely chopped parsley
- 1 clove garlic, finely chopped
- 1 teaspoon tomato paste (tomato puree)
- salt and pepper

Preheat the oven to moderately hot 200°C (400°F/Gas 6). Combine marinade ingredients in a bowl and whisk thoroughly.

Cut red capsicum (pepper) in half lengthways. Remove seeds and membrane and cut into large, flattish pieces. Grill (broil) until skin blackens and blisters. Place on a cutting board, cover with a tea towel; allow to cool. Peel, discard skin and cut flesh into thick strips. Place red capsicum (pepper) and remaining vegetables in large baking dish; coat with half the marinade. Bake for 15 minutes, turn and coat again with remaining marinade. Cook for another 15 minutes.

Cut the pasta into 24 sheets (noodles), each 10 × 16 cm (about 4 × 6⅓ inches). Make 6 individual stacks in the following order: pasta, zucchini (courgette) and sweet potato (yam), 2 teaspoons pesto and bocconcini slices, pasta, eggplant (aubergine) and red capsicum (pepper), pasta, tomatoes, 2 teaspoons pesto and bocconcini slices, pasta. Transfer the stacks to greased baking dish. Brush the tops with olive oil and sprinkle with grated Parmesan cheese. Bake for 15–20 minutes or until heated through and tender.

Serves 6

Fusilli with Sage and Garlic

- **500 g (1 lb 2 oz) fusilli**
- **60 g (2 oz) butter**
- **2 cloves garlic, crushed**

- **½ cup (10 g/⅓ oz) fresh sage leaves**
- **2 tablespoons cream**
- **freshly grated Parmesan, for serving**

Cook the fusilli in a large pan of rapidly boiling salted water until al dente. Drain and return to the pan.

While the pasta is cooking, melt the butter in a frying pan. Add the garlic and fresh sage leaves. Cook over low heat for 4 minutes, stirring frequently.

Stir in the cream and season with some salt and freshly ground black pepper, to taste. Stir the sauce through the drained pasta until thoroughly coated. Top each serving with freshly grated Parmesan.

Serves 4

Sun-Dried Tomato Sauce on Tagliatelle

- **500 g (1 lb 2 oz) tagliatelle**
- **2 tablespoons olive oil**
- **1 onion, chopped**
- **½ cup (80 g/2¾ oz) thinly sliced sun-dried tomatoes**
- **2 cloves garlic, crushed**
- **425 g (15 oz) can chopped tomatoes**
- **1 cup (125 g/4⅓ oz) pitted black (ripe) olives**
- **⅓ cup (20 g/⅔ oz) chopped fresh basil**
- **freshly grated Parmesan, for serving**

Cook the tagliatelle in a large pan of rapidly boiling salted water until al dente. Drain and return to the pan.

Meanwhile, heat the oil in a large frying pan. Add the onion and cook for 3 minutes, stirring occasionally, until soft. Add the sliced sun-dried tomato along with the crushed garlic and cook for another minute.

Add the chopped tomato, olives and basil to the pan and season with freshly ground black pepper. Bring to the boil, reduce the heat, and simmer for 10 minutes.

Add the sauce to the hot pasta and gently toss through. Serve immediately, topped with some Parmesan.

Note: Sun-dried tomatoes are available either dry or loosely packed, or in jars with olive or canola oil. The tomatoes in oil need only to be drained, but the dry tomatoes must be soaked in boiling water for 5 minutes to rehydrate and soften before using.

Serves 4

Artichoke, Egg and Sorrel Pasta

- **500 g (1 lb 2 oz) conchiglie (shell pasta)**
- **2 tablespoons oil**
- **3 cloves garlic, crushed**
- **315 g (11¼ oz) marinated artichoke hearts, halved**
- **3 tablespoons chopped fresh parsley**
- **160 g (5⅔ oz) sorrel leaves, roughly chopped**
- **4 hard-boiled eggs, chopped**
- **fresh Parmesan shavings, for serving**

Cook the conchiglie in a large pan of rapidly boiling salted water until al dente. Drain and keep warm.

While the pasta is cooking, heat the oil in a frying pan, add the garlic and cook over medium heat until golden. Add the artichoke hearts and chopped parsley and cook over low heat for 5 minutes, or until the artichoke hearts are heated through.

Transfer the pasta to a large bowl. Add the sorrel leaves, eggs and artichoke hearts and toss to combine. Serve immediately, topped with shavings of fresh Parmesan and cracked black pepper, to taste.

Serves 4

Rice

Mushroom Risotto

- 1.5 litres (1.6 US qt/1.3 UK qt) vegetable stock (broth)
- 2 cups (500 ml/17 fl oz) white wine
- 2 tablespoons olive oil
- 60 g (2 oz) butter
- 2 leeks, thinly sliced
- 1 kg (2 lb 3 oz) flat mushrooms, sliced
- 500 g (1 lb 2 oz) arborio rice
- ¾ cup (75 g/2⅔ oz) grated Parmesan, plus Parmesan shavings, to serve
- 3 tablespoons chopped fresh flat-leaf parsley
- balsamic vinegar and fresh flat-leaf parsley, to serve

Place the stock (broth) and wine in a large saucepan and keep at simmering point on the stove top.

Heat the oil and butter in a large saucepan. Add the leek and cook over medium heat for 5 minutes, or until soft and golden. Add the mushrooms to the pan and cook for 5 minutes, or until tender. Add the rice and stir for 1 minute, or until translucent.

Add ½ cup (125 ml/4¼ fl oz) hot stock (broth), stirring constantly over medium heat until the liquid is absorbed. Continue adding the stock (broth), a little at a time, stirring constantly for 20–25 minutes, or until all the rice is tender and creamy (you may not need all the stock/broth, or you may need to add a little water if you run out).

Stir in the Parmesan and chopped parsley and heat for 1 minute, or until all the cheese has melted. Serve drizzled with balsamic vinegar and topped with Parmesan shavings.

Serves 4

Pulao

- **500 g (1 lb 2 oz) basmati rice**
- **1 teaspoon cumin seeds**
- **4 tablespoons ghee or oil**
- **2 tablespoons chopped almonds**
- **2 tablespoons raisins (dark raisins) or sultanas (golden raisins)**
- **2 onions, thinly sliced**
- **2 cinnamon sticks**
- **5 cardamom pods**
- **1 teaspoon sugar**
- **1 tablespoon ginger juice**
- **15 saffron threads, soaked in 1 tablespoon warm milk**
- **2 Indian bay leaves (cassia leaves)**
- **1 cup (250 ml/8½ fl oz) coconut milk**
- **2 tablespoons fresh or frozen peas**
- **rosewater (optional)**

Wash the rice in a sieve under cold, running water until the water from the rice runs clear. Drain the rice and put in a saucepan, cover with water and soak for 30 minutes. Drain.

Place a small frying pan over low heat and dry-fry the cumin seeds until aromatic.

Heat the ghee or oil in a karhai (Indian wok) or heavy-based frying pan and fry the almonds and raisins or sultanas until browned. Remove from the pan, fry the onion in the same ghee until dark golden brown, then remove from the pan.

Add the rice, roasted cumin seeds, cinnamon, cardamom, sugar, ginger juice, saffron and salt to the pan and fry for 2 minutes, or until aromatic.

Add the bay leaves and coconut milk to the pan, then add enough water to come about 5 cm (2 inches) above the rice. Bring to the boil, cover and cook over medium heat for 8 minutes, or until most of the water has evaporated.

Add the peas to the pan and stir well. Reduce the heat to very low and cook until the rice is cooked through. Stir in the fried almonds, raisins or sultanas and onion, reserving some for garnishing. Drizzle with a few drops of rosewater if you would like a more perfumed dish. Garnish with the reserved almonds, raisins or sultanas and onion, then serve.

Serves 6

Wild Rice, Thyme and Mixed Mushroom Pilaff

- ⅔ cup (100 g/3½ oz) wild rice
- 1½ cups (375 ml/13 fl oz) vegetable stock (broth)
- 60 g (2 oz) butter
- 1 large onion, finely chopped
- 2 garlic cloves, crushed
- 1⅓ cups (265 g/9⅓ oz) long-grain rice

- 300 g (10½ oz) mixed mushrooms, sliced (e.g. button, field, Swiss brown)
- 1½ tablespoons chopped thyme
- 1 fresh bay leaf
- 2 tablespoons chopped flat-leaf (Italian) parsley
- toasted pine nuts, to serve

Rinse the wild rice and cook in a saucepan of plenty of boiling water for 25 minutes – it will only be partially cooked after this time. Drain.

When the rice is nearly done, pour the stock (broth) into a large saucepan with 1½ cups (375 ml/13 fl oz) water and bring to the boil. Reduce the heat to a simmer.

Meanwhile, melt the butter in a large heavy-based frying pan, add the onion and garlic and cook until the onion is softened but not browned. Add the white rice and stir until the rice grains are coated with butter, then stir in the mushrooms.

Add the wild rice, stock, thyme and bay leaf. Bring to the boil while stirring, then reduce the heat, cover tightly with a lid and simmer for 15 minutes, or until the rice is tender and the stock (broth) has been absorbed.

Leave to stand for 5 minutes. Remove the bay leaf. Season, add the parsley and fluff up the rice with a fork. Sprinkle with pine nuts and serve.

Serves 4

Kitcheree

- **1½ cups (300 g/10½ oz) basmati rice**
- **1½ cups (300 g/10½ oz) split mung beans (mung lentils)**
- **2 tablespoons oil**
- **1 onion, sliced**
- **3 bay leaves**
- **1 teaspoon cumin seeds**
- **2 pieces cassia bark (Chinese cinnamon)**
- **1 tablespoon cardamom seeds**
- **6 cloves**
- **¼ teaspoon black peppercorns**

Wash the rice and mung beans (mung lentils), then drain and set aside.

Heat the oil in a frying pan, add the onion, bay leaves and spices, and cook over low heat for 5 minutes, or until the onion is softened and the spices are fragrant. Add the rice and lentils, and cook, stirring, for 2 minutes. Pour in 1.25 litres (1.3 US qt/1.1 UK qt) water and salt to taste. Bring to the boil, then reduce the heat and cook, covered, over low heat for 15 minutes. Stir gently to avoid breaking the grains and cook, uncovered, over low heat for 3 minutes, or until all the moisture has evaporated. Serve hot with Indian curries.

Note: To avoid serving with the whole spices left intact, tie the spices in a piece of muslin and add it to the pan along with the boiling water. Discard when the dish is cooked.

Serves 6

Lemon and Herb Risotto with Fried Mushrooms

- 1 litre (1.1 US qt/1.75 UK pt) vegetable stock (broth)
- pinch of saffron threads
- 2 tablespoons olive oil
- 2 leeks (white part only), thinly sliced
- 2 garlic cloves, crushed
- 2 cups (440 g/15½ oz) risotto rice
- 2–3 teaspoons finely grated lemon zest
- 2–3 tablespoons lemon juice
- 2 tablespoons chopped flat-leaf (Italian) parsley
- 2 tablespoons snipped chives
- 2 tablespoons chopped oregano
- ¾ cup (75 g/2⅔ oz) freshly grated Parmesan cheese
- 100 g (3½ oz) mascarpone cheese
- 30 g (1 oz) butter
- 1 tablespoon virgin olive oil
- 200 g (7 oz) small flat mushrooms, cut into thick slices
- 1 tablespoon balsamic vinegar

Pour the stock (broth) into a saucepan and add the saffron threads. Bring to the boil, then reduce the heat, cover and keep at a low simmer.

Heat the olive oil in a large saucepan over medium heat. Add the leek, cook for 5 minutes, then add the garlic and cook for a further 5 minutes, or until golden. Add the rice and stir until well coated. Add half the lemon zest and half the juice, then add ½ cup (125 ml/4¼ fl oz) of the hot stock (broth). Stir constantly over medium heat until all the liquid has been absorbed. Continue adding more liquid, ½ cup (125 ml/4¼ fl oz) at a time until all the liquid is absorbed and the rice is tender and creamy; this will take around 25–30 minutes. (You may not need to use all the stock/broth, or you may need a little extra – every risotto will be slightly different.

Remove the pan from the heat. Stir in the herbs, Parmesan, mascarpone and the remaining lemon zest and lemon juice, then cover and keep warm.

To cook the mushrooms, melt the butter and virgin olive oil in a large frying pan, add the mushroom slices and vinegar and cook, stirring, over high heat for 5–7 minutes, or until the mushrooms are tender and all the liquid has been absorbed.

Serve the risotto in large bowls topped with the mushrooms. Garnish with sprigs of fresh herbs, if desired.

Serves 4

Asparagus and Pistachio Risotto

- 1 litre (1.1 US qt/1.75 UK pt) vegetable stock (broth)
- 1 cup (250 ml/8½ fl oz) white wine
- ⅓ cup (80 ml/2¾ fl oz) extra virgin olive oil
- 1 red onion, finely chopped
- 2 cups (440 g/15½ oz) arborio rice
- 310 g (11 oz) asparagus spears, trimmed and cut into short lengths
- ½ cup (125 ml/4⅓ fl oz) cream
- 1 cup (100 g/3½ oz) grated Parmesan
- ½ cup (40 g/1½ oz) shelled pistachio nuts, toasted and roughly chopped

Heat the stock (broth) and wine in a large saucepan and keep at simmering point on the stove top.

Heat the oil in another large saucepan. Add the onion and cook over medium heat for 3 minutes, or until soft. Add the rice and stir for 1 minute, or until translucent.

Add ½ cup (125 ml/4⅓ fl oz) hot stock (broth), stirring constantly until the liquid is absorbed. Continue adding more stock (broth), a little at a time, stirring constantly for 20–25 minutes, or until the rice is tender and creamy (you may not need to add all the stock (broth), or you may not have quite enough and will need to add a little water as well – every risotto is different). Add the asparagus during the last 5 minutes of cooking.

Remove from the heat and leave for 2 minutes, then stir in the cream and Parmesan and season well. Serve sprinkled with pistachios.

Serves 4–6

Green Pilaf with Cashews

- **200 g (7 oz) baby English (common) spinach leaves**
- **⅔ cup (100 g/3½ oz) cashew nuts, chopped**
- **2 tablespoons olive oil**
- **6 spring (green) onions (scallions), chopped**
- **2 garlic cloves, finely chopped**
- **1 teaspoon fennel seeds**
- **1½ cups (300 g/10½ oz) long-grain brown rice**
- **2 tablespoons lemon juice**
- **2½ cups (600 ml/20 fl oz) vegetable stock (broth)**
- **3 tablespoons chopped mint**
- **3 tablespoons chopped flat-leaf (Italian) parsley**

Preheat the oven to moderate 180°C (350°F/Gas 4). Shred the spinach into 1 cm (½ inch) pieces.

Put the cashew nuts on a baking tray (sheet) and roast for 5–10 minutes, or until golden brown – watch them carefully so they don't burn.

Heat the oil in a large, deep frying pan and cook the spring (green) onion over medium heat for 2 minutes, or until softened. Add the garlic and fennel seeds and cook for 1 minute, or until fragrant. Stir in the rice, mixing well to combine. Increase the heat to high, add the lemon juice, stock (broth) and 1 teaspoon salt and bring to the boil. Reduce the heat to low, cover with a tight-fitting lid and cook, without lifting the lid, for 45 minutes, or until the stock (broth) has been absorbed and the rice is cooked. Remove from the heat and sprinkle with the spinach and herbs. Stand, covered, for 8 minutes, then fork the spinach and herbs through the rice. Season. Serve sprinkled with cashews.

Serves 6

Fennel Risotto Balls with Cheesy Filling

- 1.5 litres (1.6 US qt/1.3 UK qt) vegetable stock (broth)
- 1 tablespoon oil
- 30 g (1 oz) butter
- 2 garlic cloves, crushed
- 1 onion, finely chopped
- 2 fennel bulbs, thinly sliced
- 1 tablespoon balsamic vinegar
- ½ cup (125 ml/4¼ fl oz) white wine
- 3 cups (660 g/1 lb 7 oz) risotto rice
- ½ cup (50 g/1¾ oz) freshly grated Parmesan cheese
- ½ cup (25 g/¾ oz) snipped chives
- 1 egg, lightly beaten
- 150 g (5¼ oz) sun-dried (sun-blushed) tomatoes, chopped
- 100 g (3½ oz) fresh mozzarella cheese, diced
- ½ cup (80 g/2¾ oz) frozen peas, thawed
- ½ cup (60 g/2 oz) plain (all-purpose) flour, seasoned
- 3 eggs, extra
- 2 cups (200 g/7 oz) dry breadcrumbs
- oil, for deep-frying

Pour the stock (broth) into a saucepan and bring to the boil. Reduce the heat, cover with a lid and keep at a low simmer.

Heat the oil and butter in a large saucepan and cook the garlic and onion over medium heat for 3 minutes, or until softened but not browned. Add the fennel and cook for 10 minutes, or until it starts to caramelise. Add the vinegar and wine, increase the heat and boil until the liquid evaporates. Stir in the rice until well coated.

Add ½ cup (125 ml/4¼ fl oz) hot stock (broth), stirring constantly over medium heat until the liquid is absorbed. Continue adding more stock (broth), ½ cup (125 ml/4¼ fl oz) at a time, stirring, for 20–25 minutes, or until all the stock (broth) is absorbed and the rice is tender and creamy.

Remove from the heat and stir in the Parmesan, chives, egg and tomato. Transfer to a bowl, cover and cool. Put the mozzarella and peas in a bowl and mash together. Season.

Put the flour in one bowl, the extra eggs in another and the breadcrumbs in a third. Lightly beat the eggs. With wet hands, shape the risotto into 14 even balls. Flatten each ball out, slightly indenting the centre. Put a heaped teaspoon of the pea mash into the indentation, then shape the rice around the filling to form a ball.

Roll each ball in seasoned flour, then dip in the extra egg and roll in breadcrumbs. Place on a foil-covered tray (sheet) and refrigerate for 30 minutes.

Fill a deep-fat fryer or large saucepan one-third full of oil and heat to 180°C (350°F), or until a cube of bread dropped into the oil browns in 15 seconds. Cook the risotto balls in batches for 5 minutes, or until golden and crisp and the cheese has melted inside. Drain on crumpled paper towels and season with salt. If the cheese has not melted by the end of the cooking time, cook the balls on a tray (sheet) in a (180°C/350°F/Gas 4) oven for 5 minutes. Serve with a salad.

Serves 4–6

Risotto-Stuffed Onions

- **8 onions (about 200 g/7 oz each)**
- **1 tablespoon oil**
- **20 g (⅔ oz) butter**
- **70 g (2½ oz) mushrooms, chopped**
- **½ cup (110 g/3¾ oz) arborio rice**
- **2½ cups (600 ml/20 fl oz) hot vegetable stock (broth)**
- **2 tablespoons grated Parmesan**
- **2 tablespoons chopped fresh parsley**

Preheat the oven to moderately hot 200°C (400°F/Gas 6). Trim the bases of the onions so they sit flat and cut the tops off, leaving a wide opening. Place in a baking dish, drizzle with the oil and bake for 1–1½ hours, or until golden.

Meanwhile, melt the butter in a pan, add the mushrooms and cook for 5 minutes, or until the mushrooms have softened. Add the rice and stir until well coated with the butter. Gradually stir in the hot vegetable stock (broth), about ½ cup (125 ml/4¼ fl oz) at a time, making sure the liquid has been absorbed before adding more. When all the stock (broth) has been absorbed, stir in the Parmesan and parsley.

Scoop out the flesh from the middle of each onion, leaving at least 3 outside layers on each, to hold the filling. Chop the scooped flesh and stir through the risotto mixture. Spoon the filling into the onion shells, piling a little on top. Bake for 10 minutes to heat through, then serve.

Serves 8

Brown Rice and Puy Lentils with Pine Nuts and Spinach

- 1 cup (200 g/7 oz) brown rice
- 100 ml (3½ fl oz) extra virgin olive oil
- 1 red onion, diced
- 2 garlic cloves, crushed
- 1 carrot, diced
- 2 celery stalks, diced
- 1 cup (185 g/6½ oz) Puy lentils
- 2 tomatoes, seeded and diced
- 3 tablespoons chopped coriander (cilantro)
- 3 tablespoons chopped mint
- 2 tablespoons balsamic vinegar
- 1 tablespoon lemon juice
- 2 tablespoons pine nuts, toasted
- 2 cups (90 g/3¼ oz) baby English (common) spinach leaves, washed

Bring a large saucepan of water to the boil. Add 1 teaspoon salt and the rice, and cook for 20 minutes, or until tender. Drain and refresh under cold water.

Heat 2 tablespoons of the oil in a saucepan and add the onion, garlic, carrot and celery. Cook over low heat for 5 minutes, or until softened, then add the Puy lentils and 1½ cups (375 ml/13 fl oz) water. Bring to the boil and simmer for 15 minutes, or until tender. Drain well, but do not rinse. Combine with the rice, tomato, coriander (cilantro) and mint in a large bowl.

Whisk the remaining oil with the balsamic vinegar and lemon juice, and season well with salt and freshly ground black pepper. Pour over the salad, add the pine nuts and the spinach, and toss well to combine.

Serves 6–8

Spinach Risotto Cake

- **250 g (8¾ oz) baby English (common) spinach leaves**
- **3 cups (750 ml/26 fl oz) vegetable stock (broth)**
- **100 g (3½ oz) butter**
- **1 onion, finely chopped**
- **1 garlic clove, finely chopped**
- **1 cup (220 g/7¾ oz) arborio rice**
- **155 ml (5¼ fl oz) dry white vermouth or white wine**
- **¼ teaspoon freshly grated nutmeg**
- **¼ cup (25 g/¾ oz) freshly grated Parmesan cheese, plus extra to serve**

Cook the spinach in a small amount of salted water until just wilted. Refresh in cold water and squeeze dry. Finely chop and set aside.

Pour the stock (broth) into a saucepan and bring to the boil. Reduce the heat, cover with a lid and keep at a low simmer.

Melt 75 g (2⅔ oz) of the butter in a deep heavy-based frying pan and gently cook the onion and garlic until softened but not browned. Stir in the rice until well coated. Season.

Add the vermouth to the rice and cook, stirring, until all the liquid has been absorbed. Add ½ cup (125 ml/4 fl oz) of the hot stock and stir constantly over medium heat until all the liquid is absorbed. Continue adding more stock, ½ cup (125 ml/4 fl oz) at a time until a quarter of the stock is left, then mix in the chopped spinach. Continue to add the last of the stock. When making risotto cake, it is not so essential to keep the rice al dente – if it is a little more glutinous, it will stick together better. Make sure all the liquid is absorbed or the cake may break up when you unmould it.

Remove the pan from the heat and stir in the nutmeg, Parmesan cheese and the rest of the butter.

Smear a little butter into a mould such as a 1.25 litre (40 fl oz) cake tin. Spoon the risotto into the mould, pressing it down firmly. Leave to rest for 5 minutes, then unmould and put on a warm serving plate with some Parmesan sprinkled over the top.

Serves 6

Vegetable Domburi

- 2 cups (440 g/15½ oz) Japanese short-grain rice
- 10 g (⅓ oz) dried whole shiitake mushrooms
- 2 tablespoons oil
- 1 onion, sliced
- 2 slender eggplants (aubergines), sliced on the diagonal
- 100 g (3½ oz) green beans, cut into 4 cm (1½ inch) lengths
- 5 spring (green) onions, cut into 2 cm (¾ inch) lengths
- 100 ml (3½ fl oz) Shoyu (Japanese soy sauce)
- 100 ml (3½ fl oz) mirin
- ¼ cup (60 g/2 oz) sugar
- 4 eggs, lightly beaten

Wash the rice and place in a saucepan with 2½ cups (625 ml/21 fl oz) water. Bring to the boil, reduce the heat and simmer, covered, for 15 minutes. Leave, covered, for 10 minutes.

Soak the mushrooms in 1⅔ cups (410 ml/13¾ fl oz) boiling water for 15 minutes. Drain and reserve the soaking liquid. Remove the stems and cut the caps in half.

Heat the oil in a deep frying pan. Cook the onion over medium heat for 4 minutes, or until softened but not browned. Add the eggplant (aubergine) and cook for 3–4 minutes, or until softened. Add the beans, mushrooms and spring (green) onion and cook for 2–3 minutes, or until almost cooked. Combine the Shoyu, mushroom soaking liquid, mirin and sugar, and stir through the vegetables. Simmer for 4 minutes.

Pour the egg over the vegetables, cover and simmer for 1 minute, or until partly cooked. Serve the rice in bowls, spoon on the vegetable mixture and pour on the cooking sauce.

Serves 4

Vegetable Rice Pie

- 2 large red capsicums (peppers)
- 1 cup (250 ml/8½ fl oz) dry white wine
- 1 litre (1.1 US qt/1.75 UK pt) vegetable stock (broth)
- 2 tablespoons oil
- 1 garlic cloves, crushed
- 1 leek (white part only), sliced
- 1 fennel bulb, thinly sliced
- 2 cups (440 g/15½ oz) arborio rice
- ⅔ cup (65 g/2⅓ oz) freshly grated Parmesan cheese
- 10 sheets filo (phyllo) pastry
- ¼ cup (60 ml/2 fl oz) olive oil
- 500 g (1 lb 2 oz) English common spinach leaves, blanched
- 250 g (8¾ oz) feta cheese, sliced
- 1 tablespoon sesame seeds

Cut the capsicums (peppers) in half lengthways. Remove the seeds and membrane and then cut into large, flattish pieces. Grill (broil) or hold over a gas flame until the skin blackens and blisters. Put on a cutting board, cover with a tea towel and allow to cool. Peel the skin off and cut the flesh into small pieces.

Pour the wine and stock (broth) into a large saucepan and bring to the boil. Reduce the heat, cover with a lid and keep at a low simmer.

Heat the oil and garlic in a large saucepan. Add the leek and fennel and cook over medium heat for 5 minutes, or until lightly browned. Add the rice and stir for 3 minutes, or until well coated.

Add 1 cup (250 ml/8½ fl oz) of the stock (broth) to the rice and stir constantly until the liquid is absorbed. Continue adding stock (broth), ½ cup (125 ml/4¼ fl oz) at a time, stirring constantly until all the stock (broth) has been used and the rice is tender. Remove from the heat, stir in the Parmesan and season. Cool slightly. Preheat the oven to moderate 180°C (350°F/Gas 4).

Brush each sheet of filo (phyllo) with olive oil and fold in half lengthways. Arrange like overlapping spokes on a wheel, in a 23 cm (9 inch) springform tin, with one side of each pastry sheet hanging over the side of tin.

Spoon half the rice mixture over the pastry and top with half the red capsicums (peppers), half the spinach and half the feta cheese. Repeat with the remaining ingredients.

Fold the overhanging edge of the pastry over the filling, then brush lightly with oil and sprinkle with sesame seeds. Bake for 50 minutes, or until the pastry is crisp and golden and the pie is heated through.

Serves 8

Pumpkin and Broad Bean Risotto

- 350 g (12¼ oz) pumpkin
- cooking oil spray
- 1 tablespoon olive oil
- 1 large onion, finely chopped
- 2 cloves garlic, finely chopped
- 3 cups (750 ml/26 fl oz) vegetable stock (broth)
- 1 cup (220 g/7¾ oz) arborio rice
- 200 g (7 oz) Swiss brown mushrooms, halved
- 4 tablespoons grated Parmesan
- 2 cups (310 g/11 oz) frozen broad beans, defrosted, peeled

Preheat the oven to moderately hot 200°C (400°F/Gas 6). Cut the pumpkin into small chunks, place on a baking tray (sheet) and spray lightly with oil. Bake, turning occasionally, for 20 minutes, or until tender. Set aside, covered.

Meanwhile, heat the oil in a large heavy-based pan, add the onion and garlic, cover and cook for 10 minutes over low heat. Put the stock (broth) in a different pan and keep at simmering point on the stove top.

Add the rice to the onion and stir for 2 minutes. Gradually stir in ½ cup (125 ml/4¼ fl oz) of the hot stock (broth), until absorbed. Stir in another ½ cup (125 ml/4¼ fl oz) of hot stock (broth) until absorbed. Add the mushrooms and continue adding the remaining stock (broth), a little at a time, until it is all absorbed and the rice is just tender (this will take about 25 minutes).

Stir in the cooked pumpkin and the broad beans. Sprinkle with the grated Parmesan.

Serves 4

Basmati Rice, Cashew and Pea Salad

- **40 g (1½ oz) butter or ghee**
- **½ teaspoon turmeric**
- **300 g (10½ oz) basmati rice**
- **½ teaspoon salt**
- **200 g (7 oz) fresh or frozen peas, thawed**
- **¼ cup (60 ml/2 fl oz) peanut oil**
- **1 teaspoon yellow mustard seeds**
- **1 teaspoon cumin seeds**
- **¼ cup (30 g/1 oz) dried currants**
- **1 clove garlic, crushed**
- **1–2 small green chillies, finely chopped**
- **1 teaspoon Madras curry powder**
- **100 ml (3½ fl oz) coconut cream**
- **50 g (1¾ oz) glacé (glazed) ginger, cut into thin strips**
- **¼ small red onion, finely chopped**
- **1 tablespoon chopped fresh mint leaves**
- **1 tablespoon chopped fresh coriander (cilantro)**
- **½ cup (30 g/1 oz) shredded coconut**
- **100 g (3½ oz) roasted cashew nuts, coarsely chopped**
- **2 teaspoons shredded (medium) coconut, to garnish**

Melt the butter or ghee in a heavy-based pan and stir in the turmeric. Add the rice and salt, and stir for 10–15 seconds, then pour in 1½ cups (375 ml/ 13 fl oz) of water. Stir over high heat until boiling, then reduce the heat until gently simmering. Simmer, tightly covered, and cook for 13 minutes without removing the lid. Remove the pan from the heat and leave for 10 minutes without removing the lid, then fluff gently with a fork. Add the peas, transfer to a large bowl and allow to cool.

Heat 2 teaspoons of the oil in a pan and stir in the mustard and cumin seeds. When the mustard seeds start to pop, add the dried currants, garlic, chilli and curry powder. Stir to combine, but do not brown. Stir in the coconut cream, remove from the heat and transfer to the bowl of rice and peas.

Add the ginger, onion, herbs and the remaining oil. Toss well, and set aside for at least 30 minutes. Just before serving, toss through the coconut and cashew nuts. Garnish with the shredded (medium) coconut.

Note: Rice salads often improve if made in advance. This dish may be prepared up to 24 hours in advance, but add the cashew nuts and coconut just before serving to keep them crisp.

Serves 6

Jamaican Rice with Peas

- **2 cups (400 g/14 oz) long-grain rice**
- **3 cups (750 ml/26 fl oz) coconut milk**
- **400 g (14 oz) tin kidney beans, drained and rinsed**
- **2 teaspoons finely chopped thyme**
- **4 garlic cloves, crushed**
- **large pinch of ground allspice**
- **4 whole spring (green) onions, bruised**
- **1 small red chilli**

Combine all the ingredients in a large saucepan and add enough water to come about 2.5 cm (1 inch) above the rice. Slowly bring to the boil over medium heat, cover, reduce the heat to low and simmer for about 25 minutes, or until the rice is tender and the liquid has been absorbed.

Remove the spring (green) onion and chilli, season well and serve.

Notes: As a variation, add 1 cup (155 g/5½ oz) chopped smoked ham to the other ingredients before you start to cook.

This Jamaican staple is actually rice with beans; however, beans are often referred to as peas in Jamaica. Kidney beans are commonly used, though some authentic versions contain hard-to-find gungo or pigeon peas.

Serves 6–8

Festive Coconut Rice

- 3 tablespoons oil
- 1 medium onion, cut into thin wedges
- 4 cm (1½ inch) piece fresh ginger (ginger root), grated
- 2 cloves garlic, finely chopped
- 2½ cups (500 g/1 lb 2 oz) long-grain rice
- 1 teaspoon ground turmeric
- 4 cups (1 litre 1.1 US qt/1.75 UK pt) coconut milk
- 1 teaspoon salt
- 6 curry leaves

Garnishes
- 3 hard-boiled eggs, cut into quarters
- 1 Lebanese cucumber, thinly sliced
- 2 red chillies, thinly sliced
- ½ cup (35 g/1¼ oz) crisp fried onion

Heat the oil in a large heavy-based pan; add the onion, ginger (ginger root) and garlic, and fry over low heat for 5 minutes. Add the rice and turmeric, and cook for 2 minutes, stirring well.

Place the coconut milk in a medium pan, and heat until nearly boiling. Pour the milk over the rice, stirring constantly until the mixture comes to the boil. Add the salt and curry leaves. Cover with a tight-fitting lid, reduce the heat to very low and cook for 25 minutes.

Remove the lid, stir well and leave to cool for 10 minutes. Remove the curry leaves and pile the rice onto a platter (traditionally lined with banana leaves). Arrange the egg, cucumber and chilli over the rice and scatter the fried onion over the top.

Serves 4

Sticky Rice with Mangoes

- 2 cups (400 g/14 oz) glutinous rice
- 1 tablespoon white sesame seeds, to serve
- 1 cup (250 ml/8½ fl oz) coconut milk
- ½ cup (90 g/3¼ oz) grated palm sugar or soft brown sugar
- ¼ teaspoon salt
- 2–3 mangoes, peeled, seeded and sliced
- 3 tablespoons coconut cream
- fresh mint sprigs, to garnish

Place the rice in a sieve and wash it under running water until the water runs clear. Place the rice in a glass or ceramic bowl, cover it with water and leave it to soak overnight, or for a minimum of 12 hours. Drain the rice.

Line a metal or bamboo steamer with muslin. Place the rice on top of the muslin and cover the steamer with a tight-fitting lid. Place the steamer over a pot of boiling water and steam over moderately low heat for 50 minutes, or until the rice is cooked. Transfer the rice to a large bowl and fluff it up with a fork.

Toast the sesame seeds in a dry pan over medium heat for 3 to 4 minutes, shaking the pan gently, until the seeds are golden brown; remove from the pan at once to prevent burning.

Pour the coconut milk into a small pan; add the sugar and salt. Slowly bring the mixture to the boil, stirring constantly until the sugar has dissolved. Lower the heat and simmer for 5 minutes, or until the mixture has thickened slightly. Stir the mixture often while it is simmering, and take care that it does not stick to the bottom of the pan.

Slowly pour the coconut milk over the top of the rice. Use a fork to lift and fluff the rice. Do not stir the liquid through, otherwise the rice will become too gluggy. Let the rice mixture rest for 20 minutes before carefully spooning it into the centre of 4 warmed serving plates. Arrange the mango slices around the rice mounds. Spoon a little coconut cream over the rice, sprinkle over the sesame seeds, and garnish with the mint leaves.

Serves 4

Eight-Treasure Rice

- **12 whole blanched lotus seeds (see Notes)**
- **12 jujubes (dried Chinese dates) (see Notes)**
- **20 fresh or tinned gingko nuts, shelled (see Notes)**
- **225 g (8 oz) glutinous rice**
- **2 tablespoons sugar**
- **2 teaspoons oil**
- **30 g (1 oz) slab sugar (see Notes)**
- **8 glacé (glazed) cherries**
- **6 dried longans, pitted (see Notes)**
- **4 almonds or walnuts**
- **225 g (8 oz) red bean paste (see Notes)**

Soak the lotus seeds and jujubes in bowls of cold water for 30 minutes, then drain. Remove the seeds from the jujubes. If using fresh gingko nuts, blanch in a saucepan of boiling water for 5 minutes, then refresh in cold water and dry thoroughly.

Put the glutinous rice and 300 ml (10 fl oz) water in a heavy-based saucepan and bring to the boil. Reduce the heat to low and simmer for 10–15 minutes. Stir in the sugar and oil.

Dissolve the slab sugar in 220 ml (7½ fl oz) water and bring to the boil. Add the lotus seeds, jujubes and gingko nuts and simmer for 1 hour, or until the lotus seeds are soft. Drain, reserving the liquid.

Grease a 1 litre (1.1 US qt/1.75 UK pt) heatproof bowl and decorate the base with the lotus seeds, jujubes, gingko nuts, cherries, longans and almonds. Smooth two-thirds of the rice over this to form a shell on the surface of the bowl. Fill with the bean paste, cover with the remaining rice and smooth the surface.

Cover the rice with a piece of greased foil and put the bowl in a steamer. Cover and steam over simmering water in a wok for 1–1½ hours, replenishing with boiling water during cooking.

Turn the pudding out onto a plate and pour the reserved sugar liquid over the top. Serve hot.

Notes: Eight-treasure rice is a Chinese rice pudding. It is a favourite at banquets and Chinese New Year. The eight treasures vary, but can also include other preserved fruits. You will need access to a Chinese grocer to obtain most of the ingredients.

Serves 8

Zerde

- **1 teaspoon saffron threads**
- **½ cup (125 g/4⅓ oz) medium-grain rice**
- **1 cup (250 g/8¾ oz) caster (berry) sugar**
- **2 tablespoons rosewater**
- **¼ cup (40 g/1½ oz) pine nuts, lightly toasted**
- **¼ cup (35 g/1¼ oz) pistachios, chopped**
- **pomegranate seeds, to garnish**
- **thick natural yoghurt, to serve**

Crush the saffron threads with your fingers and soak in 2 tablespoons of boiling water for 30 minutes.

Bring 1.25 litres (1.3 US qt/1.1 UK qt) water to the boil in a large saucepan, then add the rice. Reduce to a simmer and cook, stirring occasionally, for 20 minutes. Stir in the sugar, rosewater and the saffron with the soaking liquid and simmer for another 10 minutes.

Add the pine nuts and chopped pistachios and simmer for another 10 minutes. The mixture should be thick and soupy. If it is too thick, add a little more water. Serve either hot or cold (it will thicken as it cools). Garnish with pomegranate seeds. Serve with thick natural yoghurt.

Note: This delectable rice pudding from Turkey is unusual in that is made without any milk, cream or butter. If serving it cold, top it with the pomegranate seeds just before serving.

Serves 6

Stir-Fries

Stir-Fried Asian Greens and Mushrooms

- 20 stems Chinese broccoli (gai lan)
- 4 baby bok choy
- 100 g (3½ oz) shimeji or enoki mushrooms
- 100 g (3½ oz) shiitake mushrooms
- 1 tablespoon soy sauce
- 2 teaspoons crushed palm sugar
- 1 tablespoon oil
- 4 spring (green) onions, cut into short pieces
- 5 cm (2 inch) fresh ginger (ginger root), cut into thin strips
- 1–2 small red chillies, seeded and finely chopped
- 2–3 cloves garlic, crushed
- 125 g (4⅓ oz) snow peas (mange tout), halved
- 1–2 teaspoons seasoning sauce

Remove any tough outer leaves from the Chinese broccoli (gai lan) and bok choy. Cut into 4 cm (1½ inch) pieces across the leaves, including the stems. Wash thoroughly, then drain and dry thoroughly. Wipe the mushrooms with a paper towel and trim the ends. Slice the shiitake mushrooms thickly.

Combine the soy sauce and palm sugar with ¼ cup (60 ml/2 fl oz) water. Set aside.

Heat the wok until very hot, add the oil and swirl it around to coat the side. Stir-fry (scramble-fry) the spring (green) onion, ginger (ginger root), chilli and garlic over low heat for 30 seconds, without browning. Increase the heat to high and add the Chinese broccoli (gai lan), bok choy and snow peas (mange tout). Stir-fry for 1–2 minutes, or until the vegetables are wilted.

Add the prepared mushrooms and soy sauce mixture. Stir-fry (scramble-fry) over high heat for 1–2 minutes, or until the mushrooms and sauce are heated through. Sprinkle with the seasoning sauce, to taste, and serve immediately.

Serves 4

Vegetarian Phad Thai

- **400 g (14 oz) flat rice stick noodles**
- **¼ cup (60 ml/2 fl oz) soy sauce**
- **2 tablespoons lime juice**
- **1 tablespoon soft brown sugar**
- **2 teaspoons sambal oelek**
- **2 tablespoons peanut oil**
- **2 eggs, lightly beaten**
- **1 onion, cut into thin wedges**
- **2 cloves garlic, crushed**
- **1 small red capsicum (pepper), cut into thin strips**
- **6 spring (green) onions, thinly sliced on the diagonal**
- **100 g (3½ oz) fried tofu puffs, cut into 5 mm (¼ inch) wide strips**
- **½ cup (25 g/¾ oz) chopped fresh coriander (cilantro) leaves**
- **1 cup (90 g/3¼ oz) bean sprouts, tailed**
- **¼ cup (40 g/1½ oz) chopped roasted unsalted peanuts**

Soak the noodles in warm water for 15–20 minutes, or until tender. Drain, then set aside.

To make the stir-fry (scramble-fry) sauce, combine the soy sauce, lime juice, sugar and sambal oelek in a small bowl or jug.

Heat a wok over high heat and add enough peanut oil to coat the bottom and side. Add the egg and swirl to form a thin omelette. Cook for 30 seconds, or until just set. Remove from the wok, roll up, then thinly slice.

Heat the remaining oil in the wok. Add the onion, garlic and capsicum (pepper) and cook over high heat for 2–3 minutes, or until the onion softens. Add the noodles, tossing well. Stir in the slices of omelette, the spring (green) onion, tofu and half of the coriander (cilantro). Pour in the stir-fry (scramble-fry) sauce, then toss to coat the noodles. Sprinkle with the bean sprouts and top with roasted peanuts and the remaining coriander (cilantro). Serve immediately.

Serves 4

Mushroom and Water Chestnut Stir-Fry

- ¼ cup (60 ml/2 fl oz) vegetable oil
- 2 cloves garlic, julienned
- ½ cup (80 g/2¾ oz) pine nuts
- 750 g (1 lb 10 oz) mixed fresh mushrooms (e.g. Swiss brown, oyster, shiitake), sliced
- 100 g (3½ oz) snow peas (mange tout), halved
- 230 g (8¼ oz) can sliced water chestnuts, drained
- 150 g (5¼ oz) bean sprouts, tailed
- ⅓ cup (80 ml/2¾ fl oz) vegetarian oyster sauce
- 2 teaspoons sesame oil

Heat a wok over high heat, add 2 tablespoons oil and swirl to coat the side of the wok. Add the garlic and pine nuts, and cook, stirring constantly, for 1 minute, or until the pine nuts are light golden brown.

Add the mushrooms and stir-fry (scramble-fry) over high heat for 3 minutes. Add the snow peas (mange tout) and cook for a further 3 minutes, or until the vegetables are just tender, adding the remaining oil, if necessary.

Add the water chestnuts, bean sprouts, vegetarian oyster sauce and sesame oil, and cook for a further 30 seconds. Serve with rice.

Serves 4

Thai Coconut Vegetables

- 1 tablespoon oil
- 2 small onions, peeled, cut in wedges
- 1 teaspoon ground cumin
- 150 g (5¼ oz) cauliflower florets
- 1 medium red capsicum (pepper), chopped
- 2 celery sticks, sliced diagonally
- 1½ cups (185 g/6½ oz) grated pumpkin
- 1 cup (250 ml/8½ fl oz) coconut milk
- 1 cup (250 ml/8½ fl oz) vegetable stock (broth)
- 1 tablespoon sweet chilli sauce (jalapeno jelly)
- 150 g (5¼ oz) green beans
- 1 tablespoon finely chopped fresh coriander (cilantro)

Heat oil in a frying pan or wok. Add onion and cumin and stir-fry (scramble-fry) over medium heat for 2 minutes, or until the onion is golden.

Add cauliflower and stir-fry (scramble-fry) over high heat for 2 minutes. Add red capsicum (pepper), celery and pumpkin and stir-fry (scramble-fry) over high heat for 2 minutes, or until vegetables have begun to soften.

Add coconut milk, stock (broth) and chilli sauce (jalapeno jelly) and bring to boil. Reduce heat and cook, uncovered, for 8 minutes, or until the vegetables are almost tender. Trim tops and tails from beans and cut beans in half. Add to pan with coriander (cilantro), cook another 2 minutes or until beans are just tender. Serve with steamed rice.

Serves 4–6

Snow Pea Stir Fry

- 1 large onion, peeled
- 185 g (6½ oz) snow peas (mange tout)
- 1 tablespoon oil
- 1 tablespoon grated fresh ginger (ginger root)
- 1 red capsicum (pepper), cut into strips
- 1 small clove garlic, crushed
- 1 tablespoon vegetarian oyster sauce (optional)
- 1 teaspoon sugar
- pinch salt
- 1 tablespoon water

Cut the onion in half and slice thinly in rings. Remove ends and threads from the snow peas (mange tout).

Heat the oil in a frying pan or wok. Add the onion, ginger (ginger root) and red capsicum (pepper) and stir-fry (scramble-fry) over high heat 4–5 minutes or until the vegetables are just tender. Add the garlic and snow peas (mange tout) and stir-fry (scramble-fry) for 2 minutes, or until the snow peas (mange tout) become bright green.

Add the vegetarian oyster sauce, sugar, salt and water to the pan and mix through. Serve immediately.

Serves 4

Chinese-Style Stir-Fried Vegetables

- **300 g (10½ oz) baby bok choy**
- **100 g (3½ oz) snake beans**
- **2 spring (green) onions**
- **150 g (5¼ oz) broccoli**
- **1 medium red capsicum (pepper)**
- **2 tablespoons oil**
- **2 cloves garlic, crushed**
- **2 teaspoons grated fresh ginger (ginger root)**
- **1 tablespoon sesame oil**
- **2 teaspoons soy sauce**

Wash and trim the thick stalks from the bok choy, and then cut the leaves into wide strips. Slice the snake beans into 5 cm (2 inch) lengths and the spring (green) onions diagonally. Cut the broccoli into small florets and the red capsicum (pepper) into diamonds about 2.5 cm (1 inch) wide.

Heat the oil in a large heavy-based frying pan or wok. Add the garlic and ginger (ginger root) and cook over medium heat for 30 seconds, stirring constantly. Add the beans, spring (green) onions and broccoli, then stir-fry (scramble-fry) for 3 minutes.

Add the red capsicum (pepper) and stir-fry (scramble-fry) for another 2 minutes. Add the bok choy and stir-fry for 1 minute. Stir in the sesame oil and the soy sauce and toss until well combined with the vegetables. Transfer to a serving dish and serve immediately. Serve with steamed rice.

Serves 4

Pumpkin and Cashew Stir-Fry

- oil, for cooking
- 1 cup (155 g/5½ oz) raw cashew nuts
- 1 leek, white part only, sliced
- 2 teaspoons ground coriander
- 2 teaspoons ground cumin
- 2 teaspoons brown mustard seeds
- 2 cloves garlic, crushed
- 1 kg (2 lb 3 oz) butternut pumpkin (squash), cubed
- ¾ cup (185 ml/6 fl oz) orange juice
- 1 teaspoon soft brown sugar

Heat the wok until very hot, add 1 tablespoon of the oil and swirl to coat. Stir-fry (scramble-fry) the cashews until golden, then drain on paper towels. Stir-fry (scramble-fry) the leek for 2–3 minutes, or until softened. Remove from the wok.

Reheat the wok, add 1 tablespoon of the oil and stir-fry (scramble-fry) the coriander, cumin, mustard seeds and garlic for 2 minutes, or until the spices are fragrant and the mustard seeds begin to pop. Add the pumpkin (squash) and stir to coat well. Stir-fry (scramble-fry) for 5 minutes, or until the pumpkin (squash) is brown and tender.

Add the orange juice and sugar. Bring to the boil and cook for 5 minutes. Add the leek and three-quarters of the cashews and toss well. Top with the remaining cashews to serve.

Serves 4–6

Caponata

- 1 kg (2 lb 3 oz) eggplant (aubergine), cubed
- ¾ cup (185 ml/6½ fl oz) olive oil
- 200 g (7 oz) zucchini (courgette), cubed
- 1 red capsicum (pepper), thinly sliced
- 2 onions, finely sliced
- 4 celery sticks, sliced
- 400 g (14 oz) can crushed tomatoes
- 3 tablespoons red wine vinegar
- 2 tablespoons sugar
- 2 tablespoons drained capers
- 24 green olives, pitted (see Note)
- 2 tablespoons pine nuts, toasted

Put the eggplant (aubergine) in a colander, sprinkle with salt and leave to drain.

Heat 3 tablespoons of the oil in a large frying pan and fry the zucchini (courgette) and capsicum (pepper) for 5–6 minutes, or until the zucchini (courgette) is lightly browned. Transfer to a bowl. Add a little more oil to the pan and gently fry the onion and celery for 6–8 minutes, or until softened but not brown. Transfer to the bowl.

Rinse the eggplant (aubergine) and pat dry. Add ¼ cup (60 ml/2 fl oz) of the oil to the pan, increase the heat and brown the eggplant (aubergine) in batches. Keep adding more oil to each batch. Drain on paper towels and set aside.

Remove any excess oil from the pan and return the vegetables to the pan, except the eggplant (aubergine).

Add ¼ cup (60 ml/2 fl oz) water and the tomatoes. Reduce the heat and simmer for 10 minutes. Add the remaining ingredients and eggplant (aubergine) and mix well. Remove from the heat and cool. Cover and leave for 24 hours in the refrigerator. Add some pepper, and more vinegar if needed.

Note: Green olives stuffed with red pimentos (roasted red capsicum/pepper) can be used instead of pitted green olives.

Storage Time: Caponata will keep, covered, in the refrigerator for up to 5 days.

Serves 8

Tamari Roasted Almonds with Spicy Green Beans

- 2 tablespoons sesame oil
- 1 long fresh red chilli, seeded and finely chopped
- 2 cm (¾ inch) piece fresh ginger (ginger root), grated
- 2 cloves garlic, crushed
- 375 g (13¼ oz) green beans, cut into 5 cm (2 inch) lengths
- ½ cup (125 ml/4¼ fl oz) hoisin sauce
- 1 tablespoon soft brown sugar
- 2 tablespoons mirin
- 250 g (8¾ oz) tamari roasted almonds, roughly chopped (see Note)

Heat a wok over high heat, add the oil and swirl to coat. Add the chilli, ginger (ginger root) and garlic and stir-fry (scramble-fry) for 1 minute, or until lightly browned. Add the beans, hoisin sauce and sugar and stir-fry (scramble-fry) for 2 minutes. Stir in the mirin and cook for 1 minute, or until the beans are tender but still crunchy.

Remove from the heat and stir in the almonds just before serving. Serve on a bed of rice.

Note: Tamari roasted almonds are available from health-food stores. Tamari is a naturally brewed, thick Japanese soy sauce made with soy beans and rice.

Serves 4–6

Chinese Vegetables with Ginger

- 1 tablespoon oil
- 3 teaspoons grated fresh ginger (ginger root)
- 4 spring (green) onions, sliced
- 230 g (8¼ oz) canned water chestnuts, drained and sliced
- 425 g (15 oz) canned baby corn, drained
- 1 cup (45 g/1⅔ oz) finely sliced Chinese cabbage
- 125 g (4⅓ oz) bean sprouts, tails removed
- 1 tablespoon soy sauce
- 1–2 tablespoons vegetarian oyster sauce (optional)
- 2 teaspoons sesame oil

Heat the oil in a heavy-based pan or wok and add the ginger (ginger root) and spring (green) onion. Stir-fry (scramble-fry) over high heat for 1 minute. Add the water chestnuts and baby corn; stir-fry (scramble-fry) for 30 seconds.

Add the cabbage, bean sprouts and sauces; stir-fry (scramble-fry) for 1 minute. Stir in the sesame oil and toss well. Serve immediately.

Serves 4

Orange Sweet Potato, Spinach and Water Chestnut Stir-Fry

- **500 g (1 lb 2 oz) orange sweet potato (yam), peeled and cut into 1.5 cm (⅝ inch) cubes**
- **1 tablespoon vegetable oil**
- **2 cloves garlic, crushed**
- **2 teaspoons sambal oelek**
- **225 g (8 oz) can water chestnuts, sliced**
- **2 teaspoons grated palm sugar**
- **390 g (13¾ oz) English (common) spinach, stems removed**
- **2 tablespoons soy sauce**
- **2 tablespoons vegetable stock (broth)**

Cook the sweet potato (yam) in a large saucepan of boiling water for 15 minutes, or until tender. Drain well.

Heat a wok over high heat, add the oil and swirl to coat the side of the wok. Stir-fry (scramble-fry) the garlic and sambal oelek for 1 minute, or until fragrant. Add the sweet potato (yam) and water chestnuts and stir-fry (scramble-fry) over medium–high heat for 2 minutes. Reduce the heat to medium, add the palm sugar and cook for a further 2 minutes, or until the sugar has melted. Add the spinach, soy sauce and stock (broth) and toss until the spinach has just wilted. Serve with steamed rice.

Serves 4

Peppered Stir-Fried Snake Beans

- 1 tablespoon drained, canned green peppercorns
- ½ cup (15 g/½ oz) fresh coriander (cilantro) leaves and chopped stems
- 1 tablespoon oil
- 2 cloves garlic, chopped
- 220 g (7¾ oz) snake beans, cut into 4 cm (1½ inch) lengths

- 155 g/5½ oz asparagus, cut into 4 cm (1½ inch) lengths
- 1 teaspoon soft brown sugar
- 2 teaspoons water
- 1 teaspoon chopped fresh red or green chillies (optional)

Finely crush the peppercorns. Chop the coriander (cilantro) leaves and mix in a bowl with the stems and peppercorns.

Heat oil in a wok or frying pan. Add peppercorn mixture, garlic, beans, asparagus and sugar; stir-fry (scramble-fry) for 30 seconds over medium heat.

Add the water, cover and steam for 2 minutes or until the vegetables are just tender. Sprinkle with chillies and serve immediately.

Note: Snake beans have a delicious crisp texture. However, if they are not available, green beans may be substituted.

Serves 4

Tempeh Stir-Fry with Chinese Greens

- 1 teaspoon sesame oil
- 1 tablespoon peanut oil
- 2 cloves garlic, crushed
- 1 tablespoon grated fresh ginger (ginger root)
- 1 red chilli, finely sliced
- 4 spring (green) onions, sliced on the diagonal
- 300 g (10½ oz) tempeh, diced

- 500 g (1 lb 2 oz) baby bok choy leaves
- 800 g (1 lb 12 oz) Chinese broccoli (gai lan), chopped
- ½ cup (125 ml/4¼ fl oz) mushroom oyster sauce
- 2 tablespoons rice vinegar
- 2 tablespoons fresh coriander (cilantro) leaves

Heat the oils in a wok over high heat, add the garlic, ginger (ginger root), chilli and spring (green) onion and cook for 1–2 minutes, or until the onion is soft. Add the tempeh and cook for 5 minutes, or until golden. Remove and keep warm.

Add half the greens and 1 tablespoon water to the wok and cook, covered, for 3–4 minutes, or until wilted. Remove and repeat with the remaining greens and more water.

Return the greens and tempeh to the wok, add the sauce and vinegar and warm through. Top with the coriander (cilantro). Serve with rice.

Serves 4

Nori Omelette with Stir-Fried Vegetables

- 8 eggs
- 10 cm × 18 cm (4 inch × 7 inch) sheet nori
- ¼ cup (60 ml/2 fl oz) vegetable oil
- 1 clove garlic, crushed
- 3 teaspoons finely grated fresh ginger (ginger root)
- 1 carrot, cut into batons
- 2 zucchini (courgettes), halved lengthways, sliced on the diagonal
- 200 g (7 oz) mix of Swiss brown, enoki and oyster mushrooms, larger ones sliced
- 1 tablespoon Japanese soy sauce
- 1 tablespoon mirin
- 2 teaspoons yellow miso paste

Lightly beat the eggs. Roll the nori up tightly and snip with scissors into very fine strips. Add to the eggs and season to taste with salt and cracked black pepper.

Heat a wok over high heat, add 2 teaspoons of the oil and swirl to coat the side of the wok. Add ⅓ cup (80 ml/2¾ fl oz) of the egg mixture and swirl to coat the base of the wok. Cook for 2 minutes, or until set, then turn over and cook the other side for 1 minute. Remove and keep warm. Repeat with the remaining mixture, adding another 2 teaspoons of the oil each time, to make four omelettes.

Heat the remaining oil in the wok, add the garlic and ginger (ginger root) and stir-fry (scramble-fry) for 1 minute. Add the carrot, zucchini (courgettes) and mushrooms in two batches and stir-fry for 3 minutes, or until softened. Return all the vegetables to the wok. Add the soy sauce, mirin and miso paste, and simmer for 1 minute. Divide the vegetables evenly among the omelettes, roll them up and serve immediately with rice.

Serves 4

Chilli Noodles with Nuts

- 1½ tablespoons oil
- 1 tablespoon sesame oil
- 2–3 small red chillies, finely chopped
- 1 large onion, cut into thin wedges
- 4 cloves garlic, cut into paper-thin slices
- 1 red capsicum (pepper), cut into strips
- 1 green capsicum (pepper), cut into strips
- 2 large carrots, cut into thick matchsticks
- 100 g (3½ oz) green beans
- 2 celery sticks, cut into matchsticks
- 2 teaspoons honey
- 500 g (1 lb 2 oz) Hokkien noodles, gently separated
- 100 g (3½ oz) dry-roasted peanuts
- 100 g (3½ oz) honey-roasted cashews
- ¼ cup (30 g/1 oz) chopped fresh garlic chives, or 4 spring (green) onions, chopped
- sweet chilli sauce (jalapeno jelly) and sesame oil, to serve

Heat the wok over low heat, add the oils and swirl them around to coat the side. When the oil is warm, add the chilli and heat until very hot.

Add the onion and garlic and stir-fry (scramble-fry) for 1 minute, or until the onion just softens. Add the capsicum (pepper), carrot and beans and stir-fry (scramble-fry) for 1 minute. Add the celery, honey and 1 tablespoon water and season with salt and pepper. Toss well, then cover and cook for 1–2 minutes, or until the vegetables are brightly coloured and just tender.

Add the noodles and nuts and toss well. Cook, covered, for 1–2 minutes, or until the noodles are heated through. Stir in the garlic chives or spring (green) onions and serve, drizzled with the sweet chilli sauce (jalapeno jelly) and sesame oil.

Serves 4

Golden Fried Lime and Chilli Vegetables

- **2 tablespoons oil**
- **3 spring (green) onions, chopped**
- **3 cloves garlic, chopped**
- **1 tablespoon soft brown sugar**
- **2 medium eggplants (aubergines), cut into wedges**

- **2 teaspoons Golden Mountain sauce**
- **¼ Chinese cabbage, shredded**
- **2 tablespoons lime juice**
- **1 chilli, finely sliced**

Heat oil in a wok or large frying pan. Add onions and garlic and stir for 1 minute over medium heat.

Add the sugar and eggplant (aubergine) wedges to the wok and stir-fry (scramble-fry) for 3 minutes, or until the eggplant (aubergine) is golden brown.

Add the Golden Mountain sauce, cabbage and lime juice to the wok. Toss, then cover and steam for 30 seconds or until the cabbage softens slightly. Serve immediately sprinkled with sliced chilli.

Note: Thai eggplants are purple or have purple and white stripes, and come in a range of sizes. Some may be as small as a tiny pea, others the size of a golf ball or shaped like a small zucchini (courgette). Any of these may be used for this recipe, but make sure to alter the cooking time to suit the size of the eggplant. Golden Mountain sauce is an essential ingredient in Thai cooking. Buy it at Asian food stores.

Serves 4

Asian Greens with Teriyaki Tofu Dressing

- **650 g (1 lb 7 oz) baby bok choy**
- **500 g (1 lb 2 oz) choy sum**
- **440 g (15½ oz) snake beans, topped and tailed**
- **¼ cup (60 ml/2 fl oz) vegetable oil**
- **1 onion, thinly sliced**
- **⅓ cup (60 g/2 oz) soft brown sugar**
- **½ teaspoon chilli powder**
- **2 tablespoons grated fresh ginger (ginger root)**
- **1 cup (250 ml/8 fl oz) teriyaki sauce**
- **1 tablespoon sesame oil**
- **600 g (1 lb 5 oz) silken firm tofu, drained**

Cut the baby bok choy and choy sum widthways into thirds. Cut the snake beans into 10 cm (4 inch) lengths.

Heat a wok over high heat, add 1 tablespoon of the oil and swirl to coat the side of the wok. Cook the onion for 3–5 minutes, or until crisp. Remove with a slotted spoon and drain on paper towels.

Reheat the wok over high heat and add 1 tablespoon of the oil. Add half the greens and stir-fry (scramble-fry) for 2–3 minutes, or until wilted. Remove from the wok. Repeat with the remaining oil and greens. Drain any liquid from the wok.

Add the combined sugar, chilli, ginger (ginger root) and teriyaki sauce to the wok and bring to the boil. Simmer for 1 minute. Add the sesame oil and tofu and simmer for 2 minutes, turning once – the tofu will break up. Divide the greens among serving plates, then top with the dressing. Sprinkle with the fried onion.

Serves 6

Asparagus Stir-Fried with Mustard

- **480 g (17 oz) asparagus**
- **1 tablespoon oil**
- **1 red onion, sliced**
- **1 clove garlic, crushed**

- **1 tablespoon wholegrain mustard**
- **1 teaspoon honey**
- **½ cup (125 ml/4¼ fl oz) cream**

Break the woody ends off the asparagus by holding both ends of the spear and bending gently until it snaps at its natural breaking point. Cut the asparagus into 5 cm (2 inch) lengths.

Heat the wok until very hot, add the oil and swirl to coat the side. Stir-fry (scramble-fry) the onion for 2–3 minutes, or until tender. Stir in the crushed garlic and cook for 1 minute. Add the asparagus to the wok and stir-fry (scramble-fry) for 3–4 minutes, or until tender, being careful not to overcook the asparagus.

Remove the asparagus from the wok, set it aside and keep it warm. Combine the wholegrain mustard, honey and cream. Add to the wok and bring to the boil, then reduce the heat and simmer for 2–3 minutes, or until the mixture reduces and thickens slightly. Return the asparagus to the wok and toss it through the cream mixture. Serve immediately.

Variation: When asparagus is in season, white and purple asparagus are also available. Vary the recipe by using a mixture of the three colours. Do not overcook the purple asparagus or it will turn green as it cooks.

Hint: This dish can also be served on croutons, toasted ciabatta or toasted wholegrain bread as a smart starter or first course.

Serves 2

Warm Stir-Fried Salad

- 2 tablespoons olive oil
- 1 red onion, sliced
- 1 red capsicum (pepper), cut into small squares
- 2 cloves garlic, thinly sliced

- 250 g (8¾ oz) cherry tomatoes, halved
- 150 g (5¼ oz) baby English (common) spinach leaves
- ½ cup (15 g/½ oz) basil leaves
- 125 g (4⅓ oz) feta cheese, crumbled

Heat the wok until very hot, add the oil and swirl it around to coat the base and side of the wok. Add the onion, capsicum (pepper) and garlic to the wok and stir-fry (scramble-fry) for 2 minutes, or until just beginning to soften. Add the tomatoes, spinach and basil and stir-fry (scramble-fry) until the leaves have just wilted.

Transfer the salad to a serving plate and top with the crumbled feta cheese. Serve immediately.

Note: Serve as a main course with crusty bread or pasta or heap onto crostini as a starter.

Serves 2

Baked

Individual Herb Tarts

- **18 slices white bread, crusts removed**
- **40 g (1½ oz) butter, softened**

Filling
- **2 eggs**
- **2 tablespoons milk**

- **½ cup (125 ml/4¼ fl oz) cream**
- **2 teaspoons chopped fresh chives**
- **1 teaspoon chopped fresh dill**
- **1 teaspoon chopped fresh thyme**
- **1 tablespoon chopped fresh parsley**
- **2 tablespoons freshly grated Parmesan cheese**

Preheat the oven to hot 210°C (415°C/Gas 6–7). Brush two 12-cup muffin or patty (bun) pans with melted butter or oil. Cut bread into rounds using a 7 cm (2¾ inch) plain biscuit (cookie) cutter. Flatten out each round with a rolling pin.

Spread both sides of rounds with butter and gently press into muffin pan. Bake for 10 minutes or until lightly browned and crisp. Do not overcook.

To make Filling: Reduce the heat to moderate 180°C (350°F/Gas 4). Combine the eggs, milk, cream and herbs in a medium bowl and mix well. Pour the egg mixture into the bread cases and sprinkle with Parmesan cheese. Bake for 25 minutes or until the filling is lightly browned and set. Serve the tarts immediately.

Makes 18

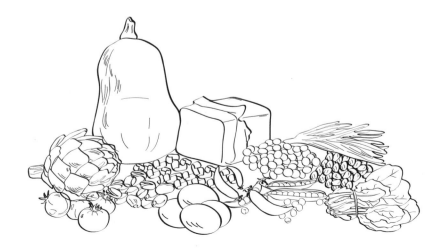

Cheese and Mushroom Pies

- **40 g (1½ oz) butter**
- **2 cloves garlic, crushed**
- **500 g (1 lb 2 oz) button mushrooms, sliced**
- **1 small red capsicum (pepper), finely chopped**
- **⅔ cup (160 g/5⅔ oz) sour cream**
- **3 teaspoons seeded mustard**
- **½ cup (65 g/2⅓ oz) finely grated Gruyère or Cheddar (American) cheese**
- **6 sheets ready-rolled puff pastry**
- **½ cup (65 g/2⅓ oz) finely grated Gruyère or Cheddar (American) cheese, extra**
- **1 egg, lightly beaten**

Preheat the oven to moderately hot 190°C (375°F/Gas 5). Lightly grease two oven trays (sheets) with melted butter or oil. Heat the butter in a large pan. Add the garlic and mushrooms, cook over medium heat, stirring occasionally, until mushrooms are tender and liquid has evaporated. Remove from heat and cool. Stir in red capsicum (pepper).

Combine the sour cream, mustard and cheese in a small bowl and mix well. Cut twelve circles with a 14 cm (5½ inch) diameter from pastry. Spread cream mixture over six of the circles, leaving a 1 cm (½ inch) border. Top each with mushroom mixture.

Sprinkle each with two teaspoons of extra grated cheese. Brush around the outer edges with beaten egg; place reserved pastry rounds on top of the filling, sealing the edges with a fork. Brush the tops of the pastry with egg. Sprinkle the remaining cheese over the pastry. Place the pies on oven trays (sheets) and bake for 20 minutes or until lightly browned and puffed.

Makes 6

Pumpkin and Hazelnut Pesto Bites

- **750 g (1 lb 10 oz) butternut pumpkin (squash)**
- **3 tablespoons oil**

- **35 g (1¼ oz) roasted hazelnuts**
- **35 g (1¼ oz) rocket (arugula)**
- **3 tablespoons grated Parmesan**

Preheat the oven to moderately hot 200°C (400°F/Gas 6). Peel the pumpkin (squash) and cut into 2 cm (¾ inch) slices, then cut into rough triangular shapes about 3 cm (1¼ inches) along the base. Toss with half the oil and some salt and cracked black pepper, until coated. Spread on a baking tray (sheet) and bake for 35 minutes, or until cooked.

For the hazelnut pesto, process the hazelnuts, rocket (arugula), 1 tablespoon of the Parmesan and the remaining oil, until they form a paste. Season with salt and cracked black pepper.

Spoon a small amount of the hazelnut pesto onto each piece of pumpkin (squash) and sprinkle with the remaining Parmesan and black pepper if desired. Serve warm or cold.

In Advance: Pesto can be made several days ahead. Pour a film of oil over the surface to prevent discoloration. Tip the oil off before using the pesto.

Makes 48

Vegetable Pasties with Rich Tomato Sauce

- 1 potato
- 1 carrot
- 1 parsnip
- 100 g (3⅓ oz) pumpkin
- 2 teaspoons oil
- 1 onion, finely chopped
- ½ cup (125 ml/4¼ fl oz) vegetable stock (broth)
- ⅓ cup (50 g/1¾ oz) fresh or frozen peas
- 1 tablespoon finely chopped fresh parsley
- 3 sheets ready-rolled puff pastry
- 1 egg, lightly beaten

Tomato Sauce
- 1 tablespoon oil
- 1 small onion, chopped
- 1 clove garlic, crushed
- 2 tomatoes, peeled and chopped
- ¼ cup (60 ml/2 fl oz) good-quality red wine
- ¼ cup (60 ml/2 fl oz) vegetable stock (broth)
- 2 tablespoons tomato paste (tomato puree)
- ½ teaspoon dried basil
- ½ teaspoon dried oregano

Preheat the oven to hot 210°C (415°F/Gas 6–7). Brush an oven tray (sheet) with melted butter or oil. Peel and cut the potato, carrot, parsnip and pumpkin into 1 cm (½ inch) cubes. Heat the oil in a frying pan and cook the onion over medium heat for 2 minutes, or until soft. Add potato, carrot, parsnip, pumpkin and stock (broth); bring to the boil. Reduce heat and simmer for 10 minutes, stirring occasionally, until the vegetables are soft and the liquid has evaporated. Stir in the peas and parsley and leave to cool.

Using a plate as a guide, cut four 13 cm (5 inch) circles from each sheet of pastry. Place 1 level tablespoon of mixture onto each round, brush the edges of pastry with water and fold the pastry over so the edges meet. Twist the edges together decoratively to seal. Brush with beaten egg, place on prepared tray (sheet) and bake for 25 minutes, until puffed and golden.

To make Tomato Sauce: Heat the oil in a small pan and add the onion and garlic. Cook over medium heat for 2 minutes, or until soft. Add the tomatoes, wine and stock (broth) and bring to boil. Reduce heat and simmer for 15 minutes, stirring occasionally. Remove from heat; cool. Process tomato mixture in a food processor until smooth. Return to pan, add tomato paste (tomato puree), basil and oregano and stir until hot. Serve hot or cold.

Makes 12

Red Lentil and Ricotta Lasagne

- ½ cup (125 g/4⅓ oz) red lentils
- 2 teaspoons olive oil
- 2–3 cloves garlic, crushed
- 1 large onion, chopped
- 1 small red capsicum (pepper), chopped
- 2 zucchini (courgette), sliced
- 1 celery stick, sliced
- 2 × 425 g (15 oz) cans chopped tomatoes
- 2 tablespoons tomato paste (tomato puree)
- 1 teaspoon dried oregano

- 350 g (12¼ oz) ricotta
- 12 dried or fresh lasagne sheets (noodles)
- 60 g (2 oz) reduced-fat Cheddar (American) cheese, grated

White Sauce
- ⅓ cup (40 g/1½ oz) cornflour (cornstarch)
- 3 cups (750 ml/26 fl oz) skim milk
- ¼ onion
- ½ teaspoon ground nutmeg

Soak the lentils in boiling water to cover for at least 30 minutes, then drain. Meanwhile, heat the oil in a large pan, add the garlic and onion and cook for 2 minutes. Add the capsicum (pepper), zucchini (courgette) and celery and cook for 2–3 minutes.

Add the lentils, tomato, tomato paste (tomato puree), oregano and 1½ cups (375 ml/13 fl oz) water. Bring slowly to the boil, reduce the heat and simmer for 30 minutes, or until the lentils are tender. Stir occasionally.

To make the white sauce, blend the cornflour (cornstarch) with 2 tablespoons of the milk in a pan until smooth. Pour the remaining milk into the pan, add the onion and stir over low heat until the mixture boils and thickens. Add the nutmeg and season with pepper, then cook over low heat for 5 minutes. Remove the onion.

Beat the ricotta with about ½ cup (125 ml/4¼ fl oz) of the white sauce. Preheat the oven to moderate 180°C (350°F/Gas 4). Spread one-third of the lentil mixture over the base of a 3 litre (3.2 US qt/2.6 UK qt) capacity ovenproof dish. Cover with a layer of lasagne sheets (noodles). Spread another third of the lentil mixture over the pasta, then spread the ricotta evenly over the top. Follow with another layer of lasagne, then the remaining lentils. Pour the white sauce evenly over the top and sprinkle with the grated cheese. Bake for 1 hour, covering loosely with foil if the top starts to brown too much. Leave to stand for 5 minutes before cutting.

Serves 6

Feta and Olive Herb Pie

- 2 teaspoons sugar
- 2 teaspoons (7 g/¼ oz) dried yeast
- 2 tablespoons olive oil
- ½ cup (60 g/2 oz) plain (all-purpose) flour
- 1 cup (125 g/4⅓ oz) self-raising flour
- 1 onion, sliced
- ½ cup (15 g/½ oz) fresh flat-leaf parsley, chopped
- 1 sprig fresh rosemary, chopped
- 3 sprigs fresh thyme, chopped
- 5 fresh basil leaves, torn
- ¼ cup (40 g/1½ oz) pine nuts, toasted
- 1 clove garlic, crushed
- 175 g (6¼ oz) feta cheese, crumbled
- ¼ cup (35 g/1¼ oz) pitted olives, chopped

Dissolve half the sugar in ½ cup (125 ml/4¼ fl oz) warm water and sprinkle the yeast over the top. Leave for 10 minutes, or until frothy (if it doesn't foam, the yeast is dead and you will need to start again), then mix with half the oil. Sift the flours and ½ teaspoon salt into a large bowl. Make a well in the centre and pour in the yeast mixture. Mix well and knead on a floured board until smooth. Cut in half, then roll each half into a 20 cm (8 inch) circle. Place one on a lightly greased baking tray (sheet), the other on a baking paper-covered baking tray (sheet). Cover the circles with a cloth and put in a warm place for 10–15 minutes, or until doubled in size.

Preheat the oven to moderately hot 200°C (400°F/Gas 6). Heat the remaining oil in a frying pan and cook the onion for 10 minutes, or until golden brown. Sprinkle with the remaining sugar and cook until caramelised. Transfer to a bowl and mix with the herbs, pine nuts, garlic, feta cheese and olives. Spread the mixture over the pastry on the greased tray (sheet). Brush the edge with water and put the second pastry circle on top, using the paper to help lift it over. Press the edges together to seal and pinch together to form a pattern. Cut a few slits in the top to allow steam to escape. Bake for 30–35 minutes, or until crisp and golden brown. Serve warm, cut into wedges.

Serves 4–6

Parmesan Tuile Cones

- **150 g (5¼ oz) Parmesan, finely grated**
- **pinch of paprika**
- **150 g (5¼ oz) ricotta cheese**
- **2 teaspoons lemon juice**
- **1½ tablespoons milk**
- **2 teaspoons fresh chopped chives, plus extra, cut into short lengths, to garnish**
- **2 fresh figs, cut into small pieces**

Preheat the oven to hot 220°C (425°F/Gas 7). Line two baking trays (sheets) with baking paper. Using a 7 cm (2¾ inch) cutter as a guide, draw circles on the paper. Invert the paper onto the trays (sheets). Place the cutter back over each round and sprinkle with 3 teaspoons of Parmesan combined with the paprika, spreading evenly to the edges.

Bake only 3–4 at a time for 3 minutes, or until melted and golden. Remove each round from the tray (sheet), using a spatula, and wrap around the end of a cream horn mould to form a cone shape. Cool. If they begin to harden too quickly, return to the oven for 10 seconds to soften again.

Beat the ricotta cheese, lemon juice and milk in a bowl until smooth. Stir in the chopped chives and salt and cracked black pepper, to taste.

Carefully spoon 2 teaspoons of the cheese mixture into each Parmesan tuile. Decorate the end of each tuile with a piece of fig and chives.

Makes 36

Harvest Pie

- **175 g (6¼ oz) butter**
- **2 cups (250 g/8¾ oz) plain (all-purpose) flour**
- **¼ cup (60 ml/2 fl oz) iced water**
- **1 tablespoon oil**
- **1 onion, finely chopped**
- **1 small red capsicum (pepper), chopped**
- **1 small green capsicum (pepper), chopped**
- **150 g (5¼ oz) pumpkin, chopped**
- **1 small potato, chopped**
- **100 g (3⅓ oz) broccoli, cut into small florets**
- **1 carrot, chopped**
- **¼ cup (30 g/1 oz) plain (all-purpose) flour**
- **1 cup (250 ml/8½ fl oz) milk**
- **2 egg yolks**
- **½ cup (60 g/2 oz) grated Cheddar (American) cheese**
- **1 egg, lightly beaten, for glazing**

Preheat the oven to moderate 180°C (350°F/Gas 4). Chop 125 g (4⅓ oz) of the butter. Sift the flour into a large bowl and add the chopped butter. Using your fingertips, rub the butter into the flour until it is fine and crumbly. Add almost all the water and use a knife to mix to a firm dough, adding more water if necessary. Turn onto a lightly floured surface and press together until smooth.

Divide the dough in half, roll out one portion and line a deep 21 cm (8¼ inch) fluted flan tin. Refrigerate for 20 minutes. Roll the remaining pastry out to a 25 cm (10 inch) diameter circle. Cut into strips and lay half of them on a sheet of baking paper, leaving a 1 cm (½ inch) gap between each strip. Interweave the remaining strips to form a lattice pattern. Cover with plastic wrap and refrigerate, keeping flat, until firm.

Cut a sheet of greaseproof paper to cover the pastry-lined tin. Spread a layer of dried beans or rice over the paper. Bake for 10 minutes, remove from oven and discard paper and beans or rice. Bake for another 10 minutes or until lightly golden; allow to cool.

Heat the oil in a frying pan. Add the onion and cook for 2 minutes or until soft. Add the capsicums (peppers) and cook, stirring, for another 3 minutes. Steam or boil remaining vegetables until just tender; drain and cool. Mix the onion, capsicums (peppers) and the other vegetables in a large bowl.

Heat the remaining butter in a small pan. Add the flour and cook, stirring, for 2 minutes. Add the milk gradually, stirring until smooth between each addition. Stir constantly over medium heat until the mixture boils and thickens. Boil for 1 minute and then remove from the heat.

Add the egg yolks and cheese and stir until smooth. Pour the sauce over the vegetables and stir to combine. Pour the mixture into the pastry case and brush the edges with egg. Using baking paper to lift, invert the pastry lattice over the vegetables, trim the edges and brush with a little beaten egg, sealing to the cooked pastry. Brush the top with egg and bake for 30 minutes or until golden brown.

Serves 6

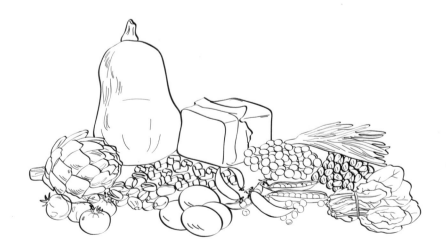

Ratatouille Tarts

- 3 cups (375 g/13¼ oz) plain (all-purpose) flour
- 170 g (6 oz) butter, chilled and chopped
- 1 eggplant (aubergine), about 500 g (1 lb 2 oz)
- ¼ cup (60 ml/2 fl oz) oil
- 1 onion, chopped
- 2 cloves garlic, crushed
- 2 zucchini (courgettes), sliced
- 1 red capsicum (pepper), chopped
- 1 green capsicum (pepper), chopped
- 250 g (8¾ oz) cherry tomatoes, halved
- 1 tablespoon balsamic vinegar
- 1 cup (125 g/4⅓ oz) grated Cheddar (American) cheese

Sift the flour into a bowl and rub in the butter with your fingertips until the mixture resembles fine breadcrumbs. Make a well and add ½ cup (125 ml/4¼ fl oz) chilled water. Mix with a flat-bladed knife, adding a little more water if necessary, until the dough just comes together. Gather into a ball and divide into 12 portions.

Grease 12 loose-based fluted flan tins measuring 8 cm (3 inches) across the base and 3 cm (1¼ inches) deep. Roll each portion of dough out on a sheet of baking paper to a circle a little larger than the tins. Lift into the tins, press into the sides, then trim away any excess pastry. Refrigerate for 30 minutes. Preheat the oven to moderately hot 200°C (400°F/Gas 6).

Put the tins on baking trays (sheets), prick the pastry bases all over with a fork and bake for 20–25 minutes, or until the pastry is fully cooked and lightly golden. Cool completely.

Meanwhile, to make the ratatouille filling, cut the eggplant (aubergine) into 2 cm (¾ inch) cubes, put into a colander and sprinkle with salt. After 20 minutes, rinse, drain and pat dry with paper towels.

Heat 2 tablespoons of the oil in a large frying pan. Cook batches of eggplant (aubergine) for 8–10 minutes, or until browned, adding more oil if necessary. Drain on paper towels. Heat the remaining oil, add the onion and cook over medium heat for 5 minutes, or until very soft. Add the garlic and cook for 1 minute, then add the zucchini (courgettes) and capsicums (peppers) and cook, stirring frequently, for 10 minutes, or until softened. Add the eggplant (aubergine) and tomatoes. Cook, stirring, for 2 minutes. Transfer to a bowl, stir in the vinegar, then cover and cool completely.

Reduce the oven to moderate 180°C (350°F/Gas 4). Divide the mixture among the tart shells with a slotted spoon, draining off any excess liquid. Sprinkle with the Cheddar (American) cheese and cook for 10–15 minutes, or until the cheese has melted and the tarts are warmed through.

Makes 12

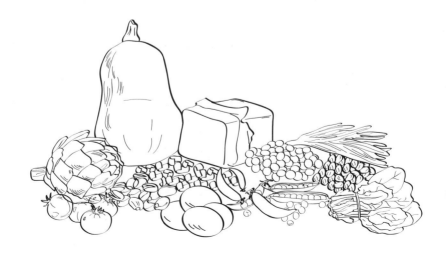

Sweet Onion Tarts

- 1 cup (125 g/4⅓ oz) plain (all-purpose) flour
- 75 g (2⅔ oz) butter, chopped
- 1 tablespoon bottled green peppercorns, drained
- 1 egg yolk
- 1 teaspoon Dijon mustard

Sweet Onion Filling
- 2 tablespoons olive oil
- 3 onions, sliced
- 1 clove garlic, sliced
- 2 teaspoons sugar
- 2 tablespoons balsamic vinegar
- 3 tablespoons raisins (dark raisins)
- 1 tablespoon olive paste
- 75 g (2⅔ oz) feta cheese

Lightly grease 20 holes in two 12-hole round-based patty (bun) tins. Sift the flour and ¼ teaspoon salt into a bowl and add the butter. Rub in with your fingertips until the mixture resembles fine breadcrumbs. Make a well in the centre. Crush the peppercorns with the back of a knife and chop finely. Add to the flour with the egg yolk, mustard and up to 2 teaspoons water. Mix with a flat-bladed knife until the mixture comes together in beads. Turn onto a lightly floured surface and press together into a ball. Wrap in plastic wrap and refrigerate for 20 minutes.

Preheat the oven to moderately hot 200°C (400°F/Gas 6). Roll the dough out on a lightly floured surface to 2–3 mm (about ⅛ inch). Cut 20 rounds with an 8 cm (3 inch) cutter. Put in the patty (bun) tins and prick with a fork. Bake for 8–10 minutes, or until golden.

For the filling, heat the oil in a heavy-based pan. Add the onion and garlic and cook, covered, over low heat for 30 minutes, or until the onion is very soft and beginning to brown. Increase the heat to moderate, add the sugar and vinegar and cook, stirring, until most of the liquid has evaporated and the onion is glossy. Stir in the raisins (dark raisins).

Spread a little olive paste into the base of each pastry case. Spoon the onion mixture over it and crumble the feta cheese on top. Serve warm or at room temperature.

Makes 20

Chilli Polenta Cake

- 1⅓ cups (165 g/5¾ oz) plain (all-purpose) flour
- 1½ teaspoons baking powder
- 1 teaspoon salt
- 1¼ cups (185 g/6½ oz) polenta (cornmeal)
- 1 cup (125 g/4⅓ oz) grated Cheddar (American) cheese
- 1 cup (250 g/8¾ oz) natural yoghurt
- ½ cup (125 ml/4¼ fl oz) milk
- 2 eggs
- ½ cup (80 g/2¾ oz) chopped red capsicum (pepper)
- 2 teaspoons chopped fresh chilli
- 60 g (2 oz) unsalted butter

Preheat oven to moderately hot 200°C (400°F/Gas 6). Sift flour, baking powder and salt into a large bowl. Mix in polenta (cornmeal) and cheese. In a separate bowl, whisk yoghurt, milk, eggs, red capsicum (pepper) and chilli. Heat a 20 cm (8 inch) ovenproof frying pan, then melt butter. Stir butter into yoghurt mixture, then pour all liquid ingredients into dry ingredients. Mix well.

Pour into hot pan; cook in the oven for 25–30 minutes or until a skewer comes out clean.

Serves 6–8

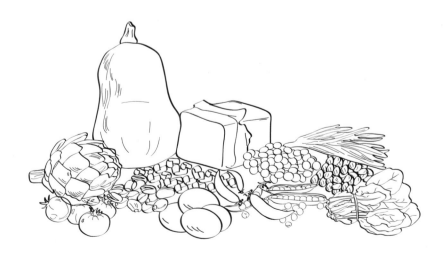

Blue Cheese and Onion Flan

- 2 tablespoons olive oil
- 1 kg (2 lb 3 oz) red onions, very thinly sliced
- 1 teaspoon soft brown sugar
- 1½ cups (185 g/6½ oz) plain (all-purpose) flour
- 100 g (3½ oz) cold butter, cubed
- ¾ cup (185 ml/6½ fl oz) cream
- 3 eggs
- 100 g (3½ oz) blue cheese, crumbled
- 1 teaspoon chopped fresh thyme leaves

Heat the oil in a heavy-based frying pan over low heat and cook the onion and sugar, stirring, for 45 minutes until caramelised.

Sift the flour into a large bowl and rub in the butter with your fingertips until the mixture resembles fine breadcrumbs. Make a well in the centre and add 3–4 tablespoons cold water. Mix with a flat-bladed knife, using a cutting action until the mixture comes together in beads. Gently gather together and lift onto a lightly floured work surface. Press into a ball, wrap in plastic wrap and refrigerate for 30 minutes.

Preheat the oven to 180°C (350°F/Gas 4). Roll out the pastry on a lightly floured surface to fit a lightly greased 22 cm (8⅔ inch) round loose-based flan tin. Invert the pastry over the tin and press in with a small ball of pastry, allowing excess to hang over the side. Trim any excess pastry, then chill for 10 minutes. Line the pastry shell with baking paper and fill with baking beads or uncooked rice. Bake on a baking tray (sheet) for 10 minutes. Remove the beads or rice and paper, then bake for 10 minutes, or until lightly golden and dry.

Cool, then gently spread the onion over the base of the pastry. Whisk the cream in a bowl with the eggs, blue cheese, thyme and some pepper. Pour over the onion and bake for 35 minutes, or until firm.

Serves 8

Mushrooms with Herb Nut Butter

- 12 large mushrooms
- 1 tablespoon olive oil
- 1 small onion, finely chopped
- ¼ cup (40 g/1½ oz) blanched almonds
- 1 clove garlic, peeled and chopped
- 1 tablespoon lemon juice
- 3 tablespoons parsley sprigs
- 3 teaspoons chopped fresh thyme or 1 teaspoon dried thyme
- 3 teaspoons chopped fresh rosemary or 1 teaspoon dried rosemary
- 1 tablespoon chopped fresh chives
- ½ teaspoon salt
- ¼ teaspoon black pepper
- 75 g (2⅔ oz) butter, chopped

Preheat oven to moderate 180°C (350°F/Gas 4). Brush a shallow baking dish with oil or melted butter. Remove stalks from mushrooms, chop stalks finely. Heat oil in a small pan, add onion. Cook over medium heat 2–3 minutes or until soft and golden. Add chopped stalks. Cook 2 minutes or until softened. Remove from heat.

Place the almonds, garlic, lemon juice, parsley, thyme, rosemary, chives, salt, pepper and butter in a food processor. Process for 20–30 seconds or until the mixture is smooth.

Place the mushroom caps in the baking dish. Spoon equal amounts of the onion and mushroom mixture into each cap and smooth the surface. Top each mushroom with the almond and herb mixture. Bake 10–15 minutes, or until mushrooms are cooked through and butter has melted.

Note: Mushrooms are best cooked just before serving. Assemble the caps up to two hours before serving and store, covered, on a flat tray (sheet), in the refrigerator.

Serves 4–6

Mini Pumpkin and Curry Quiches

- **Cream Cheese Pastry**
- **1½ cups (185 g/6½ oz) plain (all-purpose) flour**
- **125 g (4⅓ oz) cream cheese, chopped**
- **125 g (4⅓ oz) butter, chopped**

Filling
- **1 tablespoon oil**
- **2 onions, finely chopped**

- **3 cloves garlic, crushed**
- **1 teaspoon curry powder**
- **3 eggs**
- **½ cup (125 ml/4¼ oz) thick (double/heavy) cream**
- **1 cup mashed, cooked pumpkin (about 350 g/12¼ oz raw)**
- **2 teaspoons cumin seeds**

Preheat the oven to 210°C (415°F/Gas 6–7). To make the pastry, sift the flour into a large bowl and add the cream cheese and butter. Using your fingertips, rub the ingredients together for 2 minutes or until the mixture is smooth and comes together in a ball.

Turn dough onto a lightly floured surface, knead for 10 seconds or until smooth. Place, covered with plastic wrap, in the refrigerator for 30 minutes. Divide the pastry into 8 equal portions, roll out and line 8 deep, greased 10 cm (4 inch) flan tins. Bake for 15 minutes or until lightly browned. Remove from the oven. Reduce the heat to 180°C (350°F/Gas 4).

To make Filling: Heat oil in a small pan, add the onions and garlic and stir over low heat for 5 minutes or until soft. Add curry powder, stir for 1 minute. Spread over bases of pastry cases.

Combine eggs, cream and pumpkin in a large bowl, beat until combined. Pour over onion mixture, sprinkle with cumin seeds. Bake in 180°C (350°F/Gas 4) oven for 20 minutes, or until filling has set.

Makes 8

Mushroom Moussaka

- 1 eggplant (aubergine) (250 g/8¾ oz), cut into 1 cm (½ inch) slices
- 1 large potato, cut into 1 cm (½ inch) slices
- 30 g (1 oz) butter
- 1 onion, finely chopped
- 2 cloves garlic, finely chopped
- 500 g (1 lb 2 oz) flat mushrooms, sliced
- 400 g (14 oz) can chopped tomatoes
- ½ teaspoon sugar
- 40 g (1½ oz) butter, extra
- ⅓ cup (40 g/1½ oz) plain (all-purpose) flour
- 2 cups (500 ml/17 fl oz) milk
- 1 egg, lightly beaten
- 40 g (1½ oz) grated Parmesan

Preheat the oven to hot 220°C (425°F/Gas 7). Line a large baking tray (sheet) with foil and brush with oil. Put the eggplant (aubergine) and potato in a single layer on the tray (sheet) and sprinkle with salt and pepper. Bake for 20 minutes.

Melt the butter in a large frying pan over medium heat. Add the onion and cook, stirring, for 3–4 minutes, or until soft. Add the garlic and cook for 1 minute, or until fragrant. Increase the heat to high, add the mushrooms and stir continuously for 2–3 minutes, or until soft. Add the tomato, reduce the heat and simmer rapidly for 8 minutes, or until reduced. Stir in the sugar.

Melt the extra butter in a large saucepan over low heat. Add the flour and cook for 1 minute, or until pale and foaming. Remove from the heat and gradually stir in the milk. Return to the heat and stir constantly until it boils and thickens. Reduce the heat and simmer for 2 minutes. Remove from the heat and, when the bubbles subside, stir in the egg and Parmesan.

Reduce the oven to moderate 180°C (350°F/Gas 4). Grease a shallow 1.5 litre (1.6 US qt/1.3 UK qt) ovenproof dish. Spoon one third of the mushroom mixture into the dish. Cover with potato and top with half the remaining mushrooms, then the eggplant (aubergine). Finish with the remaining mushrooms, pour on the sauce and smooth the top. Bake for 30–35 minutes, or until the edges bubble. Leave for 10 minutes before serving.

Serves 4–6

Asparagus Frittata

- **6 eggs**
- **⅓ cup (35 g/1¼ oz) grated Pecorino or Parmesan**
- **¼ cup (7 g/¼ oz) fresh mint leaves, finely shredded**
- **200 g (7 oz) baby asparagus spears**
- **2 tablespoons extra virgin olive oil**

Put the eggs in a large bowl, beat well, then stir in the cheese and mint and set aside.

Trim the woody part off the asparagus, then cut the asparagus on the diagonal into 5 cm (2 inch) pieces. Heat the oil in a 20 cm (8 inch) frying pan that has a heatproof handle. Add the asparagus and cook for 4–5 minutes, until tender and bright green. Season with salt and pepper, then reduce the heat to low.

Pour the egg mixture over the asparagus and cook for 8–10 minutes. During cooking, use a spatula to gently pull the sides of the frittata away from the sides of the pan and tip the pan slightly so the egg runs underneath the frittata.

When the mixture is nearly set but still slightly runny on top, place the pan under a low grill (broiler) for 1–2 minutes, until the top is set and just browned. Serve warm or at room temperature.

Serves 4

Mexican Tomato Bake

- **2 tablespoons oil**
- **2 red (Spanish) onions, chopped**
- **2 cloves garlic, crushed**
- **6 ripe tomatoes, peeled and chopped**
- **1 green capsicum (pepper), seeded and chopped**
- **1 tablespoon red wine vinegar**
- **1 teaspoon sugar**
- **½ teaspoon ground chilli powder**
- **375 g (13¼ oz) canned corn kernels, drained**
- **125 g (4⅓ oz) plain corn (nacho) chips**
- **1¼ cups (155 g/5½ oz) grated Cheddar (American) cheese**
- **1 cup (250 g/8¾ oz) sour cream**
- **chives**

Preheat oven to warm 160°C (315°F/Gas 2–3). Heat oil in a medium pan. Add onions and garlic; cook over medium heat for 3 minutes. Add tomatoes, capsicum (pepper), vinegar, sugar and chilli. Cook, uncovered, for 6–7 minutes or until tomatoes are soft and liquid has evaporated. Stir in corn kernels over heat for 3 minutes.

Arrange layers of corn (nacho) chips, sauce and cheese in a casserole dish, finishing with cheese layer.

Spread with sour cream. Bake, uncovered, for 15 minutes. Sprinkle with chopped chives.

Serves 4–6

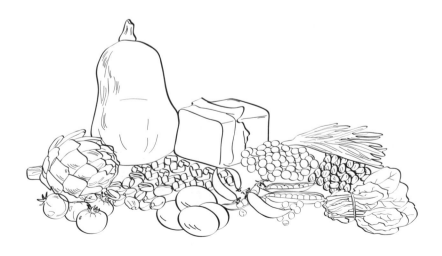

Artichoke Frittata

- **30 g (1 oz) butter**
- **2 small leeks, sliced**
- **1 clove garlic, sliced**
- **6 eggs**

- **100 g (3½ oz) bottled marinated artichoke hearts, sliced**
- **1 teaspoon chopped fresh tarragon**
- **lemon juice, for drizzling**

Heat the butter in a 20 cm (8 inch) non-stick frying pan, add the leek and garlic and cook until soft. Spread evenly over the bottom of the pan.

Lightly beat the eggs and season with salt and black pepper. Pour the eggs into the pan and arrange the artichoke slices on top. Sprinkle with the tarragon and cook over low heat until set (this will take about 10 minutes), shaking the pan occasionally to evenly distribute the egg.

Place under a hot grill (broiler) to lightly brown. Cut into wedges and drizzle with a little lemon juice.

Makes 8 wedges

Potato Baskets with Cheese

- **20 small new potatoes**
- **250 g (8¾ oz) ricotta cheese**
- **35 g (1¼ oz) Cheddar (American) cheese, grated**
- **25 g (¾ oz) Parmesan, shredded**
- **oil, for spraying or brushing**
- **15 g (½ oz) fresh chives, finely chopped, to garnish**

Preheat the oven to moderately hot 200°C (400°F/Gas 6). Boil or steam the potatoes for 10 minutes, or until just tender when tested with a skewer. (Do not overcook or the potatoes will fall apart when you are preparing them.) Drain well and cool completely.

Meanwhile, in a small bowl combine the ricotta, Cheddar (American) and Parmesan cheeses. Season, to taste, and set aside.

Cut the cooled potatoes in half and use a melon baller to scoop out the flesh, leaving a 5 mm (¼ inch) border. Discard the flesh.

Lightly spray the potato halves with oil and bake on baking trays (sheets) for 30–45 minutes, or until crisp and golden. Heat the grill (broiler) to high.

Fill each potato shell with a teaspoon of the cheese mixture and grill (broil) for 5–8 minutes, or until the tops are lightly golden and the cheese has melted. Arrange on a serving dish and garnish each with chopped chives. Serve immediately.

In Advance: The potatoes can be cooked and filled in advance, then grilled (broiled) just before serving.

Makes about 40

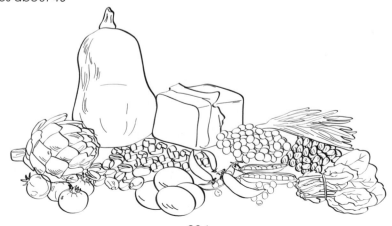

Goat's Cheese and Apple Tarts

- **2 sheets frozen puff pastry**
- **300 g (10½ oz) goat's cheese, sliced**
- **2 cooking apples**
- **2 tablespoons extra virgin olive oil**
- **1 tablespoon chopped fresh lemon thyme**

Preheat the oven to hot 210°C (415°F/Gas 6–7). While the pastry is still frozen, cut each sheet into four squares and then each square into quarters. Place slightly apart on a lightly greased baking tray (sheet). Set aside for a few minutes to thaw and then lay the cheese over the centre of each square of pastry, leaving a small border.

Core the unpeeled apples and slice them thinly. Interleave several slices over the pastry, making sure the cheese is covered completely. Lightly brush the apples with oil and sprinkle with lemon thyme and a little salt and pepper, to taste.

Bake the tarts for 20–25 minutes, or until the pastry is cooked through and golden brown at the edges. The tarts are best served immediately.

In Advance: The pastry can be topped with cheese, covered and refrigerated overnight. Top with the apple just before cooking.

Makes 32

Camembert and Potato Terrine

- **6 new potatoes, unpeeled**
- **3 green apples**
- **125 g (4⅓ oz) butter**
- **3 tablespoons olive oil**

- **200 g (7 oz) Camembert, chilled and very thinly sliced**
- **2 tablespoons chopped fresh parsley**

Par-boil the potatoes in lightly salted water for about 15 minutes. Drain and cool, then peel and cut into slices 1 cm (½ inch) thick.

Core and slice the apples into 5 mm (¼ inch) thick rounds.

Heat half the butter and half the oil in a large frying pan and cook the potato until just golden. Drain on crumpled paper towels. Heat the remaining butter and oil. Lightly fry the sliced apple until golden, then remove and drain on crumpled paper towels. Preheat the oven to moderate 180°C (350°F/Gas 4).

Line a 25 × 11 cm (10 × 4⅓ inch) terrine dish with baking paper. Arrange a layer of potato in the base of the terrine dish. Add a layer of apple, then Camembert. Sprinkle with parsley and season with salt and pepper, to taste. Build up the layers, finishing with potato.

Oil a piece of foil and cover the terrine, sealing well. Place the terrine dish in a baking dish and half fill the dish with boiling water. Bake for 20 minutes. Remove from the water-filled baking dish. Cover with foil, then put a piece of heavy cardboard, cut to fit, on top of the terrine. Put weights or food cans on top of the cardboard to compress the terrine. Refrigerate overnight. Turn out and slice, to serve.

Serves 8–10

Curries

Potato Curry with Sesame Seeds

- **4 large potatoes**
- **1 tablespoon oil**
- **1 teaspoon cumin seeds**
- **1 teaspoon coriander seeds**
- **2 teaspoons mustard seeds**
- **2 tablespoons sesame seeds**
- **½ teaspoon turmeric**
- **1 teaspoon chopped fresh chilli**
- **2 teaspoons finely grated lemon rind**
- **2 tablespoons lemon juice**
- **salt and pepper**

Boil, steam or microwave the potatoes until tender. Cool, peel and chop. Heat the oil in a large heavy-based pan over medium heat. Cook the cumin, coriander and mustard seeds for 1 minute, stirring constantly.

Add the sesame seeds; cook for 1–2 minutes, stirring until golden. Add the turmeric, chillies, potatoes, lemon rind and juice. Stir until well combined and heated through. Season, to taste, with salt and pepper.

Serves 4

Vegetable Curry

- **250 g (8¾ oz) potatoes, diced**
- **250 g (8¾ oz) pumpkin, diced**
- **200 g (7 oz) cauliflower, broken into florets**
- **150 g (5¼ oz) yellow squash, cut into quarters**
- **1 tablespoon oil**
- **2 onions, chopped**
- **3 tablespoons curry powder**
- **400 g (14 oz) can crushed tomatoes**
- **1 cup (250 ml/8½ fl oz) vegetable stock (broth)**
- **150 g (5¼ oz) green beans, cut into short lengths**
- **⅓ cup (90 g/3¼ oz) natural yoghurt**
- **¼ cup (30 g/1 oz) sultanas (golden raisins)**

Bring a saucepan of water to the boil, add the potato and pumpkin, and cook for 6 minutes, then remove. Add the cauliflower and squash, cook for 4 minutes, then remove.

Heat the oil in a large saucepan, add the onion and cook, stirring, over medium heat for 8 minutes, or until starting to brown.

Add the curry powder and stir for 1 minute, or until fragrant. Stir in the crushed tomato and vegetable stock (broth).

Add the parboiled potato, pumpkin, cauliflower and squash and cook for 5 minutes, then add the green beans and cook for a further 2–3 minutes, or until the vegetables are just tender.

Add the yoghurt and sultanas (golden raisins), and stir to combine. Simmer for 3 minutes, or until thickened slightly. Season to taste and serve with lemon wedges.

Serves 6

Dry Potato and Pea Curry

- 2 teaspoons brown mustard seeds
- 2 tablespoons ghee or oil
- 2 onions, sliced
- 2 cloves garlic, crushed
- 2 teaspoons grated fresh ginger (ginger root)
- 1 teaspoon ground turmeric
- ½ teaspoon chilli powder
- 1 teaspoon ground cumin
- 1 teaspoon garam masala
- 750 g (1 lb 10 oz) potatoes, cubed
- ⅔ cup (100 g/3½ oz) peas
- 2 tablespoons chopped mint

Heat the mustard seeds in a dry pan until they start to pop. Add the ghee or oil, onion, garlic and ginger (ginger root) and cook, stirring, until the onion is soft.

Add the turmeric, chilli powder, cumin, garam marsala and potato, and season with salt and pepper. Stir until the potato is coated with the spice mixture. Add 125 ml (4¼ fl oz) water and simmer, covered, for about 15–20 minutes, or until the potato is just tender. Stir occasionally to stop the curry sticking to the bottom of the pan.

Add the peas and stir until well combined. Simmer, covered, for 3–5 minutes, or until the potato is cooked and all the liquid is absorbed. Stir in the mint and season well.

Serves 4

Spiced Bean Curry

- **1 cup (220 g/7¾ oz) dried chickpeas (garbanzo beans)**
- **1 tablespoon oil**
- **2 onions, finely chopped**
- **2 large ripe tomatoes, chopped**
- **½ teaspoon ground coriander**
- **1 teaspoon ground cumin**
- **1 teaspoon chilli powder**
- **¼ teaspoon ground turmeric**
- **1 tablespoon channa masala (see Note)**
- **1 small white onion, sliced**
- **mint and coriander (cilantro) leaves, to garnish**

Place the chickpeas (garbanzo beans) in a bowl, cover with water and leave to soak overnight. Drain, rinse and place in a large saucepan. Cover with plenty of water and bring to the boil, then reduce the heat and simmer for 40 minutes, or until soft. Drain.

Heat the oil in a large saucepan, add the onion and cook over medium heat for 15 minutes, or until golden brown. Add the tomato, ground coriander and cumin, chilli powder, turmeric and channa masala, and 2 cups (500 ml/17 fl oz) water and cook for 10 minutes, or until the tomato is soft. Add the chickpeas (garbanzo beans), season and cook for 7–10 minutes, or until the sauce thickens. Garnish with sliced onion and fresh mint and coriander (cilantro) leaves.

Note: Channa (chole) masala is a spice blend available at Indian grocery stores. Garam masala can be used as a substitute but the flavour will be a little different.

Serves 6

Dhal

- **200 g (7 oz) red lentils**
- **4 cups (1 litre/1.1 US qt/ 1.75 UK pt) water**
- **4 cm (1½ inch) piece fresh ginger (ginger root), cut into 3 slices**
- **½ teaspoon ground turmeric**
- **½ teaspoon salt**
- **3 tablespoons ghee or oil**
- **2 cloves garlic, crushed**
- **1 medium onion, finely chopped**
- **pinch of asafoetida, optional**
- **1 teaspoon cumin seeds**
- **1 teaspoon ground coriander**
- **¼ teaspoon chilli powder**
- **1 tablespoon chopped fresh coriander (cilantro) leaves**

Place the lentils and water in a medium pan, and bring to the boil. Reduce heat to low, add the ginger (ginger root) and turmeric, and simmer, covered, for 1 hour or until the lentils are tender. Stir every 5 minutes during the last 30 minutes to prevent the lentils sticking to the pan. Remove the ginger (ginger root) and stir in the salt.

Heat the ghee in a frying pan; add the garlic and onion, and cook over medium heat for 3 minutes or until the onion is golden. Add the asafoetida, if using, cumin seeds, coriander and chilli powder, and cook for 2 minutes.

Add the onion mixture to the lentils and stir gently to combine. Serve sprinkled with fresh coriander (cilantro).

Serves 4–6

212

Curry-Flavoured Noodles

- **250 g (8¾ oz) thick fresh noodles**
- **¼ cup (60 ml/2 fl oz) oil**
- **2 cloves garlic, sliced**
- **1 onion, finely sliced**
- **1 red capsicum (pepper), cut into long, thin strips**
- **1 small cucumber, unpeeled, cut into thin 4 cm (1½ inch) strips**
- **2 teaspoons mild curry powder**
- **½ cup (125 ml/4¼ fl oz) vegetable stock (broth)**
- **2 teaspoons dry sherry**
- **1 tablespoon soy sauce**
- **½ teaspoon sugar**
- **3 spring (green) onions, sliced diagonally**

Add the noodles to a large pan of boiling water and cook until just tender; drain.

Heat the oil in a wok or pan. Add the garlic, onion and red capsicum (pepper) and stir over medium heat for 3 minutes. Add the cucumber and curry powder and stir over medium heat for another 3 minutes.

Add the combined stock (broth), sherry, soy sauce and sugar, stir until the mixture boils. Add the noodles and spring (green) onions, stir over low heat for 3 minutes or until ingredients are well combined and heated through.

Serves 4

Curried Lentils

- 1 cup (250 g/8¾ oz) red lentils
- 2 cups (500 ml/17 fl oz) vegetable stock (broth)
- ½ teaspoon ground turmeric
- 50 g (1¾ oz) ghee
- 1 onion, chopped
- 2 cloves garlic, finely chopped
- 1 large green chilli, seeded and finely chopped
- 2 teaspoons ground cumin
- 2 teaspoons ground coriander
- 2 tomatoes, chopped
- ½ cup (125 ml/4¼ fl oz) coconut milk

Rinse the lentils and drain well. Place the lentils, stock (broth) and turmeric in a large heavy-based pan. Bring to the boil, reduce the heat and simmer, covered, for 10 minutes, or until just tender. Stir occasionally and check the mixture is not catching on the bottom of the pan.

Meanwhile, heat the ghee in a small frying pan and add the onion. Cook until soft and golden and add the garlic, chilli, cumin and coriander. Cook, stirring, for 2–3 minutes until fragrant. Stir the onions and spices into the lentil mixture and then add the tomato. Simmer over very low heat for 5 minutes, stirring frequently.

Season to taste and add the coconut milk. Stir until heated through. Serve with naan bread or rice.

Serves 4

Pea, Egg and Ricotta Curry

- **4 hard-boiled eggs**
- **½ teaspoon ground turmeric**
- **3 tablespoons ghee or oil**
- **1 bay leaf**
- **2 small onions, finely chopped**
- **1 teaspoon finely chopped garlic**
- **1½ teaspoons ground coriander**
- **1½ teaspoons garam masala**
- **½ teaspoon chilli powder, optional**
- **½ cup (125 g/4⅓ oz) chopped, canned, peeled tomatoes**
- **1 tablespoon tomato paste (tomato puree, double concentrate)**
- **½ cup (125 ml/4¼ fl oz) water**
- **125 g (4⅓ oz) baked ricotta, cut in 1 cm (½ inch) cubes**
- **¼ teaspoon salt**
- **1 tablespoon yoghurt**
- **½ cup (80 g/2¾ oz) frozen peas**
- **2 tablespoons finely chopped fresh coriander (cilantro) leaves**

Peel the eggs and coat them with the turmeric.

Melt the ghee in a large pan and cook the eggs over moderate heat for 2 minutes until they are light brown, stirring constantly. Set aside.

Add the bay leaf, onion and garlic to the pan and cook over moderately high heat, stirring frequently, until the mixture is well reduced and pale gold. Lower the heat if the mixture is browning too quickly. Add the ground coriander, garam masala and chilli powder, if using, and cook until fragrant.

Add the tomato, tomato paste (tomato puree) and water; cover and simmer for 5 minutes. Return the eggs to the pan with the ricotta, salt, yoghurt and peas, and cook for 5 minutes. Remove the bay leaf, sprinkle with coriander (cilantro) and serve immediately.

Serves 4

Red Vegetable Curry

- **225 g (8 oz) bamboo shoots or tips, drained**
- **2 cups (500 ml/17 fl oz) coconut milk**
- **2 tablespoons Thai red curry paste**
- **1 onion, finely chopped**
- **4 kaffir lime leaves**
- **2 potatoes, roughly chopped**
- **200 g (7 oz) pumpkin, chopped**
- **150 g (5¼ oz) green beans, chopped**
- **1 red capsicum (pepper), chopped**
- **3 small zucchini (courgettes), chopped**
- **2 tablespoons chopped fresh basil leaves**
- **2 tablespoons lime juice**
- **3 teaspoons soft brown sugar**

Cut the bamboo shoots in half, discard the tough ends and set the shoots aside. Combine the coconut milk and curry paste in a large wok or pan with ½ cup (125 ml/4¼ fl oz) water. Bring to the boil, stirring occasionally.

Add the onion and kaffir lime leaves and allow to boil for 3 minutes.

Add the potato and pumpkin to the wok and cook over medium heat for 8 minutes, or until the pumpkin is nearly cooked. Add the beans, capsicum (pepper) and zucchini (courgettes) and simmer for another 5 minutes. Add ½ cup (125 ml/4¼ fl oz) of water if the curry is too thick. Add the bamboo shoots and basil. Add the lime juice and sugar and season to taste. Serve with steamed rice.

Serves 4

Mixed Vegetables in Mild Curry Sauce

- 250 g (8¾ oz) peeled pumpkin
- 2 medium orange sweet potatoes (yams)
- 125 g (4⅓ oz) yellow squash
- 125 g (4⅓ oz) green beans
- 125 g (4⅓ oz) cabbage
- 6 teaspoons oil
- 1 large onion, finely sliced
- 1 clove garlic, crushed
- ½ cup (100 g/3½ oz) peeled and chopped tomato
- 1 red chilli, chopped
- 3 strips lemon rind
- 4 kaffir lime leaves, dried or fresh
- 2 teaspoons grated palm sugar or soft brown sugar
- 1 teaspoon salt
- 1 tablespoon vegetarian fish sauce or soy sauce
- 1⅔ cups (410 ml/13¾ fl oz) coconut milk
- 1 cup (250 ml/8½ fl oz) vegetable stock (broth)
- 2 teaspoons lemon juice

Cut the pumpkin into small wedges and the sweet potato (yam) into 2 cm (¾ inch) pieces. Quarter the squash; top and tail the beans, halving them if long; and cut the cabbage into 1 cm (½ inch) wide shreds.

Heat the oil in a medium pan; add the onion and garlic and cook over medium heat until soft and slightly golden.

Add the tomato, chilli, lemon rind, lime leaves, sugar, salt, sauce, coconut milk, stock (broth) and lemon juice; cook for 5 minutes until the flavour has intensified.

Add the sweet potato (yam) and pumpkin to the sauce and cook for 8 minutes. Add the beans, cabbage and squash and cook for 6 minutes. Serve with steamed rice.

Note: The sauce can be prepared a few hours ahead and reheated. Cook the vegetables just before serving.

Serves 4

Pineapple Curry

- 1 medium pineapple
- 1 teaspoon cardamom seeds
- 1 teaspoon coriander seeds
- 1 teaspoon cumin seeds
- ½ teaspoon whole cloves
- 2 tablespoons oil
- 2 spring (green) onions, cut in
  2 cm (¾ inch) pieces
- 2 teaspoons grated fresh ginger
  (ginger root)
- 4 candlenuts, roughly chopped
- 1 cup (250 ml/8½ fl oz) water
- 1 teaspoon sambal oelek
- 1 tablespoon chopped fresh mint

Peel and halve the pineapple, remove the core, and cut the pineapple into 2 cm (¾ inch) chunks.

Grind the cardamom seeds, coriander seeds, cumin seeds and cloves in a mortar and pestle.

Heat the oil in a medium pan; add the spring (green) onion, ginger (ginger root), candlenuts and spice mixture, and stir-fry (scramble-fry) over low heat for 3 minutes.

Add the water, sambal oelek, mint and pineapple and bring to the boil. Reduce the heat to low, cover and simmer for 10 minutes, or until the pineapple is tender but still holding its shape. Serve as an accompaniment.

Note: If the pineapple is a little tart, add 1 to 2 teaspoons sugar. A 450 g (15¾ oz) can of drained pineapple pieces can be used instead of fresh pineapple.

Serves 4

Green Curry with Sweet Potato

- 1 tablespoon oil
- 1 onion, chopped
- 1–2 tablespoons green curry paste (see Note)
- 1 eggplant (aubergine), quartered and sliced
- 1½ cups (375 ml/13 fl oz) coconut milk
- 1 cup (250 ml/8½ fl oz) vegetable stock (broth)
- 6 kaffir lime leaves
- 1 orange sweet potato (yam), cubed
- 2 teaspoons soft brown sugar
- 2 tablespoons lime juice
- 2 teaspoons lime rind

Heat the oil in a large wok or frying pan. Add the onion and green curry paste and cook, stirring, over medium heat for 3 minutes. Add the eggplant (aubergine) and cook for a further 4–5 minutes, or until softened.

Pour in the coconut milk and vegetable stock (broth), bring to the boil, then reduce the heat and simmer for 5 minutes. Add the kaffir lime leaves and sweet potato (yam) and cook for 10 minutes, or until the eggplant (aubergine) and sweet potato (yam) are very tender.

Mix in the sugar, lime juice and lime rind until well combined with the vegetables. Season to taste with salt and serve with steamed rice.

Note: Strict vegetarians should be sure to read the label and choose a green curry paste that doesn't contain shrimp paste. Alternatively, you can make your own curry pastes.

Serves 4–6

Hot Vegetable Curry with Spiced Noodles

- 2 tablespoons oil
- 1½ cups (375 ml/13 fl oz) coconut milk
- 200 g (7 oz) green beans, cut into short lengths
- 2 small zucchini (courgette), thickly sliced
- 1 eggplant (aubergine), cubed
- 200 g (7 oz) pumpkin, cubed
- 5 kaffir lime leaves
- 2 tablespoons lime juice
- ¼ cup (15 g/½ oz) chopped fresh coriander (cilantro)
- ½ cup (30 g/1 oz) chopped fresh basil

Curry Paste
- 5 red chillies, seeded and chopped
- 1 stem lemon grass, sliced
- 1 tablespoon chopped galangal (Thai ginger)
- 2 garlic cloves, crushed
- 1 small onion, chopped
- 1 tablespoon chopped fresh coriander (cilantro)
- 10 black peppercorns
- 2 tablespoons lime juice
- 2 teaspoons oil

Spiced Noodles
- 2 tablespoons oil
- 1 small onion, chopped
- 1 clove garlic, crushed
- ½–1 teaspoon dried chilli flakes
- ½ teaspoon garam masala
- 200 g (7 oz) thin egg noodles

To make the curry paste, blend all the ingredients in a food processor or blender to make a smooth paste.

Heat the oil in a pan and stir-fry (scramble-fry) the curry paste for 2 minutes. Add the coconut milk and ½ cup (125 ml/4¼ fl oz) water and bring to the boil. Reduce the heat and add the vegetables, kaffir lime leaves and lime juice. Cook, covered, until tender. Add the coriander (cilantro) and basil.

To make the spiced noodles, heat the oil in a pan. Cook the onion and garlic over low heat for 5 minutes. Add the chilli flakes and garam masala and cook for 2 minutes. Meanwhile, cook the noodles in boiling water until tender and drain. Add to the onion mixture and toss well. Serve with the vegetable curry.

Serves 4–6

Lentil and Cauliflower Curry Stacks

- 60 g (2 oz) ghee or butter
- 2 onions, thinly sliced
- 2 tablespoons Madras curry paste
- 2 cloves garlic, crushed
- 180 g (6⅓ oz) button mushrooms, sliced
- 1 litre (1.1 US qt/1.75 UK pt) vegetable stock (broth)
- 300 g (10½ oz) brown or green lentils
- 400 g (14 oz) can chopped tomatoes
- 2 cinnamon sticks
- 300 g (10½ oz) cauliflower, cut into small florets
- oil, for deep-frying
- 18 small (8 cm/3 inch) pappadums
- plain yoghurt and fresh coriander (cilantro), to serve

Heat the ghee in a large pan over medium heat and cook the onion for 2–3 minutes, or until soft. Add the curry paste, garlic and mushrooms and cook for 2 minutes, or until soft.

Add the stock (broth), lentils, tomato and cinnamon and mix well. Bring to the boil and cook for 40 minutes, or until the lentils are tender. Add the cauliflower in the last 10 minutes and cover. If the curry is too wet, continue to cook, uncovered, until the excess liquid has evaporated. Season to taste with salt and cracked black pepper. Remove the cinnamon.

Meanwhile, fill a deep heavy-based saucepan one third full of oil and heat until a cube of bread dropped into the oil browns in 15 seconds. Cook the pappadums in batches for 10 seconds, or until golden brown and puffed all over. Drain on crumpled paper towels and season with salt.

To assemble, place a pappadum on each serving plate and spoon on a little of the curry. Place a second pappadum on top and spoon on some more curry. Cover with the remaining pappadum and top with a spoonful of yoghurt. Garnish with coriander (cilantro) sprigs and serve immediately (the pappadums will become soggy if left to stand for too long.)

Serves 6

Sweet Vegetable Curry

- 2 medium carrots
- 1 medium parsnip
- 1 medium potato
- 2 tablespoons oil
- 2 medium onions, chopped
- 1 teaspoon ground cardamom
- ¼ teaspoon ground cloves
- 1½ teaspoons cumin seeds
- 1 teaspoon ground coriander
- 1 teaspoon ground turmeric
- 1 teaspoon brown mustard seeds
- ½ teaspoon chilli powder
- 2 teaspoons grated fresh ginger (ginger root)
- 1⅓ cups (350 ml/11¾ fl oz) vegetable stock (broth)
- ¾ cup (185 ml/6½ fl oz) apricot nectar
- 2 tablespoons fruit chutney
- 1 medium green capsicum (pepper), cut into 2 cm (¾ inch) squares
- 200 g (7 oz) small button mushrooms
- 300 g (10½ oz) cauliflower, cut into small florets
- ¼ cup (45 g/1⅔ oz) ground almonds

Cut the carrots, parsnip and potato into 2 cm (¾ inch) pieces.

Heat the oil in a large heavy-based pan; add the onion and cook over medium heat for 4 minutes, or until just soft. Add the cardamom, cloves, cumin seeds, ground coriander, turmeric, mustard seeds, chilli powder and ginger (ginger root), and cook, stirring, for 1 minute or until aromatic.

Add the carrot, parsnip, potato, stock (broth), nectar and chutney. Cook, covered, over medium heat for 25 minutes, stirring occasionally.

Stir in the green capsicum (pepper), mushrooms and cauliflower. Simmer for 10 minutes more or until the vegetables are tender. Stir in the ground almonds and serve with rice.

Serves 4

Tempeh
and
Tofu

Thai Tempeh

Thai Marinade
- 2 stems lemon grass, finely chopped
- 2 kaffir lime leaves, shredded
- 2 small red chillies, seeded and finely chopped
- 3 cloves garlic, crushed
- 2 teaspoons sesame oil
- ½ cup (125 ml/4¼ fl oz) lime juice
- 2 teaspoons shaved palm sugar
- ½ cup (125 ml/4¼ fl oz) soy sauce

- 600 g (1¼ lb) tempeh, cut into twelve 5 mm (¼ inch) slices
- 3 tablespoons peanut oil
- 1 tablespoon shaved palm sugar
- 100 g (3½ oz) snow pea (mange tout) sprouts or watercress
- kaffir lime leaves, finely shredded

To make the Thai marinade, mix the lemon grass, lime leaves, chilli, garlic, sesame oil, lime juice, sugar and soy sauce in a non-metallic bowl. Add the tempeh. Cover and marinate overnight in the fridge, turning occasionally.

Drain the tempeh, reserving the marinade. Heat half the peanut oil in a frying pan over high heat. Cook the tempeh in batches, turning once, for 5 minutes, or until crispy, adding more oil when needed. Drain on paper towels. Heat the reserved marinade with the palm sugar in a saucepan until syrupy.

Put a slice of tempeh on each serving plate and top with some snow pea (mange tout) sprouts. Continue the layers, finishing with the tempeh on top. Drizzle with the reserved marinade and sprinkle with lime leaves.

Serves 4

Tofu Triangles

- 150 g (5½ oz) firm tofu
- 2 spring (green) onions, chopped
- 3 teaspoons chopped fresh coriander (cilantro) leaves
- ½ teaspoon grated orange rind
- 2 teaspoons soy sauce
- 1 tablespoon sweet chilli sauce (jalapeno jelly)
- 2 teaspoons grated fresh ginger (ginger root)
- 1 teaspoon cornflour (cornstarch)

- ½ cup (125 ml/4 fl oz) seasoned rice vinegar
- ¼ cup (60 g/2 oz) sugar
- 1 small Lebanese cucumber, finely diced
- 1 small red chilli, thinly sliced
- 1 spring (green) onion, extra, thinly sliced on the diagonal
- 2 sheets puff pastry
- 1 egg, lightly beaten

Drain the tofu, then pat dry and cut into small cubes.

Put the spring (green) onion, coriander (cilantro), rind, soy and chilli sauces (jalapeno jelly), ginger (ginger root), cornflour (cornstarch) and tofu in a bowl and gently mix. Cover, then refrigerate for 3–4 hours.

To make a dipping sauce, put the vinegar and sugar in a small saucepan and stir over low heat until the sugar dissolves. Remove from the heat and add the cucumber, chilli and extra spring (green) onion. Cool completely.

Preheat the oven to 220°C (425°F/Gas 7). Cut each pastry sheet into four squares. Drain the filling and divide into eight. Place one portion in the centre of each square and brush the edges with egg. Fold into a triangle and seal the edges with a fork.

Put the triangles on two lined baking trays (sheets), brush with egg and bake for 15 minutes. Serve with the dippping sauce.

Serves 4

Marinated Tofu

- ½ cup (125 ml/4¼ fl oz) peanut oil
- 2 cloves garlic, crushed
- 1 teaspoon grated fresh ginger (ginger root)
- 2 stems lemon grass, white part only, finely chopped
- 1 small fresh red chilli, finely chopped
- 2 tablespoons vegetarian fish sauce or soy sauce
- 2 tablespoons lime juice
- 1 tablespoon soft brown sugar
- 500 g (1 lb 2 oz) fried tofu puffs, halved on the diagonal

Combine all the ingredients in a flat non-metallic dish. Toss the tofu until coated in the marinade, then cover with plastic wrap and refrigerate overnight.

Heat a lightly oiled wok over high heat and stir-fry (scramble-fry) the tofu in batches for 1–2 minutes, or until browned. Serve hot.

Serves 4

Crunchy Stuffed Tofu Puffs

- **12 deep-fried tofu puffs**
- **1 cup (90 g/3¼ oz) bean sprouts, scraggly ends removed**
- **¼ cup (40 g/1½ oz) unsalted roasted peanuts, chopped**
- **1 carrot, grated**
- **1 tablespoon chopped fresh coriander (cilantro) leaves**

Chilli (Pepper) Sauce
- **2 small red chillies, finely chopped**
- **2 cloves garlic, crushed**
- **2 teaspoons soft brown sugar**
- **1 tablespoon soy sauce**
- **1 tablespoon vinegar**
- **½ cup (125 ml/4¼ fl oz) boiling water**

Cut the tofu puffs in half. Cut a small slit in each half and open it up carefully to form a pocket.

Place the bean sprouts, peanuts, carrot and coriander (cilantro) in a bowl, and toss until well mixed. Fill each pocket with a portion of the mixture. Serve drizzled with a little Chilli (Pepper) Sauce, and offer the rest of the sauce for dipping.

To make Chilli (Pepper) Sauce: Combine all the ingredients in a small pan, bring to the boil, reduce heat and simmer for 5 minutes or until the sauce thickens slightly.

Note: Tofu puffs are cubes of tofu which have been deep-fried and are puffed and golden. They are available from Asian food shops.

Makes 24

Stir-Fried Crisp Tofu in a Hot Bean Sauce

- **500 g (1 lb 2 oz) firm tofu, cut into small cubes**
- **2 tablespoons peanut oil**
- **¼ cup (60 ml/2 fl oz) soy sauce**
- **2 teaspoons finely grated fresh ginger (ginger root)**
- **oil, for cooking**
- **¾ cup (125 g/4⅓ oz) rice flour**
- **2 onions, cut into thin wedges**
- **2 cloves garlic, finely chopped**
- **2 teaspoons soft brown sugar**
- **½ red capsicum (pepper), cut into short, thin strips**
- **5 spring (green) onions, cut into short pieces**
- **2 tablespoons dry sherry**
- **2 teaspoons finely grated orange rind**
- **2 tablespoons hot bean paste**

Place the tofu in a glass or ceramic bowl with the peanut oil. Add the soy sauce and ginger (ginger root), cover and refrigerate for 30 minutes.

Drain the tofu, reserving the marinade, and toss several pieces at a time in the rice flour to coat heavily. Heat the wok until very hot, add about ¼ cup (60 ml/2 fl oz) of the oil and swirl it around to coat the side. Add the tofu to the hot oil and stir-fry (scramble-fry) over medium heat for 1½ minutes, or until golden all over. Remove from the wok and drain on paper towels. Repeat with the remaining tofu. Keep warm. Drain any oil from the wok.

Reheat the wok and stir-fry (scramble-fry) the onion, garlic and sugar for 3 minutes, or until golden. Add the capsicum (pepper), spring (green) onion, sherry, orange rind, bean paste and the reserved tofu marinade. Stir and bring to the boil. Return the tofu to the wok, toss to heat through, and serve.

Serves 4

Spiced Tempeh

- **2 small dried red chillies**
- **8 black peppercorns**
- **2 cloves garlic**
- **2 tablespoons chopped fresh coriander (cilantro) stems and leaves**
- **⅓ cup (80 ml/2¾ fl oz) vegetable oil**
- **100 g (3½ oz) tempeh, thinly sliced**
- **250 g (8¾ oz) slender eggplants (aubergines), cut into 2 cm (¾ inch) chunks**
- **1 tablespoon soy sauce**
- **1 tablespoon vegetarian fish sauce or extra soy sauce**
- **1 teaspoon grated palm sugar**
- **1 tablespoon lime juice**

Soak the chillies in a bowl of boiling water for 20 minutes. Drain, remove the seeds and finely chop the flesh.

Put the peppercorns, garlic and coriander (cilantro) in a food processor and process to a smooth paste – add a little water if needed.

Heat a wok over high heat, add the oil and swirl to coat. Add the paste and chilli and stir-fry (scramble-fry) for 10 seconds. Add the tempeh and stir-fry (scramble-fry) for a further 2 minutes, or until golden brown. Remove the tempeh.

Add the eggplant (aubergine) to the wok and stir-fry (scramble-fry) for 6 minutes, or until golden brown. Add the sauces, palm sugar, lime juice and tempeh and cook, stirring, for a further 30 seconds. Serve immediately with rice.

Serves 6

229

Barbecue Vegetable and Tofu Kebabs

- 500 g (1 lb 2 oz) firm tofu, cubed
- 1 red capsicum (pepper), cubed
- 3 zucchini (courgettes), thickly sliced
- 4 small onions, cut into quarters
- 300 g (10½ oz) button mushrooms, cut into quarters
- ½ cup (125 ml/4¼ fl oz) tamari
- ½ cup (125 ml/4¼ fl oz) sesame oil
- 2.5 cm (1 inch) piece ginger (ginger root), peeled and grated
- ½ cup (175 g/6¼ oz) honey

Peanut Sauce
- 1 tablespoon sesame oil
- 1 small onion, finely chopped
- 1 clove garlic, crushed
- 2 teaspoons chilli paste
- 1 cup (250 g/8¾ oz) smooth peanut butter
- 1 cup (250 ml/8½ fl oz) coconut milk
- 1 tablespoon soft brown sugar
- 1 tablespoon tamari
- 1 tablespoon lemon juice
- ¼ cup (40 g/1½ oz) peanuts, roasted and chopped
- ¼ cup (40 g/1½ oz) sesame seeds, toasted

Soak 12 bamboo skewers in water for 2 hours. Thread the tofu, capsicum (pepper), zucchini (courgettes), onions and mushrooms alternately onto the skewers. Lay out in a large flat dish.

Combine the tamari, oil, ginger (ginger root) and honey in a non-metallic bowl. Pour over the kebabs. Leave for 30 minutes. Cook on a hot barbecue or in a chargrill (charbroil) pan, basting and turning, for 10–15 minutes, or until tender. Remove and keep warm.

To make the peanut sauce, heat the oil in a large frying pan over medium heat and cook the onion, garlic and chilli paste for 1–2 minutes, or until the onion is soft. Reduce the heat, add the peanut butter, coconut milk, sugar, tamari and lemon juice and stir. Bring to the boil, then reduce the heat and simmer for 10 minutes, or until just thick. Stir in the peanuts. If the sauce is too thick, add water. Serve with the kebabs, sprinkled with sesame seeds.

Serves 4

Steamed Tofu with Soy

- **2 tablespoons soy sauce**
- **2 tablespoons kecap manis (Indonesian soy sauce)**
- **1 teaspoon sesame oil**
- **500 g (1 lb 2 oz) firm tofu, drained**
- **1½ teaspoons julienned fresh ginger (ginger root)**
- **3 spring (green) onions, thinly sliced on the diagonal**
- **1 cup (50 g/1¾ oz) chopped fresh coriander (cilantro) leaves**
- **1–2 tablespoons crisp fried shallots**

Combine the soy sauce, kecap manis (Indonesian soy sauce) and oil in a bowl. Cut the tofu in half widthways, then into triangles. Place on a heatproof plate and pour the sauce over the top. Marinate for 30 minutes, turning the tofu once.

Sprinkle the ginger (ginger root) over the tofu. Place the plate on a wire rack over a wok of simmering water. Cover and steam for 3–4 minutes. Sprinkle with the spring (green) onion and coriander (cilantro), then cover and steam for 3 minutes. Sprinkle with the crisp fried shallots.

Serves 4

Green Tofu Curry

- 2 tablespoons oil
- 1 onion, sliced
- 400 ml (13½ fl oz) can coconut cream
- 4–5 kaffir lime leaves, torn
- 500 g (1 lb 2 oz) firm tofu, cut into 2 cm (¾ inch) cubes
- 1 tablespoon lime juice
- 1 tablespoon shredded fresh Thai basil

Curry Paste
- 10 small fresh green chillies
- 50 g (1¼ oz) red Asian shallots, peeled
- 2 cloves garlic
- 1 cup (50 g/1¾ oz) finely chopped coriander (cilantro) stems and roots
- 1 stem lemon grass (white part only), chopped
- 2 tablespoons grated fresh galangal (Thai ginger)
- 1 tablespoon ground coriander
- 1 teaspoon ground cumin
- 1 teaspoon black peppercorns
- ½ teaspoon ground turmeric
- 1 tablespoon lime juice

To make the curry paste, place all the ingredients in a food processor and process until smooth.

Heat the oil in a frying pan, add the onion and cook for 5 minutes, or until soft. Add 4 tablespoons curry paste (or more for a stronger flavour) and cook, stirring, for 2 minutes. Stir in the coconut cream and 1 cup (250 ml/8½ fl oz) water, and season with salt. Bring to the boil and add the lime leaves and tofu. Reduce the heat and simmer for 8 minutes, stirring often. Stir in the lime juice and Thai basil, and serve.

Note: The recipe for the curry paste makes 1 cup, but you will only need ⅓ cup. Freeze the remaining paste in two portions to use at a later date.

Serves 6

Tofu in Black Bean Sauce

- ⅓ cup (80 ml/2¾ fl oz) vegetable stock (broth)
- 2 teaspoons cornflour (cornstarch)
- 2 teaspoons Chinese rice wine
- 1 teaspoon sesame oil
- 1 tablespoon soy sauce
- 2 tablespoons peanut oil
- 450 g (15¾ oz) firm tofu, cut into 2 cm (¾ inch) cubes
- 2 cloves garlic, very finely chopped
- 2 teaspoons finely chopped fresh ginger (ginger root)
- 3 tablespoons black beans, rinsed and very finely chopped
- 4 spring (green) onions, sliced on the diagonal (white and green parts)
- 1 red capsicum (pepper), cut into 2 cm (¾ inch) chunks
- 300 g (10½ oz) baby bok choy, chopped crossways into 2 cm (¾ inch) pieces

Combine the vegetable stock (broth), cornflour (cornstarch), Chinese rice wine, sesame oil, soy sauce, ½ teaspoon salt and freshly ground black pepper in a small bowl.

Heat a wok over medium heat, add the peanut oil and swirl to coat. Add the tofu and stir-fry (scramble-fry) in two batches for 3 minutes each batch, or until lightly browned. Remove with a slotted spoon and drain on paper towels. Discard any bits of tofu stuck to the wok or floating in the oil.

Add the garlic and ginger (ginger root) and stir-fry (scramble-fry) for 30 seconds. Toss in the black beans and spring (green) onion and stir-fry for 30 seconds. Add the capsicum (pepper) and stir-fry (scramble-fry) for 1 minute. Add the bok choy and stir-fry (scramble-fry) for a further 2 minutes. Return the tofu to the wok and stir gently. Pour in the sauce and stir gently for 2–3 minutes, or until the sauce has thickened slightly. Serve immediately with steamed rice.

Serves 4

Tofu Burgers

- 1 tablespoon olive oil
- 1 red onion, finely chopped
- 200 g (7 oz) Swiss brown mushrooms, finely chopped
- 350 g (12¼ oz) hard tofu (see Note)
- 2 large cloves garlic
- 3 tablespoons chopped fresh basil
- 2 cups (200 g/7 oz) dry wholemeal breadcrumbs
- 1 egg, lightly beaten
- 2 tablespoons balsamic vinegar
- 2 tablespoons sweet chilli sauce (jalapeno jelly)
- 1½ cups (150 g/5¼ oz) dry wholemeal (whole wheat) breadcrumbs, extra
- olive oil, for shallow-frying
- 6 wholemeal (whole wheat) or wholegrain bread rolls
- ½ cup (125 g/4⅓ oz) mayonnaise
- 100 g (3½ oz) semi-dried tomatoes
- 60 g (2 oz) rocket (arugula) leaves
- sweet chilli sauce (jalapeno jelly), to serve

Heat the oil in a frying pan and cook the onion over medium heat for 2–3 minutes, or until soft. Add the mushrooms and cook for a further 2 minutes. Cool slightly.

Blend 250 g (8¾ oz) of the tofu with the garlic and basil in a food processor until smooth. Transfer to a large bowl and stir in the onion mixture, breadcrumbs, egg, vinegar and sweet chilli sauce (jalapeno jelly). Grate the remaining tofu and fold through the mixture, then refrigerate for 30 minutes. Divide the mixture into six and form into patties, pressing together well. Coat them in the extra breadcrumbs.

Heat 1 cm (½ inch) oil in a deep frying pan and cook the patties in two batches for 4–5 minutes each side, or until golden. Turn carefully to prevent them breaking up. Drain on crumpled paper towels and season with salt.

Halve the bread rolls and toast under a hot grill (broiler). Spread mayonnaise over both sides of each roll. Layer semi-dried tomatoes, a tofu patty and rocket (arugula) leaves in each roll and drizzle with sweet chilli sauce (jalapeno jelly).

Note: Hard tofu (not to be confused with 'firm' tofu) is quite rubbery and firm and won't break up during cooking. It's perfect for patties, stir-frying (scramble-frying) and pan-frying.

Serves 6

Stir-Fry with Mushrooms and Cashews

- 1 tablespoon peanut oil
- 1 teaspoon sesame oil
- 1 tablespoon grated fresh ginger (ginger root)
- 1 fresh red chilli, thinly sliced
- 2 cloves garlic, crushed
- 4 spring (green) onions, sliced on the diagonal
- 300 g (10½ oz) shiitake mushrooms, sliced
- 800 g (1 lb 12 oz) broccolini, cut into 2 cm pieces, chopped
- 500 g (1 lb 2 oz) baby bok choy leaves
- ½ cup (125 ml/4¼ fl oz) vegetarian oyster sauce
- 2 tablespoons rice vinegar
- 2 tablespoons fresh coriander (cilantro) leaves
- ¼ cup (40 g/1½ oz) toasted cashew nuts

Heat a wok over high heat, add the oils and swirl to coat the side of the wok. Add the garlic, ginger (ginger root), chilli and spring (green) onion and cook for 1–2 minutes, or until the onion is soft. Add the tempeh and cook for 5 minutes, or until golden. Remove from the wok.

Add half the greens and mushrooms and 1 tablespoon water to the wok and cook, covered, for 3–4 minutes, or until the greens have wilted. Remove from the wok and repeat with the remaining greens and mushrooms and a little more water.

Return the greens and tempeh to the wok, add the sauce and vinegar and warm through. Top with the coriander (cilantro) and nuts. Serve with rice.

Serves 4

Tofu and Vegetables

- 125 g (4⅓ oz) rice vermicelli
- ¾ cup (185 ml/6½ fl oz) oil
- 1 tablespoon soy sauce
- 1 tablespoon sherry
- 1 tablespoon vegetarian oyster sauce (optional)
- ½ cup (125 ml/4¼ fl oz) vegetable stock (broth)
- 2 teaspoons cornflour (cornstarch)
- 2 teaspoons water
- 1 tablespoon oil, extra
- 1 clove garlic, crushed
- 1 teaspoon grated fresh ginger (ginger root)
- 375 g (13¼ oz) firm tofu, cut into small cubes
- 2 medium carrots, cut into matchsticks
- 250 g (8¾ oz) snow peas (mange tout), trimmed
- 4 spring (green) onions, finely sliced
- 425 g (15 oz) canned straw mushrooms, drained

Break the vermicelli into short lengths. Heat half the oil in a wok. Cook the vermicelli in batches in the wok over medium heat until crisp, adding more oil when necessary. Drain on paper towels.

Combine the soy sauce, sherry, vegetarian oyster sauce and stock (broth) in a small bowl. Blend the cornflour (cornstarch) with the water in a small bowl.

Heat the wok; add the extra oil and the garlic and ginger (ginger root) and cook over high heat for 1 minute. Add the tofu and stir-fry (scramble-fry) for 3 minutes. Remove the tofu from the wok. Add the carrots and snow peas (mange tout) to the wok and stir-fry (scramble-fry) for 1 minute. Add the combined sauces and vegetable stock (broth); cover and cook for another 3 minutes, or until the vegetables are just cooked.

Return the tofu to the wok. Add the spring (green) onions, mushrooms and blended cornflour (cornstarch). Stir until the sauce has thickened, then remove from the heat. Serve with the crisp vermicelli.

Serves 4–6

Tofu Salad

- **2 teaspoons Thai sweet chilli sauce**
- **½ teaspoon grated fresh ginger (ginger root)**
- **1 clove garlic, crushed**
- **2 teaspoons soy sauce**
- **2 tablespoons oil**
- **250 g (8¾ oz) firm tofu**
- **105 g (3⅔ oz) snow peas (mange tout), cut into 3 cm (1¼ inch) lengths**
- **2 small carrots, cut into matchsticks**
- **105 g (3⅔ oz) red cabbage, finely shredded**
- **2 tablespoons chopped peanuts**

Place the chilli sauce, ginger (ginger root), garlic, soy sauce and oil in a small screw-top jar and shake well. Cut the tofu into 2 cm (¾ inch) cubes. Place the tofu in a medium bowl, pour the marinade over and stir. Cover with plastic wrap and refrigerate for 1 hour.

Place the snow peas (mange tout) in a small pan, pour boiling water over and leave to stand for 1 minute, then drain and plunge into iced water. Drain well.

Add the snow peas (mange tout), carrots and cabbage to tofu and toss lightly to combine. Transfer to a serving bowl or individual plates, sprinkle with peanuts and serve immediately.

Serves 4

Tofu, Snow Pea and Mushroom Stir-Fry

- ¼ cup (60 ml/2 fl oz) peanut oil
- 600 g (1 lb 5 oz) firm tofu, drained, cut into 2 cm (¾ inch) cubes
- 2 teaspoons sambal oelek or chilli paste
- 2 cloves garlic, finely chopped
- 300 g (10 oz) snow peas (mange ½ tout), trimmed
- 400 g (14 oz) fresh Asian mushrooms (e.g. shiitake, oyster or black fungus), sliced
- ¼ cup (60 ml/2 fl oz) kecap manis (Indonesian soy sauce)

Heat a wok over high heat, add 2 tablespoons of the peanut oil and swirl to coat the side of the wok. Add the tofu in two batches and stir-fry (scramble-fry) each batch for 2–3 minutes, or until lightly browned on all sides, then transfer to a plate.

Heat the remaining oil in the wok, add the sambal oelek, garlic, snow peas (mange tout), mushrooms and 1 tablespoon water and stir-fry (scramble-fry) for 1–2 minutes, or until the vegetables are almost cooked but still crunchy.

Return the tofu to the wok, add the kecap manis (Indonesian soy sauce) and stir-fry (scramble-fry) for another minute, or until heated through. Serve immediately with steamed jasmine rice.

Serves 4

Tofu Kebabs with Miso Pesto

- **1 large red capsicum (pepper), cubed**
- **12 button mushrooms, halved**
- **6 pickling onions, quartered**
- **3 zucchini (courgettes), cut into chunks**
- **450 g (15¾ oz) firm tofu, cubed**
- **½ cup (125 ml/4¼ fl oz) light olive oil**
- **3 tablespoons light soy sauce**
- **2 cloves garlic, crushed**
- **2 teaspoons grated fresh ginger (ginger root)**

Miso Pesto
- **½ cup (90 g/3¼ oz) unsalted roasted peanuts**
- **2 cups (60 g/2 oz) firmly packed fresh coriander (cilantro) leaves**
- **2 tablespoons white miso paste**
- **2 cloves garlic**
- **100 ml (3½ oz) olive oil**

If using wooden skewers, soak them in water for 30 minutes to prevent scorching. Thread the vegetables and tofu alternately onto 12 skewers, then place in a large non-metallic dish.

Mix together the olive oil, soy sauce, garlic and ginger (ginger root), then pour half over the kebabs. Cover and leave to marinate for 1 hour.

To make the miso pesto, finely chop the peanuts, coriander (cilantro) leaves, miso paste and garlic in a food processor. Slowly add the olive oil while the machine is still running and blend to a smooth paste.

Cook the kebabs on a hot, lightly oiled barbecue flatplate or grill (broiler), turning and brushing with the remaining marinade, for 4–6 minutes, or until the edges are slightly brown. Serve with the miso pesto.

Serves 4

239

Tofu with Carrot and Ginger Sauce

- 2 × 300 g (10½ oz) packets firm tofu, drained
- ½ cup (125 ml/4¼ fl oz) orange juice
- 1 tablespoon soft brown sugar
- 1 tablespoon soy sauce
- 2 tablespoons chopped fresh coriander (cilantro) leaves
- 2 cloves garlic, crushed
- 1 teaspoon grated fresh ginger (ginger root)

- 2–3 tablespoons oil
- 1 kg (2 lb 3 oz) baby bok choy, quartered lengthways

Carrot and Ginger Sauce
- 300 g (10½ oz) carrots, chopped
- 2 teaspoons grated fresh ginger (ginger root)
- ⅔ cup (170 ml/5¾ fl oz) orange juice
- ½ cup (125 ml/4¼ fl oz) vegetable stock (broth)

Slice each block of tofu into six lengthways. Place in a single layer in a flat non-metallic dish. Mix the juice, sugar, soy sauce, coriander (cilantro), garlic and ginger (ginger root) in a jug, then pour over the tofu. Cover and refrigerate overnight, turning once.

Drain the tofu, reserving the marinade. Heat the oil in a large frying pan and cook the tofu in batches over high heat for 2–3 minutes each side, or until golden. Remove and keep warm. Put the marinade in a saucepan and bring to the boil over medium heat. Reduce the heat and gently simmer for 1 minute. Remove from the heat and keep warm.

Heat a wok, add the bok choy and 1 tablespoon water and cook, covered, over medium heat for 2–3 minutes, or until tender. Remove and keep warm.

Put all the sauce ingredients in a saucepan, bring to the boil, then reduce the heat and simmer, covered, for 5–6 minutes, or until the carrot is tender. Transfer to a food processor and blend until smooth.

To serve, divide the bok choy among six plates. Top with some of the carrot and ginger sauce, then the warm tofu and drizzle with a little of the marinade before serving.

Serves 6

Sweet and Sour Tofu

- ⅓ cup (80 ml/2¾ fl oz) rice vinegar
- 2 tablespoons light soy sauce
- 1½ tablespoons caster (berry) sugar
- 2 tablespoons tomato sauce (ketchup)
- 1½ cups (375 ml/13 fl oz) vegetable stock (broth)
- 600 g (1 lb 5 oz) firm tofu
- 3–4 tablespoons vegetable oil
- 1 large carrot, julienned
- 2 cups (180 g/6⅓ oz) bean sprouts or soy bean sprouts, tailed
- 1 cup (95 g/3⅓ oz) sliced button mushrooms
- 6–8 spring (green) onions, sliced on the diagonal
- 100 g (3½ oz) snow peas (mange tout), cut in half on the diagonal
- 1 tablespoon cornflour (cornstarch) dissolved in 2 tablespoons water

Combine the vinegar, soy sauce, sugar, tomato sauce (ketchup) and stock in a small bowl.

Cut the tofu in half horizontally, then cut into 16 triangles in total. Heat a wok over high heat, add 2 tablespoons of the oil and swirl to coat. Add the tofu in batches and stir-fry (scramble-fry) over medium heat for 2 minutes on each side, or until crisp and golden. Drain on paper towels and set aside. Keep warm.

Wipe the wok clean, then reheat it over high heat. Add the remaining oil and swirl to coat. Add the carrot, bean sprouts, mushrooms, spring (green) onion and snow peas (mange tout) and stir-fry (scramble-fry) for 1 minute. Add the sauce and stir for a further 1 minute. Add the cornflour (cornstarch) paste and cook until the sauce thickens. Divide the tofu among the serving bowls and spoon some sauce over the top. Serve with steamed rice on the side.

Serves 4

Sweet and Sour Tofu with Noodles

- 100 g (3½ oz) deep-fried tofu puffs (see Note)
- 2 tablespoons oil
- 1 onion, sliced
- 1 red capsicum (pepper), cut into squares
- 3 cloves garlic, crushed
- 2 teaspoons grated fresh ginger (ginger root)
- 500 g (1 lb 2 oz) thin Hokkien noodles
- ¾ cup (120 g/4¼ oz) small chunks fresh pineapple
- ¼ cup (60 ml/2 fl oz) pineapple juice
- ¼ cup (60 ml/2 fl oz) hoisin sauce
- ¼ cup (15 g/½ oz) roughly chopped fresh coriander (cilantro)

Slice the tofu puffs into three, then cut each slice into two or three pieces.

Heat the wok until very hot, add the oil and stir-fry (scramble-fry) the onion and capsicum (pepper) for 1–2 minutes, or until beginning to soften. Add the garlic and ginger (ginger root), stir-fry (scramble-fry) for 1 minute, then add the tofu and stir-fry (scramble-fry) for 2 minutes.

Add the noodles and pineapple chunks and toss until the mixture is combined and heated through. Add the pineapple juice, hoisin sauce and chopped coriander (cilantro), and toss well. Serve immediately.

Note: Deep-fried tofu puffs are available from the refrigerated section in Asian grocery stores and some supermarkets. They have a very different texture to ordinary tofu.

Serves 4

Tofu with Chilli Sauce and Cashews

- ⅓ cup (80 ml/2¾ fl oz) peanut oil
- 12 red Asian shallots, chopped
- 8 cloves garlic, chopped
- 8 fresh long red chillies, chopped
- 2 red capsicums (peppers), chopped
- 1 tablespoon tamarind puree
- 1 tablespoon soy sauce
- 100 g (3½ oz) palm sugar, grated
- 2 tablespoons kecap manis (Indonesian soy sauce)

- 1 tablespoon peanut oil
- 6 spring (green) onions, cut into 3 cm (1¼ inch) lengths
- 750 g (1 lb 10 oz) silken firm tofu, cut into 3 cm (1¼ inch) cubes
- ¾ cup (25 g/¾ oz) fresh Thai basil
- ⅔ cup (100 g/3½ oz) roasted salted cashews

To make the chilli sauce, heat half the oil in a frying pan. Add the shallots and garlic and cook over medium heat for 2 minutes. Transfer to a food processor, add the chilli and red capsicum (pepper) and process until smooth. Heat the remaining oil in the pan, add the shallot mixture and cook over medium heat for 2 minutes. Stir in the tamarind, soy sauce and sugar and cook for 20 minutes.

To make the stir-fry (scramble-fry) sauce, combine 2–3 tablespoons of the chilli sauce with the kecap manis (Indonesian soy sauce) in a small bowl or jug.

Heat the oil in a non-stick wok over high heat and swirl to coat the side of the wok. Add the spring (green) onion and cook for 30 seconds. Remove. Add the tofu, stir-fry (scramble-fry) for 1 minute, then add the stir-fry (scramble-fry) sauce. Cook for 3 minutes, or until the tofu is coated and heated through. Return the spring (green) onion to the wok, add the basil and cashews and cook until the basil has wilted.

Serves 4

Deep-Fried Spiced Tofu

- **375 g (13¼ oz) firm tofu**
- **½ cup (90 g/3¼ oz) rice flour**
- **2 teaspoons ground coriander**
- **1 teaspoon ground cardamom**
- **1 clove garlic, crushed**
- **½ cup (125 ml/4¼ fl oz) water**
- **oil, for deep-frying**

Drain the tofu and cut it into 1 cm (½ inch) thick slices.

Combine the flour, coriander, cardamom and garlic in a bowl; add the water and stir until smooth.

Heat the oil in a large pan. Dip the tofu slices into the spice mixture and coat thickly. Place the tofu slices into the oil, 3 at a time, and cook over medium heat for about 2 minutes, or until crisp and golden brown. Drain on paper towels.

Note: Serve the tofu with stir-fried (scramble-fried) vegetables and any sauce of your choice; for example, peanut, chilli or soy sauce – the tofu soaks up the flavours.

Serves 4

Desserts

Chocolate Mousse Flan

- **250 g (8¾ oz) plain chocolate biscuits (cookies), finely crushed**
- **125 g (4⅓ oz) butter, melted**

- **⅔ cup cream (170 ml/5¾ fl oz), extra, whipped**
- **2 egg whites**

Filling
- **200 g (7 oz) dark cooking (bitter sweet) chocolate, chopped**
- **2 tablespoons cream**
- **2 egg yolks**
- **2 teaspoons agar agar powder**

Topping
- **1½ teaspoons instant coffee**
- **1 cup (250 ml/8½ fl oz) cream**
- **1 tablespoon caster (berry) sugar**
- **cocoa powder, for dusting**

Brush a 28 cm (11 inch) round fluted flan tin with melted butter or oil. Line the base with paper. Mix the biscuit (cookie) crumbs and butter and press into the tin. Refrigerate until firm.

To make the filling, put the chocolate and cream in a small pan. Stir over low heat until smooth. Cool slightly, then stir in the yolks. Sprinkle the agar agar powder over 1 tablespoon water in a small bowl and leave until spongy, then stir. Cool slightly and stir into the filling. Fold in the whipped cream.

Beat the egg whites until soft peaks form. Fold into the filling and spread over the biscuit (cookie) base. Refrigerate until set. Just before serving, remove from the tin and spread with the topping.

To make the topping, dissolve the coffee in 3 teaspoons water. Stir in the cream and sugar. Beat until soft peaks form, then spread over the flan. Dust with sifted cocoa powder to serve.

Serves 10

Vanilla Bavarois

- 2¾ cups (685 ml/23 fl oz) milk
- 1 vanilla bean
- 1 cinnamon stick
- 6 egg yolks

- ⅔ cup (160 g/5⅔ oz) caster (berry) sugar
- 3 teaspoons agar agar powder
- ¾ cup (185 ml/6½ fl oz) cream

Gently heat the milk, vanilla bean and cinnamon stick in a pan until almost boiling. Remove from the heat and set aside to infuse for 5 minutes. Remove the cinnamon stick and vanilla bean.

Whisk together the egg yolks and sugar until thick and pale. Gradually whisk in the milk. Pour into a large clean pan and stir continuously over low heat until the mixture thickens. Do not boil. Remove from the heat. Cover the surface with plastic wrap to prevent a skin forming.

Place 2 tablespoons water in a small heatproof bowl, sprinkle the agar agar powder in an even layer over the surface and leave to go spongy. Bring a large pan filled with about 4 cm (1½ inches) water to the boil, remove from the heat, carefully lower the agar agar powder bowl into the water (it should come halfway up the side of the bowl) and stir until dissolved. Whisk into the custard. Cover as before and leave to cool.

Beat the cream until soft peaks form and fold into the cold custard. Spoon into four 250 ml (8½ fl oz) ramekins or moulds, tap the bases gently on a worktop to remove air bubbles, then refrigerate overnight.

To unmould, tilt each ramekin slightly on its side. Use your finger to gently pull the bavarois away from the edge, allowing air to enter and break the suction. Turn the bavarois out onto a plate. If it does not come out straight away, wipe a cloth dipped in hot water over the outside of the mould. Garnish with pieces of fresh fruit if you wish.

Serves 4

Hot Chocolate Soufflé

- **170 g (6 oz) caster (berry) sugar**
- **450 ml (15½ fl oz) milk**
- **70 g (2½ oz) plain (all-purpose) flour**
- **1 egg**
- **4 eggs, separated**

- **40 g (1½ oz) butter, melted**
- **¼ cup (30 g/1 oz) cocoa powder, sifted**
- **1 tablespoon caster (berry) sugar,**
  extra icing (powdered) sugar,
  to serve

Grease a 1.25 litre (1.3 US qt/1.1 UK qt) soufflé dish and preheat the oven to moderately hot 200°C (400°F/Gas 6).

Put the sugar and 1 cup (250 ml/8½ fl oz) milk in a pan and stir over low heat until the sugar dissolves. Put the flour, egg and the remaining milk in a bowl and whisk to combine. Pour the hot milk mixture into the bowl and mix well with a whisk. When smooth, return the mixture to the pan and stir over low heat until it boils and thickens. Combine the egg yolks and butter with the cocoa and add to the pan, mixing well. Transfer to a bowl, cover the surface with plastic wrap and allow to cool completely.

In a large clean dry bowl, beat the egg whites until soft peaks form, then add the extra sugar. Continue beating until well combined and the egg whites are glossy. Carefully combine one spoonful of the egg whites with the chocolate mixture, then add the remaining egg white and fold in gently with a metal spoon.

Fill the soufflé dish to three-quarters full and place on an oven tray (sheet). Cook in a hot oven for 25–30 minutes, or until puffed up and firm to the touch. Dust with icing (powdered) sugar before serving.

Serves 8

Tropical Cheesecake

- **145 g (5 oz) plain sweet biscuits (cookies)**
- **¼ cup (25 g/¾ oz) desiccated (fine) coconut**
- **90 g (3¼ oz) unsalted butter, melted**

Filling
- **½ cup (125 ml/4¼ fl oz) fresh orange juice**
- **6 teaspoons agar agar powder**
- **350 g (12¼ oz) cream cheese, softened**
- **⅓ cup (90 g/3¼ oz) caster (berry) sugar**
- **2 tablespoons lemon juice**
- **425 g (15 oz) can mangoes, drained and chopped, or 2 fresh mangoes, chopped**
- **450 g (15¾ oz) can unsweetened crushed pineapple, drained**
- **1¼ cups (315 ml/11 fl oz) cream**
- **extra whipped cream, kiwi fruit and mango wedges, to decorate**

Lightly grease a 20 cm (8 inch) diameter springform tin and line the base with baking paper. Put the biscuits (cookies) in a food processor and chop until they are finely crushed. Add the coconut and butter and process until well combined. Spoon into the tin, press firmly over the base, then refrigerate.

Put the fresh orange juice in a small heatproof bowl, sprinkle the agar agar powder in an even layer over the surface and leave to go spongy. Bring a large pan filled with about 4 cm (1½ inches) water to the boil, then remove from the heat. Carefully lower the agar agar powder bowl into the water (it should come halfway up the side of the bowl), then stir until the agar agar powder has dissolved. Allow to cool.

Beat the softened cream cheese and caster (berry) sugar in a bowl for 3 minutes, or until smooth. Beat in the lemon juice and gently fold in the mango and crushed pineapple. Fold in the dissolved agar agar powder.

Whip the cream into peaks. Fold into the mixture with a metal spoon. Pour into the tin, smooth and chill overnight. Decorate with extra cream and slices of fruit.

Serves 8

Spanish Rice Pudding

- **1.25 litres (1.3 US qt/1.1 UK qt) milk**
- **1 cup (220 g/7¾ oz) arborio rice**
- **1 large strip of orange zest, pith removed**
- **1 cinnamon stick**
- **1 teaspoon natural vanilla extract**
- **⅔ cup (145 g/5 oz) caster (berry) sugar**
- **orange zest, to garnish (optional)**

Put the milk, rice, orange zest, cinnamon stick, vanilla, sugar and a pinch of salt in a large saucepan and stir over high heat until the sugar is dissolved. Allow to just come to the boil, then reduce the heat to a simmer.

Cook the rice mixture over low heat, stirring regularly, for 50 minutes, or until the rice is tender but not mushy. Stirring not only helps to ensure the rice mixture does not stick to the bottom of the pan but it also helps to produce a very creamy texture.

Lift out the zest and cinnamon stick from the pan with some tongs and serve the rice pudding warm or cold, garnished with some thin strips of orange zest.

Note: In Spanish, this dish is called Arroz con leche and it is found not only in Spain but also in Spanish–influenced countries. The Spanish often dust the surface of the pudding with cinnamon just before serving – use only a little or you risk overpowering the subtle flavour.

Serves 6

Poached Pears in Saffron Citrus Syrup

- **1 vanilla bean, split lengthways**
- **½ teaspoon firmly packed saffron threads**
- **¾ cup (185 g/6½ oz) caster (berry) sugar**
- **2 teaspoons grated lemon rind**
- **4 pears, peeled**
- **biscotti, to serve (see Note)**

Place the vanilla bean, saffron threads, sugar, lemon rind and 2 cups (500 ml/17 fl oz) water in a large saucepan and mix together well. Heat, stirring, over low heat until the sugar has dissolved. Bring to the boil, then reduce to a gentle simmer.

Add the pears and cook, covered, for 12–15 minutes, or until tender when tested with a metal skewer. Turn the pears over with a slotted spoon halfway through cooking. Once cooked, remove from the syrup with a slotted spoon.

Remove the lid and allow the saffron citrus syrup to come to the boil. Cook for 8–10 minutes, or until the syrup has reduced by half and thickened slightly. Remove the vanilla bean and drizzle the syrup over the pears. Serve with biscotti.

Note: Biscotti are available in a wide variety of flavours. You can buy biscotti at gourmet food stores, delicatessens and supermarkets.

Serves 4

251

Chocolate Tarts

- 2 cups (250 g/8¾ oz) plain (all-purpose) flour
- 2 tablespoons custard powder
- 125 g (4⅓ oz) unsalted butter, chilled and cubed
- 1 egg yolk
- 2–3 tablespoons iced water

Filling
- 250 g (8¾ oz) cream cheese, at room temperature

- ½ cup (125 g/4⅓ oz) caster (berry) sugar
- 1 egg
- 125 g (4⅓ oz) dark (semi-sweet) chocolate, melted
- 3 tablespoons ground almonds
- 100 g (3½ oz) white chocolate, melted

Preheat the oven to 180°C (350°F/Gas 4). Lightly grease two 12-cup shallow patty (bun) tins. Mix the flour, custard powder and butter in a food processor for 30 seconds, or until fine and crumbly. Add the egg yolk and almost all of the water and process for 20 seconds or until the mixture just comes together, adding the rest of the water if necessary. Turn out onto a lightly floured surface and gather into a smooth ball. Wrap in plastic and refrigerate for 20 minutes.

Divide the dough in two; wrap one portion and set aside. Roll the other half between two sheets of baking paper until 3 mm (⅛ inch) thick. Cut rounds with a 7 cm (2¾ inch) fluted cutter to line the tins. Repeat with the other portion of pastry. Refrigerate the trays while preparing the filling.

Beat the cream cheese and sugar until light and creamy. Add the egg and cooled melted chocolate. Beat until no streaks are visible. Stir in the almonds. Spoon into the pastry cases. Bake for 15 minutes or until just beginning to firm (the filling will set on standing.) Cool on a rack. Drizzle with white chocolate and leave to set.

Makes 24

Banana Cream Pie

- **375 g (13¼ oz) shortcrust (pie) pastry**
- **90 g (3¼ oz) dark (semi-sweet) chocolate chips (bits/morsels)**
- **4 egg yolks**
- **½ cup (125 g/4⅓ oz) caster (berry) sugar**
- **½ teaspoon vanilla essence**

- **2 tablespoons custard powder**
- **2 cups (500 ml/17 fl oz) milk**
- **40 g (1½ oz) unsalted butter, softened**
- **1 teaspoon brandy or rum**
- **3 large ripe bananas, thinly sliced**
- **60 g (2 oz) dark (semi-sweet) chocolate, grated**

Roll out the pastry between two sheets of baking paper to line an 18 cm (7 inch) pie tin, pressing it firmly into the side and trimming away the excess. Refrigerate for 20 minutes.

Preheat the oven to 190°C (375°F/Gas 5). Line the pastry with baking paper and spread with baking beads or rice. Bake for 10 minutes, remove the paper and beads or rice and bake for 10–12 minutes, until the pastry is dry and lightly golden.

While the pastry is still hot, place the chocolate chips (bits/morsels) in the base. Leave for 5 minutes to melt, then spread over the crust with the back of a spoon.

To make the filling, beat the egg yolks, sugar, vanilla and custard powder with electric beaters for 2–3 minutes, or until pale and thick. Bring the milk to boiling point in a small pan, then remove from the heat and gradually pour into the egg and sugar mixture, stirring well. Return to the pan and bring to the boil, stirring. Cook for 2 minutes, or until thickened. Remove from the heat and stir in the butter and brandy. Cool completely.

Arrange the banana over the chocolate, then pour the custard over the top. Refrigerate until ready to serve. Decorate with banana slices and the grated chocolate.

Serves 6–8

Passionfruit Mousse

- 5–6 passionfruit
- 6 eggs, separated
- ¾ cup (185 g/6½ oz) caster (berry) sugar
- ½ teaspoon finely grated lemon rind
- 3 tablespoons lemon juice
- 1 tablespoon agar agar powder
- 1¼ cups (315 ml/11 fl oz) cream, lightly whipped
- ¾ cup (40 g/1½ oz) flaked or shredded (medium) coconut, toasted

Cut the passionfruit in half and scoop out the pulp. Strain, then measure out 3 tablespoons of juice and set aside. Add the seeds and pulp to the remaining juice and set aside. Put the egg yolks, ½ cup (125 g/4⅓ oz) of the sugar, lemon rind, lemon juice and strained passionfruit juice in a heatproof bowl. Place the bowl over a pan of simmering water and, using electric beaters, beat for 10 minutes, or until thick and creamy. Remove from the heat and transfer to a glass bowl.

Sprinkle the agar agar powder over ½ cup (125 ml/4⅓ fl oz) water in a small bowl and leave until spongy. Place the bowl in a pan of just boiled water (the water should come halfway up the bowl) and stir until dissolved. Add the agar agar powder to the mousse mixture and mix well. Mix in the passionfruit pulp and leave until cold, then gently fold in the whipped cream.

Using electric beaters, whisk the egg whites until soft peaks form and gradually whisk in the remaining sugar, beating until the sugar has dissolved. Fold the egg whites into the mousse mixture quickly and lightly. Spoon into eight 1-cup (250 ml/8½ fl oz) ramekins or elegant stemmed wine glasses, and refrigerate for 2 hours, or until set. Sprinkle with the coconut just before serving.

Serves 8

Figs with Orange Cream and Raisins

- 1 cup (150 g/5¼ oz) raisins (dark raisins)
- 75 ml (2½ fl oz) tawny port
- 1 tablespoon custard powder
- 1 cup (250 ml/8½ fl oz) skim milk
- 1 tablespoon sugar
- 100 g (3½ oz) ricotta
- 200 g (7 oz) low-fat fromage frais
- rind strips and juice of 1 orange
- 1 teaspoon ground cinnamon
- 8 fresh figs

Soak the raisins (dark raisins) in the tawny port for 1 hour, or until plumped up.

In a small saucepan, blend the custard powder with the skim milk, add the sugar and stir over low heat until dissolved. Increase the heat and stir until the custard boils and thickens. Remove from the heat immediately, pour into a small bowl and cover with plastic wrap. Cool completely. Transfer to an electric mixer, add the ricotta and fromage frais and beat until smooth.

Warm the raisin mixture with the orange rind, juice and cinnamon in a small pan. Cover and keep warm.

Starting from the top, cut the figs into quarters, slicing only two-thirds of the way down so they hold together. Transfer to ramekins or a serving dish or platter. Place 2 heaped tablespoons of the custard cream mixture into the centre of each fig, top with a spoonful of the warm raisin and orange mixture and serve at once.

Serves 4

Walnut Pie with Caramel Sauce

- 2 cups (250 g/8¾ oz) plain (all-purpose) flour
- 180 g (6⅓ oz) unsalted butter, chilled and cubed
- ⅓ cup (40 g/1½ oz) icing (powdered) sugar
- 1 egg yolk
- 3–4 tablespoons iced water
- 1 egg yolk, lightly beaten, to glaze
- icing (powdered) sugar and walnuts, to garnish

Filling
- 2 eggs
- 210 g (7⅓ oz) caster (berry) sugar
- 150 g (5¼ oz) walnuts, finely chopped

Caramel Sauce
- 40 g (1½ oz) unsalted butter
- 1¼ cups (230 g/8¼ oz) soft brown sugar
- 2 teaspoons vanilla essence
- 200 ml (6¾ fl oz) cream

Sift the flour and ½ teaspoon salt into a large bowl and rub in the butter with your fingertips until the mixture resembles fine breadcrumbs. Mix in the icing (powdered) sugar. Make a well, add the egg yolk and almost all the water and mix with a flat-bladed knife, using a cutting action, until the mixture comes together in beads.

Gather the dough together and lift onto a lightly floured work surface. Press together into a ball and flatten slightly into a disc. Wrap in plastic and refrigerate for 20 minutes.

Preheat the oven to 180°C (350°F/Gas 4). Grease a fluted 36 × 11 cm (14¼ × 4⅓ inch) pie tin. Beat the eggs and sugar with a spoon or whisk for 2 minutes. Stir in the walnuts.

Divide the dough into two portions, with one slightly larger than the other. Roll the larger portion out between two sheets of baking paper until large enough to line the base and sides of the pie tin. Refrigerate, covered in plastic wrap, while you roll out the remaining portion of pastry until it is large enough to cover the top of the tin.

Pour the walnut filling into the pastry case, brush the rim with the egg yolk and position the lid in place, pressing the edges to seal. Trim the edge. Make a steam hole in the top. Brush with egg yolk and bake for 30–35 minutes. Leave to cool for at least 1 hour (do not refrigerate).

To make the caramel sauce, place the butter, sugar, vanilla and cream in a saucepan and cook, stirring, for 5 minutes, or until thick. Dust the pie with the icing (powdered) sugar and sprinkle with walnuts. Drizzle with the caramel sauce to serve.

Serves 8

Caramelised Pineapple Gratin

- **800 g (1 lb 12 oz) ripe pineapple, cut into 1.5 cm (⅝ inch) cubes**
- **¼ cup (60 ml/2 fl oz) dark rum**
- **2 tablespoons unsalted butter**
- **1 teaspoon vanilla essence**
- **¼ cup (45 g/1⅔ oz) soft brown sugar**
- **½ teaspoon ground ginger**
- **300 g (10½ oz) sour cream**
- **¼ cup (60 ml/2 fl oz) cream**
- **1 teaspoon finely grated lemon rind**
- **½ cup (95 g/3⅓ oz) soft brown sugar, to sprinkle, extra**

Place the pineapple, rum, butter, vanilla, sugar and ginger in a saucepan and cook, stirring occasionally, for 8–10 minutes, or until caramelised. Remove from the heat.

Divide the pineapple among four individual gratin dishes and allow it to cool slightly.

Combine the sour cream, cream and lemon rind in a bowl, then spoon evenly over the pineapple. Sprinkle the extra brown sugar over each gratin.

Cook the gratins under a hot grill (broiler) for 4–5 minutes, or until the sugar has melted and caramelised. Take care not to burn them. Serve immediately.

Serves 4

Chocolate Fudge Pecan Pie

- 1¼ cups (150 g/5¼ oz) plain (all-purpose) flour
- 2 tablespoons cocoa powder
- 2 tablespoons soft brown sugar
- 100 g (3½ oz) unsalted butter, chilled and cubed
- 2–3 tablespoons iced water

Filling
- 2 cups (200 g/7 oz) pecans, chopped
- 100 g (3½ oz) dark (semi-sweet) chocolate, chopped
- ½ cup (90 g/3¼ oz) soft brown sugar
- ⅔ cup (170 ml/5¾ fl oz) glucose (corn) syrup
- 3 eggs, lightly beaten
- 2 teaspoons vanilla essence

Grease an 18 cm (7 inch) pie dish. Sift the flour, cocoa and sugar into a bowl and rub in the butter until the mixture resembles fine crumbs. Make a well, add the water and mix with a knife, adding more water if necessary.

Press the dough into a ball and refrigerate for 20 minutes. Roll out between two sheets of baking paper to fit the dish, trimming away the excess. Refrigerate for 20 minutes.

Preheat the oven to 180°C (350°F/Gas 4). Cover the pastry with baking paper and spread with a layer of baking beads or rice. Bake for 15 minutes. Remove the paper and beads or rice and bake for 15–20 minutes, or until dry. Cool completely.

Put the dish on a tray (sheet). Spread the pecans and chocolate in the shell. Whisk the sugar, glucose (corn) syrup, eggs and vanilla. Pour into the shell and bake for 45 minutes. Cool completely.

Serves 6

Creamy Lime Tart

- 1¼ cups (155 g/5½ oz) plain (all-purpose) flour
- ½ cup (95 g/3⅓ oz) ground almonds
- 90 g (3¼ oz) butter, chopped

Filling
- 6 egg yolks
- ½ cup (125 g/4⅓ oz) caster (berry) sugar
- 100 g (3½ oz) butter, melted
- ⅓ cup (80 ml/2¾ fl oz) lime juice
- 2 teaspoons finely grated lime rind
- 2 teaspoons agar agar powder
- ½ cup (125 ml/4¼ fl oz) cream, whipped
- ½ cup (125 g/4⅓ oz) sugar
- rind of 4 limes, finely shredded

Preheat the oven to 180°C (350°F/Gas 4). Sift the flour into a large bowl and add the almonds and butter. Rub in the butter until fine and crumbly. Add 1–2 tablespoons cold water and mix to a firm dough, adding more if necessary. Turn out onto a lightly floured surface and roll out to fit a 23 cm (9 inch) fluted flan tin. Trim the edge and refrigerate for 20 minutes.

Line with baking paper and beads or dried beans or rice and bake for 20 minutes. Remove the paper and beads beans or rice and bake the pastry shell for a further 20 minutes, or until lightly golden. Cool completely.

To make the filling, put the egg yolks, sugar, butter, lime juice and rind in a heatproof bowl. Whisk together to dissolve the sugar. Place the bowl over a pan of simmering water and stir constantly for 15 minutes, or until thickened. Leave to cool slightly.

Put the agar agar powder and 1 tablespoon water in a small bowl. Leave until spongy, then stir until dissolved. Stir into the lime curd. Cool to room temperature, stirring occasionally.

Fold the cream through the lime curd and pour into the pastry case. Refrigerate for 2–3 hours until set, removing 15 minutes before serving. Put the sugar in a small pan with 3 tablespoons water. Stir without boiling until the sugar has completely dissolved. Bring to the boil, add the lime rind and simmer for 3 minutes. Remove the rind and dry on a rack then use to decorate the tart.

Serves 12

Mocha Ice Cream

- ½ cup (40 g/1½ oz) espresso coffee beans
- 3 cups (750 ml/26 fl oz) cream
- 250 g (8¾ oz) good-quality dark cooking (bitter sweet) chocolate, chopped
- ¾ cup (185 g/6½ oz) caster (berry) sugar
- 6 egg yolks
- 1 cup (250 ml/8½ fl oz) milk

Line a rectangular tin with plastic wrap and freeze. Combine the coffee beans and cream in a pan. Stir over medium heat until the mixture just starts to boil. Add the chocolate, remove from the heat and set aside for 1 minute before stirring.

Combine the sugar and egg yolks in a large bowl, whisk until slightly thickened, then whisk in the milk. Gradually add the coffee mixture with the beans and whisk until smooth. Strain the mixture and discard the beans.

Return the mixture to the pan and stir over low heat until the mixture thickens and will coat the back of a spoon. Do not boil. Remove from the heat and set aside to cool.

Put the mixture into the prepared tin and freeze until just firm. Transfer to a large chilled bowl and beat with electric beaters until thick. Return to the tin and cover with plastic wrap and freeze again until firm. Repeat, beating once more before transferring to a container for storage in the freezer. Cover the surface with plastic wrap or baking paper. Serve in scoops with frosted rose petals (see Note) or store in the freezer for up to 7 days.

Note: To frost rose petals, lightly whisk 1 egg white, dip clean dry petals in egg white (or brush lightly with a paintbrush), then sprinkle with sugar. Shake off the excess sugar and place on a paper-lined tray (sheet) to dry.

Serves 4–6

Profiteroles with Dark Chocolate Sauce

- **60 g (2 oz) butter, chopped**
- **¾ cup (90 g/3¼ oz) plain (all-purpose) flour**
- **3 eggs, lightly beaten**

White Chocolate Filling
- **¼ cup (30 g/1 oz) custard powder**
- **1 tablespoon caster (berry) sugar**
- **1½ cups (375 ml/13 fl oz) milk**

- **150 g (5¼ oz) white chocolate melts, chopped**
- **1 tablespoon triple sec liqueur**

Dark Chocolate Sauce
- **125 g (4⅓ oz) dark (semi-sweet) chocolate, chopped**
- **½ cup (125 ml/4¼ fl oz) cream**

Preheat the oven to hot 210°C (415°F/Gas 6–7). Line a baking tray (sheet) with baking paper. Put the butter and ¾ cup (185 ml/6½ fl oz) water in a pan. Bring to the boil, then remove from the heat. Add the flour all at once. Return to the heat and stir until the mixture forms a smooth ball. Set aside to cool slightly. Transfer to a bowl and, while beating with electric beaters, gradually add the eggs a little at a time, beating well after each addition, to form a thick, smooth, glossy paste.

Spoon 2 heaped teaspoons of the mixture onto the tray (sheet) at 5 cm (2 inch) intervals. Sprinkle lightly with water and bake for 12–15 minutes, or until the dough is puffed. Turn off the oven. Pierce a small hole in the base of each profiterole with the point of a knife and return the profiteroles to the oven. Leave them to dry in the oven for 5 minutes.

For the filling, combine the custard powder and sugar in a pan. Gradually add the milk, stirring until smooth, then continue to stir over low heat until the mixture boils and thickens. Remove from the heat and add the white chocolate and liqueur. Stir until the chocolate is melted. Cover the surface with plastic wrap and allow to cool. Stir the custard until smooth, then spoon into a piping bag fitted with a 1 cm (½ inch) plain nozzle. Pipe the filling into each profiterole. Serve with the warm chocolate sauce.

For the dark (semi-sweet) chocolate sauce, combine the chocolate and cream in a small saucepan. Stir over low heat until the chocolate is melted and the mixture is smooth. Serve warm.

Note: The profiteroles can be made a day ahead. Fill just before serving. You can also make miniature profiteroles, using 1 teaspoon of the mixture. Dip the tops of the cooked profiteroles in melted chocolate. When set, fill them with whipped cream.

Serves 4–6

Ice Cream Bombe

- 1 large mango, finely chopped
- 1 cup (160 g/5⅔ oz) canned pineapple pieces, drained
- ¼ cup (60 ml/2 fl oz) triple sec liqueur
- 250 g (8¾ oz) fresh strawberries, pureed
- 400 g (14 oz) can condensed milk
- 2½ cups (600 ml/20 fl oz) cream
- 80 g (2¾ oz) dessert nougat, chopped
- ¼ cup (35 g/1¼ oz) roughly chopped unsalted pistachios
- strawberries, extra, halved, to garnish

Toffee Bark
- ⅓ cup (90 g/3¼ oz) caster (berry) sugar

Lightly grease a 2 litre (2.1 US qt/1.75 UK qt) pudding basin and line with plastic wrap, allowing it to hang over the side of the basin. Put in the freezer until ready to use. Drain the mango and pineapple in a sieve.

Mix the liqueur, strawberry puree and condensed milk in a large bowl. Whisk the cream to soft peaks, then add to the bowl and continue whisking until thick. Fold in the drained fruits, nougat and pistachios. Pour the mixture into the pudding basin, cover with plastic wrap and freeze overnight, or until firm.

To serve, remove the plastic wrap from the base and invert the pudding onto a chilled serving plate. Remove the bowl, but leave the plastic wrap and refrigerate for 15–25 minutes to soften slightly.

For the toffee bark, line a baking tray (sheet) with baking paper. Heat the sugar over low heat in a heavy-based saucepan for 2–3 minutes, or until melted and golden. Carefully pour onto the tray (sheet). Tilt the tray (sheet) to get a thin, even layer of toffee over the paper and cool slightly. While still pliable, drape the paper over a rolling pin and allow to cool for 30–60 seconds before peeling away strips of toffee in large irregular shapes. Cool. To serve, remove the plastic and decorate the bombe with toffee bark and strawberries.

Note: Dessert nougat is a soft nougat available at confectionery shops and some delicatessens.

Serves 8

Lemon Grass Infused Fruit Salad

- ¼ cup (60 g/2 oz) caster (berry) sugar
- 2.5 cm × 2.5 cm (1 inch × 1 inch) piece fresh ginger (ginger root), thinly sliced
- 1 stem lemon grass, bruised and halved

- 1 large passionfruit
- 1 Fiji red pawpaw (560 g/1 lb 4 oz)
- ½ honeydew melon (800 g/1 lb 12 oz)
- 1 large mango (500 g/1 lb 2 oz)
- 1 small fresh pineapple (1 kg/2 lb 3 oz)
- 12 fresh lychees
- 3 tablespoons shredded fresh mint

Place the sugar, ginger (ginger root) and lemon grass in a small saucepan, add ½ cup (125 ml/4¼ fl oz) water and stir over low heat to dissolve the sugar. Boil for 5 minutes, or until reduced to ⅓ cup (80 ml/2¾ fl oz) and cool. Strain the syrup and add the passionfruit pulp.

Peel and seed the pawpaw and melon. Cut into 4 cm (1½ inch) cubes. Peel the mango and cut the flesh into cubes, discarding the stone. Peel, halve and core the pineapple and cut into cubes. Peel the lychees, then make a slit in the flesh and remove the seed.

Place all the fruit in a large serving bowl. Pour on the syrup, or serve separately if preferred. Garnish with the shredded mint.

Note: If fresh lychees are not available, canned ones are fine.

Serves 4

Ginger and Lychee Jelly

- **565 g (1 lb 4 oz) can lychees**
- **2 cups (500 ml/17 fl oz) clear apple juice (no added sugar)**
- **⅓ cup (80 ml/2¾ fl oz) strained lime juice**
- **2 tablespoons caster (berry) sugar**
- **3 cm × 3 cm (1¼ inch × 1¼ inch) piece fresh ginger (ginger root), peeled and thinly sliced**
- **4 agar agar sheets (about 7 g/¼ oz)**
- **fresh mint leaves, to garnish**

Drain the syrup from the lychees and reserve 1 cup (250 ml/8½ fl oz) of the syrup. Discard the remaining syrup. Place the reserved syrup, apple juice, lime juice, sugar and ginger (ginger root) in a large saucepan. Bring to the boil, then reduce the heat and simmer for 5 minutes. Strain into a heatproof bowl.

Place the agar agar sheets in a large bowl of cold water and soak for 2 minutes, or until they soften. Squeeze out the excess water, then add the agar agar sheets to the syrup. Stir until the agar agar sheets has completely dissolved. Allow to cool.

Pour 2 tablespoons of the jelly (jello) mixture into each of six 150 ml (5 fl oz) stemmed wine glasses, and divide the lychees among the wine glasses. Refrigerate the glasses until the jelly (jello) has set. Spoon the remaining jelly (jello) over the fruit and refrigerate again until set. Before serving, garnish with mint leaves.

Note: Sprinkle 1 tablespoon slivered almonds among the jelly (jello), if desired.

Serves 6

Strawberry Trifle

- 2 × 85 g (3 oz) packets agar agar powder and red colouring crystals
- 1 cup (250 ml/8½ fl oz) brandy or rum
- 1 cup (250 ml/8½ fl oz) milk
- 2 × 250 g (8¾ oz) packets thin sponge finger biscuits (ladyfingers)

- 500 g (1 lb 2 oz) strawberries, sliced
- 750 ml (26 fl oz) carton custard
- 1¼ cups (315 ml/11 fl oz) cream, whipped

Mix the jelly (jello) crystals with 1¾ cups (440 ml/15 fl oz) of boiling water and stir to dissolve. Pour into a shallow tin and refrigerate until the jelly (jello) has just set but is not firm.

Combine the brandy and milk in a dish. Dip half the biscuits (ladyfingers) in the brandy mixture then place in a single layer in a 3-litre (3.2 US qt/2.6 UK qt) glass or ceramic dish. Spoon half the jelly (jello) over the biscuits (ladyfingers). Scatter with half the strawberries and then half of the custard.

Dip the remaining sponge fingers in the brandy mixture and place evenly over the custard, followed by the remaining jelly (jello) and custard. Spread the whipped cream evenly over the custard and top with the remaining strawberries. Cover and refrigerate for 4 hours before serving.

Serves 8

Raspberry Mousse

- **3 teaspoons agar agar powder**
- **1 cup (250 g/8¾ oz) low-fat vanilla yoghurt**
- **2 × 200 g (7 oz) tubs low-fat fromage frais**
- **4 egg whites**
- **150 g (5¼ oz) raspberries, mashed**
- **fresh raspberries and mint leaves, for serving**

Sprinkle the agar agar powder in an even layer onto 1 tablespoon water in a small bowl and leave to go spongy. Bring a small pan of water to the boil, remove from the heat and place the bowl in the pan. Stir until clear.

In a large bowl, stir the vanilla yoghurt and fromage frais together, then add the agar agar powder and mix well.

Using electric beaters, beat the egg whites until stiff peaks form, then fold through the yoghurt mixture. Transfer half to a separate bowl and fold the mashed raspberries through.

Divide the raspberry mixture into the bases of 4 long glasses or serving bowls. Top with the vanilla mixture. Refrigerate for several hours, or until set. Decorate with fresh raspberries and mint leaves.

Serves 4

Lemon Granita

- 1¼ cups (315 ml/11 fl oz) lemon juice
- 1 tablespoon lemon zest
- 200 g (7 oz) caster (berry) sugar

Place the lemon juice, lemon zest and caster (berry) sugar in a small saucepan and stir over low heat for 5 minutes, or until the sugar is dissolved. Remove from the heat and leave to cool.

Add 2 cups (500 ml/17 fl oz) water to the juice mixture and mix together well. Pour the mixture into a shallow 30 × 20 cm (12 × 8 inch) metal container and place in the freezer until the mixture is beginning to freeze around the edges. Scrape the frozen sections back into the mixture with a fork. Repeat every 30 minutes until the mixture has even-size ice crystals. Beat the mixture with a fork just before serving. To serve, spoon the lemon granita into six chilled glasses.

Serves 6

Apple Sago Pudding

- ⅓ cup (90 g/3¼ oz) caster (berry) sugar
- ½ cup (100 g/3½ oz) tapioca (or sago)
- 600 ml (20 fl oz) fat-reduced milk
- ⅓ cup (55 g/2 oz) sultanas (golden raisins)
- 1 teaspoon vanilla essence
- pinch ground nutmeg
- ¼ teaspoon ground cinnamon
- 2 eggs, lightly beaten
- 3 small ripe apples (about 250 g/ 8¾ oz), peeled, cored and very thinly sliced
- 1 tablespoon soft brown sugar

Preheat the oven to moderate 180°C (350°F/Gas 4). Grease a 1.5 litre (1.6 US qt/ 1.3 UK qt) ceramic soufflé dish. Place the sugar, tapioca (or sago), milk, sultanas (golden raisins) and ¼ teaspoon salt in a saucepan and heat, stirring often. Bring to the boil, then reduce the heat and simmer for 5 minutes.

Stir in the vanilla essence, nutmeg, cinnamon, egg and the apple slices, then pour into the prepared dish. Sprinkle with the brown sugar and bake for 45 minutes, or until set and golden brown.

Note: If you prefer, you can use skim milk instead of fat-reduced milk.

Serves 4

Golden Syrup Dumplings

- **1 cup (125 g/4⅓ oz) self-raising flour**
- **40 g (1½ oz) cold butter, chopped**
- **1 egg**
- **1 tablespoon milk**
- **1 cup (250 g/8¾ oz) sugar**
- **40 g (1½ oz) butter, extra**
- **2 tablespoons golden (corn) syrup**
- **¼ cup (60 ml/2 fl oz) lemon juice**

Sift the flour into a bowl and add a pinch of salt. Using your fingertips, rub the butter into the flour until the mixture resembles fine breadcrumbs, and make a well in the centre. Using a flat-bladed knife, stir the combined egg and milk into the flour mixture to form a soft dough.

To make the syrup, place 2 cups (500 ml/17 fl oz) water in a large pan with the sugar, butter, golden (corn) syrup and lemon juice. Stir over medium heat until combined and the sugar has dissolved.

Bring to the boil, then gently drop dessertspoons of the dough into the syrup. Reduce the heat to a simmer and cook, covered, for 20 minutes, or until a knife inserted into a dumpling comes out clean. Spoon onto serving plates, drizzle with syrup, and serve immediately with whipped cream.

Serves 4

Plum and Almond Slice

- **160 g (5⅔ oz) butter**
- **⅔ cup (160 g/5⅔ oz) caster (berry) sugar**
- **2 eggs**
- **½ cup (60 g/2 oz) plain (all-purpose) flour**
- **⅓ cup (40 g/1½ oz) cornflour (cornstarch)**

- **2 tablespoons rice flour**
- **1½ tablespoons thinly sliced glacé (glazed) ginger**
- **825 g (1 lb 13 oz) can plums in syrup, drained and halved (see Note)**
- **1 cup (100 g/3½ oz) flaked almonds**
- **1 tablespoon warmed honey**

Preheat the oven to 180°C (350°F/Gas 4). Lightly grease a 20 cm (8 inch) square tin and line with baking paper, extending over the top edge of the tin on all sides.

Using electric beaters, beat the butter and sugar in a mixing bowl until light and creamy. Add the eggs one at a time, beating well. Fold the sifted flours into the mixture with the ginger. Spread into the tin. Arrange the plums on top, pressing them in. Scatter with the almonds, pressing in gently, then drizzle with the honey.

Bake for 1 hour 10 minutes, or until firm and golden (cover with foil if over-browning). Cool before cutting.

Note: If in season, use 7 ripe blood plums instead of canned. They may bleed more than the canned.

Makes 9 pieces

Dressings
and
Sauces

Classic White Sauce

- **1 cup (250 ml/8½ fl oz) milk**
- **1 slice of onion**
- **1 bay leaf**
- **6 peppercorns**

- **30 g (1 oz) butter**
- **1 tablespoon plain (all-purpose) flour**
- **salt and white pepper**

Combine milk, onion, bay leaf and peppercorns in a small pan. Bring to the boil; remove the pan from heat and set aside to infuse for 10 minutes. Strain the milk and discard all the flavourings.

Melt the butter in a small pan and add the flour. Stir over medium heat for 1 minute, or until the mixture is golden and bubbling. Remove from heat, add milk very slowly, a little at a time, and stir between each addition until mixture is completely smooth. When all the milk has been added, return to heat, keep stirring over medium heat until mixture boils and thickens.

Boil for another minute and remove from the heat. Season with salt and white pepper.

Note: Infusing the milk with onion, bay leaves and peppercorns adds flavour. Plain milk may be used, particularly if adding other flavourings.

Variation – Parsley Sauce: Add 3 tablespoons finely chopped fresh parsley to the finished sauce and stir to combine. Other fresh herbs such as chives, dill or tarragon may be added, or try different combinations of your favourite herbs.

Makes about 250 ml (8½ fl oz)

272

Tomato Sauce

- **1.5 kg (3 lb 5 oz) large ripe tomatoes**
- **1 tablespoon olive oil**
- **1 medium onion, finely chopped**
- **2 cloves garlic, crushed**
- **1 teaspoon dried oregano leaves**

- **2 tablespoons tomato paste (tomato puree)**
- **1 teaspoon sugar**
- **salt and pepper**

Mark a small cross on the base (opposite stem end) of each tomato. Place in a small bowl and cover with boiling water for 2 minutes; drain and cool. Peel the skin down from the cross and discard. Finely chop the flesh.

Heat the oil in a medium pan. Add the onion and cook, stirring, over medium heat 3 minutes or until soft. Add garlic and cook for 1 minute. Add tomato, oregano, tomato paste (tomato puree) and sugar.

Bring to the boil, reduce heat and simmer, uncovered, for about 15 minutes or until the sauce has thickened slightly. Season, to taste.

Note: This will keep, covered, for up to 2 days in the refrigerator, or freeze for up to 2 months. Reheat in a pan or in the microwave. Serve hot over pasta, or use as a pizza sauce.

Serves 4

Basic Hollandaise

- **175 g (6¼ oz) butter**
- **2 tablespoons water**
- **4 egg yolks**

- **1 tablespoon lemon juice**
- **salt and white pepper**

Melt the butter in a small pan. Skim any froth from the top and discard; cool the melted butter. Combine water and egg yolks in another small pan. Using a wire whisk, beat for about 30 seconds until the mixture is pale and creamy.

Place the pan over very low heat and continue whisking for 3 minutes or until thick and foamy; remove from the heat. (Make sure the pan does not get too hot or you will end up with scrambled eggs.)

Add the cooled butter slowly, a little at a time at first, whisking well between each addition. Keep adding the butter in a thin stream, whisking continuously, until all the butter has been used. Try to avoid using the milky white whey in the bottom of the pan, but don't worry if a little gets in. Stir in the lemon juice and season with salt and white pepper.

Variation – Processor Method: Use the same quantities of ingredients as for making basic hollandaise, but place the yolks, water and juice in a food processor and blend for 10 seconds. Melt the butter; skim off the froth. With the motor running, add the melted hot butter to the processor in a thin stream. Transfer to a bowl and season, to taste.

Makes about 315 ml (11 fl oz)

Cumberland Sauce

- **2 oranges**
- **1 lemon**
- **225 g (8 oz) redcurrant jelly**

- **2 teaspoons Dijon mustard**
- **2 tablespoons red wine vinegar**
- **1 cup (250 ml/8½ fl oz) port**

Remove the orange and lemon rind with a zester. Place the rind in a small pan with 1 cup (250 ml/8½ fl oz) water and bring to the boil. Cook for 5 minutes, then strain the liquid, keeping the rind.

Squeeze the juice from the oranges and lemon and place in a pan. Add the jelly, mustard, vinegar, port and reserved rind. Slowly bring to the boil, stirring as the jelly melts. Reduce the heat to simmer gently for 15 minutes. Season to taste and serve at room temperature or cover with plastic wrap and refrigerate for up to a week.

Serves 8

Chilli Spiced Mango Sauce

- 1 large ripe mango
- 1 tablespoon oil
- 1 red onion, finely sliced
- 3 cloves garlic, finely chopped
- 4 cm (1½ inch) piece fresh ginger (ginger root), finely chopped
- 2–3 red chillies, seeded and finely chopped
- 1 tablespoon honey
- ¼ teaspoon ground cinnamon
- pinch of ground cardamom
- pinch of ground nutmeg
- pinch of ground cloves
- ¼ cup (60 ml/2 fl oz) dark rum
- ¼ cup (60 ml/2 fl oz) lime juice
- ¼ cup (7 g/¼ oz) coriander (cilantro) leaves, chopped

Peel the mango and dice the flesh. Heat the oil in a frying pan and add the onion, garlic, ginger (ginger root) and chilli. Cook for about 3–4 minutes, or until the onion is soft.

Add the mango, honey, cinnamon, cardamom, nutmeg and cloves. Mix well and bring to the boil. Simmer gently for 5 minutes. Add the rum and simmer for a further 5 minutes. Add the lime juice, coriander (cilantro) and salt and pepper to taste.

Serves 4

Preserved Lemons

- **8–12 small thin-skinned lemons**
- **1 cup (315 g/11¼ oz) rock salt**
- **2 cups (500 ml/17 fl oz) lemon juice (8–10 lemons)**
- **½ teaspoon black peppercorns**
- **1 bay leaf**
- **olive oil**

Scrub the lemons under warm running water with a soft bristle brush to remove the wax coating. Cut into quarters, leaving the base attached at the stem end. Gently open each lemon, remove any visible seeds and pack 1 tablespoon of the salt against the cut edges of each lemon. Push the lemons back into shape and pack tightly into a 2 litre (2.1 US qt/1.75 UK qt) jar that has a clip or tight-fitting lid. Depending on the size of the lemons, you may not need all 12. They should be firmly packed and fill the jar.

Add 1 cup (250 ml/8½ fl oz) of the lemon juice, the peppercorns, bay leaf and remaining rock salt to the jar. Fill the jar to the top with the remaining lemon juice. Seal and shake to combine all the ingredients. Leave in a cool, dark place for 6 weeks, inverting the jar each week. (In warm weather, store the jar in the refrigerator.) The liquid will be cloudy initially, but will clear by the fourth week.

To test if the lemons are preserved, cut through the centre of one of the lemon quarters. If the pith is still white, the lemons aren't ready. In this case, re-seal and leave for another week before testing again. The lemons should be soft-skinned and the pith should be the same colour as the skin.

Once the lemons are preserved, cover the brine with a layer of olive oil. Replace the oil each time you remove some of the lemon pieces. Refrigerate after opening.

Fills a 2 litre (2.1 US qt/1.75 UK qt) jug

Quick and Easy Cranberry Sauce

- **250 g (8¾ oz) whole cranberry sauce**
- **1 teaspoon grated orange rind**
- **3 tablespoons orange juice**
- **1 teaspoon ground ginger**
- **½ teaspoon ground cardamom**
- **¼ teaspoon ground allspice**

Mix together the cranberry sauce, grated orange rind and juice, ginger, cardamom and allspice in a small pan.

Bring the cranberry mixture to the boil over medium heat, stirring occasionally. Reduce the heat and leave to simmer for 2 minutes. Allow the sauce to cool to room temperature before serving.

Serves 4–6

Harissa

- **125 g (4⅓ oz) dried red chillies, stems removed**
- **1 tablespoon dried mint**
- **1 tablespoon ground coriander**
- **1 tablespoon ground cumin**
- **1 teaspoon ground caraway seeds**
- **10 cloves garlic, chopped**
- **½ cup (125 ml/4¼ fl oz) olive oil**

Roughly chop the chillies, then cover with boiling water and soak for 1 hour. Drain, place in a food processor and add the mint, spices, garlic, 1 tablespoon of oil and ½ teaspoon salt. Process for 20 seconds, scrape down the side of the bowl, then process for another 30 seconds. Add 2 tablespoons oil and process again. Repeat and process until a thick paste forms.

Spoon the paste into a clean jar (see Note), cover with a thin layer of olive oil and seal. Label and date.

Notes: To prepare a storage jar, preheat the oven to very slow 120°C (250°F/Gas ½). Wash the jar and lid in hot soapy water and rinse with hot water. Put the jar in the oven for 20 minutes, or until fully dry. Do not dry with a tea towel.

This hot chilli (pepper) sauce will keep in the fridge for up to six months. It is delicious with tagines and couscous, or can be added to salad dressings, marinades and pasta sauces for extra flavour.

Fills a 600 ml (20 fl oz) jar

Spiced Coconut Sauce

- **40 g (1½ oz) bunch coriander (cilantro–roots, stems and leaves)**
- **2 teaspoons oil**
- **3 cm (1¼ inch) fresh ginger (ginger root), peeled and grated**
- **2 stalks lemon grass (white part only), finely chopped**
- **2 small red chillies, finely chopped**
- **1 clove garlic, finely chopped**
- **3 tablespoons coconut cream, plus extra if necessary**
- **2 tablespoons rice vinegar**
- **1 teaspoon soft brown sugar**

Finely chop the coriander (cilantro), keeping the roots, stems and leaves separate. Heat the oil in a frying pan over low heat and cook the ginger (ginger root), lemon grass, chilli, coriander (cilantro) root and garlic, stirring constantly, for 3 minutes, or until aromatic. Add the coconut cream, stirring well. Increase the heat to high and bring the sauce to a rapid boil. Cook for about 1 minute until the mixture looks oily (this is the coconut cream separating or 'cracking'). Do not let the sauce burn. Add another 2 tablespoons of coconut cream if the sauce becomes too thick.

Transfer to a bowl and add the coriander (cilantro) stem and leaves, rice vinegar and sugar. Stir well and add salt and more sugar, to taste. Serve at room temperature.

Serves 2–4

Potato and Oil Puree

- **1 kg (2 lb 3 oz) floury potatoes (such as russet, spunta and pontiac), cut into large chunks**
- **200 ml (6¾ fl oz) vegetable stock (broth)**

- **2 garlic cloves, peeled and bruised**
- **2 sprigs of fresh thyme**
- **150 ml (5 fl oz) extra-virgin olive oil**

Cook the potatoes in boiling salted water until tender but still firm. While the potatoes are cooking, heat the stock (broth) in a small saucepan with the garlic and thyme. Bring to simmering point, then remove from the heat and allow to infuse.

Drain the potatoes well and pass them through a mouli or mash with a potato masher. Strain the stock, return to the saucepan, add the olive oil and reheat gently. Place the potato puree in a bowl and add the stock (broth) in a thin steady stream, stirring continuously with a flat wooden spoon. Season with salt and pepper, then beat well until the puree is smooth.

Serves 4

Avocado Salsa

- 1 medium red (Spanish) onion
- 2 large avocados
- 1 tablespoon lime juice
- 1 medium tomato
- 1 small red capsicum (pepper)
- 1 teaspoon ground coriander
- 1 teaspoon ground cumin
- 3 tablespoons chopped fresh coriander (cilantro) leaves
- 2 tablespoons olive oil
- 4–5 drops hot chilli (pepper) sauce

Finely chop the onion. Cut the avocados in half; remove the seed and carefully peel. Finely chop the flesh; place in a medium bowl and toss lightly with lime juice.

Cut the tomato in half horizontally, squeeze gently to remove seeds; chop finely. Remove seeds and membrane from capsicum (pepper), chop finely.

Place the ground coriander and cumin in a small pan; stir over medium heat for 1 minute to enhance fragrance and flavour; cool. Add all the ingredients to the avocado in a bowl and gently combine, so that the avocado retains its shape and is not mashed. Refrigerate until required and serve at room temperature with corn (nacho) chips.

Serves 6

Algerian Spiced Jam

- **2 eggplants (aubergines), about 400 g (14 oz), cut into 1 cm (½ inch) slices**
- **olive oil, for frying**
- **2 garlic cloves, crushed**

- **1 teaspoon sweet paprika**
- **1½ teaspoons ground cumin**
- **½ teaspoon sugar**
- **1 tablespoon lemon juice**

Sprinkle the eggplant (aubergine) slices with salt and drain in a colander for 30 minutes. Rinse well, squeeze gently and pat dry. Heat about 5 mm (¼ inch) of the oil in a large frying pan and fry the slices in batches over medium heat until golden brown on both sides. Drain on paper towels, then chop finely. Put in a colander until most of the oil has drained off, then transfer to a bowl and add the garlic, paprika, cumin and sugar.

Wipe out the pan, add the eggplant (aubergine) mixture and stir constantly over medium heat for 2 minutes. Transfer to a bowl, stir in the lemon juice and season. Serve at room temperature.

Serves 6–8

Pawpaw Sauce

- **250 g (8¾ oz) ripe pawpaw or papaya**
- **3 tablespoons cream**
- **1 tablespoon dry white wine**
- **2 teaspoons wholegrain mustard**
- **2 spring (green) onions, finely chopped**

Cut the pawpaw or papaya in half, discarding the seeds and peel. Chop the flesh finely and place in a bowl with all of the juices from the fruit.

Add the cream, wine, mustard and spring (green) onion to the pawpaw. Season to taste with salt and pepper and whisk well. Cover and leave to stand for 20 minutes before serving.

Serves 4

Index

288